Transnational Audiences

Global Media and Communication

Transnational Audiences

Media Reception on a Global Scale

ADRIAN ATHIQUE

polity

The right of Adrian Athique to be identified as Author of this Work has been asserted in accordance with the UK Copyright, Designs and Patents Act 1988.

First published in 2016 by Polity Press

Polity Press
65 Bridge Street
Cambridge CB2 1UR, UK

Polity Press
350 Main Street
Malden, MA 02148, USA

ISBN-13: 978-0-7456-7021-8
ISBN-13: 978-0-7456-7022-5(pb)

A catalogue record for this book is available from the British Library.

Library of Congress Cataloging-in-Publication Data

Athique, Adrian, author.
    Transnational audiences : media reception on a global scale / Adrian Athique.
      pages cm
    Includes bibliographical references and index.
    ISBN 978-0-7456-7021-8 (hardback) -- ISBN 978-0-7456-7022-5 (pbk.) 1. Mass media and globalization. 2. Mass media and culture. 3. Transnationalism. I. Title.
    P94.6.A885 2016
    302.23--dc23
                                                                          2015034095

Typeset in 11 on 13pt Adobe Garamond Pro by
Servis Filmsetting Ltd, Stockport, Cheshire
Printed and bound in the UK by CPI Group (UK) Ltd, Croydon, CR0 4YY

The publisher has used its best endeavours to ensure that the URLs for external websites referred to in this book are correct and active at the time of going to press. However, the publisher has no responsibility for the websites and can make no guarantee that a site will remain live or that the content is or will remain appropriate.

Every effort has been made to trace all copyright holders, but if any have been inadvertently overlooked the publisher will be pleased to include any necessary credits in any subsequent reprint or edition.

For further information on Polity, visit our website:
politybooks.com

Contents

Acknowledgements

This book was written across time and space, and there are many friends and colleagues to whom I owe thanks. Kate Bowles and John Robinson were always in my thoughts as I wrote. My gratitude is due to colleagues working with me on the empirical programmes running alongside this discussion. Their patience, generosity and practical insights have all been invaluable. Without space to list them all here, I would like to thank Vibodh Parthasarathi, S.V. Srinivas, Jozon Lorenzana, Devi Leena Bose, Jinna Tay, Chetna Monga and Douglas Hill for their forbearance to date and into the future. For kind invitations to join larger discussions around the disciplines of media and cultural studies, I would also like to thank Karina Ayeyard, Joost De Bruin, Stephen Epstein, Craig Hight, Peter Lunt, Albert Moran, Anna Pertierra, Hari Ramaswami, Susan Turnbull and Graeme Turner. Thanks are also due to Tom O'Regan, Brian Yecies, Pete Randles and Nicola Evans who have engaged with me on these topics over many years. Andrea Drugan and Elen Griffiths saw this project home, as I worked into the gaps between managing various departments, missed deadlines and double-handled my fieldwork commitments. They kept me in line with exceeding grace. My daughter, Kaya, kept me in one piece.

1   Media Reception on a Global Scale

Almost twenty years ago, Ella Shohat and Robert Stam observed that 'The centrifugal forces of the globalizing process, and the global reach of the media, virtually oblige the contemporary media theorist to move beyond the restrictive framework of the nation-state' (1996: 145). Certainly, few would now argue that an analysis of either the aesthetics or the reception of any media source can be presented convincingly within the closed frame of a strictly national history. Nonetheless, the need to make such a statement in the first place reflects the longstanding dominance of a national paradigm in media analysis, corresponding with the heyday of the nation-state system and terrestrial broadcast technologies in the second half of the twentieth century. In reconsidering those logics, media studies has increasingly embraced a new 'transnational' paradigm conceived in opposition to the long-running national canons of media content and academic expertise (Ezra et al. 2006; Durovicova and Newman 2009; Shohat and Stam 2003). Even so, we must recognize from the outset that national frameworks for media analysis were never oblivious to the global dimension. It is more precisely the case that national media models relied on the foundational notion of a world structured by national components which, taken collectively, constituted the 'international'. For decades, the international film festival showcase was the perfect example of this display of nationally marked aesthetics, considered to be favourable to a comparative understanding of discrete cultural formations (Chaudhuri 2005; Goldsmith and Lealand 2012). The great transnational shift that took place over the turn of the millennium was prompted by a fundamental reconsideration of this paradigm.

New forms of mediation (or, in a fuller sense, what Andreas Hepp would call 'mediatization') were a central factor in this re-evaluation, as they became embedded within the political, economic and technical functions of the world system (Couldry and Hepp 2013; Hepp and Krotz 2014). This was to be expected, since one of the foundational claims of modernity rests upon the newfound capacity to collapse time and distance within a world-spanning technical apparatus. In that respect, Anthony Giddens' characterization of the technical impetus of globalization is typical in terms of his explicit recognition of changing media technologies as a driving force within the matrix of globalization. As Giddens put it: 'Instantaneous electronic communication isn't just a way in which news or information is conveyed more quickly. Its existence alters the very texture of our lives' (2002: 11). Arjun Appadurai, similarly, subscribed to the view that 'electronic mediation transforms pre-existing worlds of communication and conduct' (1996: 3). For Manuel Castells (1996) it was the rise of information technology, and global computer networking in particular, that informed his formulation of globalization in the form of a network society. Fundamentally, Castells' new world order was structured by the exchanges of knowledge, people and wealth taking place between the 'nodes' where information, and thus economic power, is increasingly concentrated. A global network society takes the spatial form of increasingly inter-connected global cities joined together by dense 'flows' of information. Taking this lead, the emerging discourse on 'transnational' mediation has tended to emphasize the insistent cultural flows that escape and/or circumvent fixed territories and national structures (for example, Curtin and Shah 2010; Hudson and Zimmerman 2015; Madianou and Miller 2012).

Nonetheless, even now, there is still a strong tendency to position examples of transnational media exchange as exciting anomalies to the general theory, and everyday experience, of communication. Arguably, this is an unsatisfactory framing for contemporary media experiences and, indeed, it is somewhat questionable when set against a serious historical viewpoint. Of necessity, then, I will revisit the theoretical field in the first section of this book, with a mind to clarifying the various concerns and imperatives that predispose our enquiry. Many of the core principles of social communications research rest upon the unique combination of culture and polity that has arisen in parallel with the mass media. The centrality of cultural nationalism, in particular, has far-reaching implications for sociological inquiry. The ubiquitous logics of this pairing determine the 'majority positions' through which we commonly seek to conceptualize and identify a diverse world. Bearing this in mind, chapters 2 through to 4 will examine the underlying claims that demarcate the national, the international and the transnational. In the process, we will begin to illuminate the imagined worlds that we habituate in the course of our daily lives. Some historical grounding is required here, since the temporal evolution of this 'worlding' process has interacted closely with successive waves of social change, with the evolution of intellectual reason and with a constantly shifting geopolitical situation. Equally, the changing forms and potentials of media systems over the past century have themselves frequently recast the terms of the debate. Thus, I will also make some effort, over the course of the book as a whole, to account for the continuities and ruptures stemming from successive phases of remediation.

In this dimension, social change and technological developments necessarily interact, with neither historical timeline being entirely independent of the other. The prevailing structures of mediation and the nature of the media material itself (that is, what commercial managers like to call 'content') are also significant factors in the disjointed discussions taking place around transnational communication. Given the diversity of interests and approaches, the varying conceptualization of audiences for different forms and functions of media has given rise to an array of ideal types that have been given empirical substance through a bewildering series of demographics and datasets. From spectators to users and from households to flashmobs, all of these placeholders for human participation are necessarily implicated in the routine conduct of various methodologies. As such, the second section of this book will canvas some of the major themes, critical concerns and seminal works in transnational audience research. In doing so, I will illustrate how the investigation of transnational audiences has been centred upon particular audience formations, encountered here over three chapters as 'diasporas', 'crossovers' and 'proximities'. Each of those chapters presents a brief sample of historical and contemporary studies, with the larger purpose of establishing the impetus, salience and future direction of these particular enquiries. This section will also begin to explore the differences in form and formation that have engendered distinctive approaches to transnational phenomena emerging from film, music, television and Internet applications. Thus, throughout the second, and also the third, section of the book, I will explore transnational audience formations with reference to media phenomena from around the globe.

This book does not, however, provide a thorough empirical account of transnational audiences. That far larger task belongs to the academy as a whole. Nonetheless, I would urge readers new to the field to engage with the more substantive empirical studies listed at the end of each chapter. Paying attention to detailed case studies will assist greatly in demonstrating the practical application (and origins) of the concerns canvassed in this book. These works will also provide the most effective demonstration of the linkages between particular media forms and certain academic disciplines, and of how the methodological toolkits in use tend to favour particular lines of questioning around the intent, structure and operation of global media systems. With this in mind, in the third and final section of the book, I will engage more explicitly with the methodological and epistemological concerns arising from contemporary media applications. Whereas my attention in the middle section is given to the evolution of audience formations that have intrigued researchers over a reasonable period of time, the final section will concentrate instead upon new audience formations that did not exist in the previous generation, and which bring to light new questions, new challenges and new opportunities for future research. In the final chapter itself, I will seek to explicate certain ways of thinking about the transnational through which all of the audience formations explored in this book can be understood as parts of a larger whole. In a nutshell, then, the purpose of this book is to survey the theoretical foundations of transnational communication and to evaluate our present understanding of this proposition using some cogent examples of media configurations operating across our increasingly interlaced world.

Transnational Cultures

Before we begin that journey, however, there is some intrinsic value in elaborating on the title of this book and the terminology it invokes. Steven Vertovec has described 'transnationalism' as broadly referring to the 'multiple ties and interactions linking people or institutions across the borders of nation-states' (1999: 447). Within the existing literature, Vertovec identifies six major strands of enquiry into transnationalism: as a social morphology, a type of consciousness, a mode of cultural reproduction, an avenue of capital, a site of political engagement and as a reconstruction of place and locality (1999: 449–56). Although the media, and telecommunications in particular, are seen as crucial in all of these strands, narrative media forms are seen to be most influential in two instances: as a 'mode of cultural reproduction' and as a 'reconstruction of place or locality'. In terms of the former:

> transnationalism is often associated with a fluidity of constructed styles, social institutions and everyday practices. They are often described in terms of syncretism, creolization, bricolage, cultural translation and hybridity. Fashion, music, film and visual arts are some of the most conspicuous areas in which such processes are observed . . . an increasingly significant channel for the flow of cultural phenomena and the transformation of identity is through global media and communications. (Vertovec 2009: 7)

In this instance, transnationalism occurs through practices of cultural mixing enacted within the representative arts. A contemporary artistic transnationalism can be seen explicitly in the more conscious examples of cultural borrowing, such as a Thai 'Western' movie like *Tears of the Black Tiger* (2001) or the Hollywood remakes of the Japanese *Ring* films. It can be seen objectively in the worldwide adoption of American and European television formats or the take up of Indian 'Bollywood' styles by African video productions. It can also be seen implicitly in the circulation of media products intended for multinational audiences, such as the success of the Korean 'K wave' across a large part of East Asia in the 2000s or the development of the transatlantic popular music industries in the 1960s. Transnational culture takes many forms, from the bland universalism of electronic games to the conscious fusion of contemporary music. It can stem from both imitation and appropriation, which may be a conscious artistic decision by a producer (as with Tarantino's *Kill Bill* films) or a cumulative action by consumers, as in the British adoption of Jamaican music cultures. In all these cases, transnational popular cultures are symptomatic of global connectivity and a greater awareness of cultural diversity. Within those contexts, there are important distinctions (in Bourdieu's sense of the term) to be made between the self-conscious cosmopolitanism of 'world cinema' and the continuous spread and revival of post-war youth culture in different times and settings (Bourdieu 1984).

In Vertovec's summary, it is important to note his conclusion that transnational popular cultures have implications for socialization at a very personal level. The assumption that media usage influences personal identity in some fundamental fashion has been the orthodox view of popular culture since the 1970s. This has shaped our approaches to all forms of media audiences to the extent that we now rarely question the socializing effect of media consumption and its determining role in the making of each generation. Equally, the literature on transnationalism tends to suggest the passing of what were previously discrete cultural spheres defined by the established parameters of national spaces. If we apply these lines of thinking to a rise in artistic transnationalism, then it does appear reasonable to assume that national aesthetics and idioms are threatened with disruption by the mixing and merging of cultural codes. Indeed, this has been a major concern in media sociology for the past hundred years, where the international tastes of the global elite have long been taken to be potentially damaging for the lower social orders. Consequently, the spectre of cultural confusion and the loss of our distinctive human heritages is frequently overlaid with anxieties about political loyalties and public morality. Such concerns also arise around the second strand of transnationalism in which Vertovec sees the media as being particularly significant, that is, in the 'reconstruction of place or locality', where:

> a high degree of human mobility, telecommunications, films, video and satellite TV, and the Internet have contributed to the creation of trans-local understandings . . . some analysts have proposed that transnationalism has changed people's relations to space primarily by creating transnational 'social

fields' or 'social spaces' that connect or position some actors in more than one country. (Vertovec 2009: 12)

The critical status of place is obviously central to any exploration of transnational media. What is also significant here is the recognition of the dual function of modern media. They provide the modes of representation through which wider social relations are expressed as well as the means of communication through which personal social networks are maintained. As such, the emergence of transnational social spaces is linked closely to mediated geographies with both symbolic and practical functions. Our everyday perceptions of the larger world are framed by the ubiquitous circulation of media artefacts, while our personal access to global communications systems facilitates the globalization of our personal domain. Both aspects of transnational communication bring distant societies into sensory proximity, as Marshall McLuhan famously noted in his evocation of the 'Global Village' during the 1960s (McLuhan and Fiore 1968). A sense of place and a relative perception of location is also where media mobility meets human mobility, which is the other most frequently cited symptom of transnational cultures. Media become active not only in negating space but also in bridging temporal divides. When we relocate we use media to maintain contact with those we have left behind, thus taking our past with us as an active participant in our new situation. The transnational circulation of media content often cohabits with the itinerancy of contemporary life, marking a double movement through the fields of global culture.

Identifying Audiences

The broad discussion of transnationalism in the media tends to draw evidence from the dispersal of media content. On the face of it, there is good reason to focus upon the supply side, since audiences are notoriously elusive and have posed a perennial challenge for media scholars, sociologists and market researchers alike. In the formative years of mass communications, the enduring conception of the crowd provided the putative biological mass which served as the consumer of media content and arbiter of public opinion. Amidst the concrete of urbanization and mass transport, dynamic crowd formations have since continued to provide the commercial basis for evolving forms of spectacle from circus to cinema to rock concerts. Nonetheless, for observers seeking to understand the composition and motivation of any crowd there are obvious practical challenges, given its ephemeral condition and the inherent diversity of a social body coalescing around mass appeal.

By its nature, each crowd is indelibly linked by its very nature to a particular place and time, which makes the mobility of media content the only means by which crowds in different locales can be conceived collectively as a mass audience. Thus, prior to the advent of the World Wide Web, there was no real foundation for the idea of a transnational crowd formation. So we had a world of audiences, but no framework for an international audience in the singular sense. It is also significant that the crowd has always been indelibly linked to mass entertainments and emotive behaviours, and has long stood in obvious contrast to the individualized and dispassionate concept of the reader that underpinned the European enlightenment (and the subsequent pursuit of progress through global markets).

The individual, therefore, is well catered for in modernist thinking, even if those particular configurations of culture, class and cognition have proved themselves to be poor travellers in a wider world. In the heyday of print-capitalism, however, the classical notion of the audience as crowd was powerfully juxtaposed by entirely new concepts for identifying the dispersed and anonymous publics facilitated by modern media technologies that spanned time and space (Innis 1952). Looking at the content of mass circulation books and newspapers from that period, it is obvious that communication by print engendered a conscious conceit to address a worldwide audience (Anderson 1991). For those at the receiving end, it is a doxa of modernist thinking that the spread of reading powerfully transformed our everyday sense of being in the world. At the same time, this new kind of transnational audience remained largely invisible as any kind of collective body, appearing only in sales figures and library lending records. A set of dispersed and mediated communes required new forms of shorthand for understanding the enlarged public sphere (which were steadily codified within the 'enlightened' discipline of sociology) (Habermas 1989). From the middle of the twentieth century onwards, mass broadcasting gave rise to a new generation of audience formations that also dispensed with the physicality of the crowd, and thereby required new social categories such as 'listeners' and 'viewers'. Here the primary unit was the household, where public life was now deemed to have interpenetrated the domestic domain. For those seeking to construct a viable commercial basis for broadcast media via advertising, the disaggregated audience became a pressing concern that was tackled with a panoply of focus groups, consumer surveys and ratings mechanisms (Balnaves et al. 2011).

By such means, market researchers constructed an empirical account of media audiences that compensated for their disembodiment, but it is also significant that they did so during the high tide of nationalist economic models. As such, audiences were recast at the national level by those seeking to understand the vagaries of voting patterns, consumer tastes and social mores. With the audience broken down into 'housewives', 'teenagers', 'pensioners' and other types, there was still a general assumption of the national specificity of such groups, which took primacy over their local conditions. In this formulation, audiences outside of the national space became of interest primarily as export opportunities and, to a lesser extent, for the comparative purpose of experts in social communication. By the 1970s, the widespread use of ideal types and quantification to produce both market knowledge and social knowledge was being challenged by scholars seeking a more nuanced understanding of media power in the modern age, most notably by cultural studies with its focus on the meaning (rather than the act) of media consumption and the promotion of anthropological methods and thick description (Turner 2002). The goal here was to understand communication as a two-way, rather than top-down, process (Hall 1980). Audiences were recast from a 'passive' mode into an 'active' category where viewers consciously subverted ideological structures within media content in light of their own social experience (Morley 1980). In the early body of work, much was invested in the notion of working-class subcultures as resistant audiences who worked to counter a privileged mode of national communication (Hall and Jefferson 1977; Hebdige 1979).

Over time, the very British concerns of early cultural studies work underwent a series of translations into the contexts of other societies, and came under the influence of a hyper-liberal doctrine that tended to promote individualism over the more stable categories of community favoured by early ethnographic studies of audiences (Fiske 1989; Gauntlett 2007; Jenkins 1992). As a consequence, the natural correlation between social movement theory and active audience approaches (both products of the 1960s) eventually coalesced in the model of a networked consumer society (Arvidsson 2005; Castells 1997; Jenkins 2008). Thus, in broad terms, we have seen a parallel transition in both sociology and audience studies from approaches largely derived from the primacy of social structure and physical proximity to approaches largely derived from the primacy of individual agency and mediated relationships (Cavanagh 2007; Napoli 2010). At heart, this remarkable convergence between the conceptual evolution of the audience concept and the concept of community was itself the result of deepening mediation (Athique 2013: 49–63). The technological (and ideological) foundations of the IT revolution proved to be critical in reprogramming the co-ordinates of media sociology, as it was significantly recast through the adoption of computational metaphors (for example, Rainie and Wellman 2012). From the mid-1990s onwards, the global scope of the World Wide

Web has also served to ensure that online audiences are inherently transnational. Across this vast canvas, the combination of 'multimedia' performance, the 'many to many' potentials of networked computing, and the rise of mobile and locative media has engendered a bewildering array of audience configurations that are yet to be adequately described (Goggin 2010; Nightingale 2011).

In a classic case of wood amongst trees, our understanding of increasingly diverse audience formations in the digital era has tended to centre around either the residual categories of a generic 'user' or, even worse, around the loose deployment of a 'virtual community' that has become endemic in most areas of media studies (following Rheingold 1993). The continuing primacy of the concept of community (however virtual, elective and segregated it may have become) in an era of remediation and footloose populations is indicative of a long-term obsession with the role of media in maintaining bonds within groups of similar individuals. Philip Schlesinger has observed that this 'inherently internalist' tendency is an enduring legacy of the social communication theory that formed the basis of modern media studies (2000: 24). Thus, despite the laborious attention now paid to the subcultures *within* national audiences, there is still

> no general principle for analysing the interaction between communicative communities, for assessing cultural and communicative flows in a global system . . . because that is not where the theoretical interest lies. Social communication theory is therefore about how shared cultural and communicative practices strengthen the identity of a group by creating boundaries. (Schlesinger 2000: 21)

So, remarkably, amidst the fanfare of globalization we don't yet have a firm framework for understanding forums comprised of an inherently diverse membership, which is precisely what transnational communication facilitates. In the era of satellite television, playback formats, mobile communication and the World Wide Web, our long-term investment in strictly national media cultures (taken to be 'held in common') has been more or less forced to accommodate the rise of narrowcast media and niche audiences across the media spectrum (and with it, across the social spectrum). Nonetheless, this diversification of the audience still tends to take place within a pluralized re-jigging of the national frame.

In parallel with technological change, the steady relocation of 'ethnic' migrants into the developed nations has further highlighted the inherent diversity of national populations, as well as underscoring the mobility of cultural idioms aided by a raft of new technologies. The post-1970s understanding of cultural practices in everyday life as major sites of identity formation imbued with political significance (as reflected by the notion that the 'personal is political') has quickly drawn the attention of Caucasian governments increasingly concerned with managing the 'risks' of diversity. All of these factors have contributed to the impetus for a wide range of studies focusing upon the media usage of minority populations, and the resulting configurations of social identity and their attendant implications for assessing processes of assimilation or alienation (Brinkerhoff 2009; Cunningham and Sinclair 2000; Gillespie 1995). From the perspective of those who grew up amongst the novel conditions of the United Nations, it is easy to see why the accelerating dispersal of media content across a global geography has been so readily seen as destabilizing the analytical coherence of cultural identities. To suggest, however, that transnational media audiences can only be exemplified by Internet-enabled migrants is to miss the far bigger picture of transnationalism in the 'mainstream'. Accordingly, the analytical turn towards transnational modes of media analysis necessarily requires a broader reassessment of the nature of media reception taking place across so many different locations and contexts.

The Point of Reception

The increasing attention being paid to transnational flows in contemporary media studies is highly valuable in that it explicitly recognizes the inherent mobility of media content as well as the organic solidarity of audiences operating outside a strictly national framework. Nonetheless, any formulation of audiences as social bodies has to be supported by a general theory of social communication that explains the encounter between the symbolic-technological structures of media and the volition of human beings. It may be useful, then, if we define the environmental conditions of transnational reception at variance with those of a 'resident' audience of the kind implicitly presumed in studies conjoining a national media with a 'domestic audience'. Resident audiences are generally seen as being keen to consume content that is simultaneously 'about here and about us'. The term 'resident' is itself, of course, a variable and contested term; a signifier shaped by the social, cultural, geographic and bureaucratic territories in which it is deployed. There is nevertheless a broad unifying context to the word which implies *belonging* in not only a symbolic but also a physically located sense. A media audience might therefore be considered 'resident' under conditions of reception where viewers perceive what is on-screen as somehow coterminous with the society in which they live. This is an allegorical function served effectively by both fantastic and 'realist' narrative and, indeed, this was the normative viewing position promoted during the heydey of national media systems (and it applies equally to network news, Batman or AOL).

A 'non-resident' mode of media consumption, by contrast, is more useful for identifying audiences within the conditions of reception that fall outside of this viewing position. Non-resident audiences are engaged with media content in a context where the diegetic world cannot reasonably be claimed to be 'about here and about us'. In much of the world, where imports make up the bulk of media content and where media systems interface with a wide range of transnational territories, it is non-resident experiences of media consumption that are actually the most common. Nonetheless, non-resident media inevitably cohabit with 'resident' media reception in our daily experience. You may watch foreign films with intensely local advert breaks, or you may keep an eye on the local weather while communicating across the World Wide Web. As such, the transnational and the national are unlikely to be mutually exclusive. In practice, any social body defined through media-use is likely to be shaped by transnational patterns of cultural consumption and association, since what most characterizes contemporary media is its multiple sources and its intertextuality.

In her recent work, Shani Orgad has drawn upon Arjun Appadurai, Charles Taylor and Cornelius Castoriadis to argue that the globalizing tendencies of media content in the contemporary world serve to simulate a 'global imagination' amongst audiences (Appadurai 1996; Castoriadis 1987; Taylor 2002). The driving force in Orgad's argument is not the complexities of reception, but rather the semiotics of representation. Thus, the global imagination is described as 'intimately intertwined with the act of representation: the capacity to imagine relies upon a repertoire of symbolic resources (representations) available to be drawn upon. In turn, representation, through signs, makes the absent present, which is the essence of imagining' (2012: 41). By this account, the flow of global communications (from rotating television news to the global backdrops of Hollywood spectaculars and contemporary backpackers armed with smartphones) all serve to inculcate a set of relativities around which we make sense of our place in the world. Thus, our personalized understanding of our social relationships, responsibilities and potentials is constructed in relation to our capacity to comprehend our place, and other places, in a global totality. As a catalyst, the increasing proximity and density of a 'global village' on screen feeds into a 'global consciousness' that expresses itself through the production of media representations that address this interlaced narrative (McLuhan and Fiore 1968; Robertson 1992). Essentially, this is a 'circuit of communication' argument, where

> Global imagination refers to both the faculty to and the process of forming mental images and concepts of the world, and of ourselves and others traversing this global social space. It relies on making this space present through signs and symbols. In other words, global imagination is cultivated by a process of ongoing construction of views, images, understandings, desires and scripts about the world. (Orgad 2012: 51)

There are two components here. The first is a recognition of the 'mental maps' through which individuals understand their existence within a society, in this case a polyglot global society. The second component is an assertion that this capacity is inculcated by discursive prompts carried via a textual system. Both should interest us in terms of understanding media reception, but such a strong textual determinism has generally been eschewed in audience studies for quite a long time. Although various modes of representation will construct an articulation of the global through certain conventions, the larger processes of social identification are inherently dialogic. The production of meaning is therefore highly dependent upon the experiences of the audiences that encounter any work of representation. Thus, for audience researchers, the exploration of any given 'global imagination' has to encompass representation as only part of a broader pattern of social communication. Culture is not a closed system. Within the larger system of meaning-making, various works of representation serve to mediate the social process, at times both formally and informally, but they cannot encapsulate that larger process. Accordingly, the orientation of any global imagination cannot be grasped independently of the highly variable contexts of social situation, reception and response (see Canclini 2014). A distinction, therefore, has to be maintained between global imagination and 'mediated worlds'. The former is a fundamental cognitive process, while the latter are communicative envelopments of various kinds.

Taking this view, we have to assume that the global imagination cannot be deduced solely, or even primarily, from systems of representation in the fashion emphasized by semioticians. In order to illustrate this point better, there may be some merit in revisiting C. Wright Mills' pioneering conceptualization of sociological imagination as a human attribute. According to Mills, the sociological imagination is the set of cognitive processes where two opposing scales of social reality – individual experience and social structures – become comprehensible. Mills therefore defined sociological imagination as 'the vivid awareness of the relationship between experience and the wider society . . . the capacity to shift from one perspective to another . . . the capacity to range from the most impersonal and remote transformations to the intimate features of the human self – and to see the relationship between the two' (Mills 1959: 8). It is this human capacity to correlate structure and experience that allows us to identify and understand the relationship between wider social forces and our personal actions. Thus, the imagination is intrinsic to human consciousness and behaviour in our 'natural' state, regardless of its increasing mediation through various modes of representation and interpersonal communication. Self-orientation is something that people do naturally as social animals. Indeed, this is why their personalized insights make audience research valuable and interesting, and why it produces essentially collaborative knowledge. Without the intellectual capacity to situate ourselves in complex relative terms, globalization could be no more than mechanical and would not enter our consciousness to the extent that it presently does.

The application of the concept of 'sociological imagination' within the academy tends to be quite different. In sociology, the term is often inflected by the power relations between the research expert and the research subject. That is, a well-developed 'sociological imagination' can be associated more narrowly with the particular role of the sociologist, which 'requires us . . . to "think ourselves away" from the familiar routines of our daily lives' (Giddens and Sutton 2013: 5). Arguably, however, the real value of Wright's concept is precisely opposite to this kind of 'sociological imagination'. Wright's location of social understanding in our personal experience leads us towards a more mundane, but larger, concept of 'social imagination'. Here, the imaginative self-orientation of research subjects takes us deep into their social understanding and consequently reveals much about the embedding of symbolic and abstract relationships, both near and far, within the fabric of their everyday lives. It is social imagination in this sense that makes the lives of individuals both functionally plausible and meaningful, thereby reminding us that identity is as much an external matter (of relations) as an internal one (of selfhood). Active at all scales, this process of relative identification implies a personalised global imagination. Equally, in establishing our unique relationship to other individuals, groups and cultures, social imagination is by its very nature an open-ended and dynamic process. The balance between adaptive independence and cumulative interdependence of thought prompts us to consider transnational communication as a consequence, rather than an effect, of mediation.

Global Scale

Going beyond symbolic structures and the orientation of individual subjectivities, it is also worth noting that there is no aspect or practice of culture that is not firmly located in the material domain. This is particularly important for audience studies, since media reception, by whatever means, always takes place somewhere particular, whether this is in the lodgings of a rural migrant to Shanghai or beneath the electronic billboards of Times Square. The time and place of imagining are critical, as is the embodiment of the individual recipient and the particularities of their life-world in material, temporal and relational terms. While other areas of media studies may be adequately focused upon the semiotics of content or the dimensions of certain markets, the primary interest of reception studies must always be the point of contact. This may be less apparent at the overarching scale at which this survey will take place, but it remains a central concern for any empirical researcher within the field. As Nick Couldry observes: 'accumulating more accounts of media from more places will not be enough unless we can grasp the variety of everyday media practices on the ground' (2012: 157). Conversely, the richness of point samples from reception studies will only illuminate our understanding when they become situated within a coherent cultural geography, where the larger point 'is not to track minor variations in media use but to grasp the overall span of media cultures on a global scale and the dynamics that shape that diversity' (2012: 159).

In that context, the invocation of the global itself must be understood critically. In making the claim that our daily experience of living in the world is undergoing radical transformation, globalization theorists have been compelled to link patterns of technological connections and economic transactions with the shifting conduct of human beings. Although they are commonly conflated in the process, I think it is important to maintain a distinction between the 'transnational' and 'globalization'. Globalization is a term that denotes increasing interactivity and exchange and the collapse of the barriers of distance and ideology which have previously served to frustrate the triumph of a universal capitalist order. The transnational on the other hand denotes cultural practices which take place across the national boundaries that have structured the discussion of human geography for the past century. Transnational phenomena do not of themselves necessarily imply, as does the term globalization, any particular ideological cohesion or historical volition. Nonetheless, the identification of the condition of globalization is itself predicated upon establishing the existence of such transnational exchanges, as well as providing evidence of their increase (either in numerical terms or in terms of their significance or influence). It is probably fair to say that this case has been made successfully in the empirical research of the past two decades. It would be unreasonable to claim, however, that the new conceptual relationships between globalization and mass media have entirely overwritten the discursive power of the national.

Two reasons for this immediately spring to mind. Both serve to indicate that we live in a world which is increasingly *trans*national, rather than post-national. At a practical level, the official production and circulation of media content as an economic activity continues to operate within a system of exchange where national governments at least nominally regulate, subsidize, censor and/or tax the production, distribution and exhibition of media products. This authority may be at times coerced and is increasingly subverted, but almost all media producers still need to carry passports, request filming permits, obtain broadcast and journalism licences. Media providers must operate within at least one, but typically several, national economic systems. The Internet is a complex jurisdiction in this regard, but certainly not immune to national authorities (as the Megaupload case has demonstrated). The second (epistemological) reason is that the contemporary experience of globalization continues to be framed by the linguistic and semantic dominance of the nation state. The invocation of 'national interest' remains an everyday feature of our 'globalized' world. As such, we should never underestimate the national in transnational, where the discourse of 'national interest' is fostered by the aggressive pursuit of particularity in some instances, while in others the selfsame 'national interest' is invoked to promote various international coalitions or a selective (and typically commercial) cosmopolitanism. Thus, while it is undeniable that the functional reality of a more interconnected globe sits uneasily within the discursive logic of nationalism, it is equally clear that national imaginaries continue to provide key staging grounds for transnational politics.

Needless to say, in a globalizing world of this kind, marked by what Shohat and Stam describe as 'the entrenched asymmetries of international power' (2000: 381), the globalization of cultural production has received both utopian and dystopian readings. We will consider some, by no means all, of these readings in subsequent chapters. At the individual scale, these debates have tended to focus upon the subjective complexities of cultural influence, hybrid identities and the customizable field of mediation made possible by the intense personalization of digital platforms (for example, Hegde 2011; Kraidy 2005; Goggin 2011). The lived experience of 'globalization' at this level often brings to light intense anxieties around ethnic coherence, political loyalty, cultural disorientation and social dislocation. No doubt, there is a lot of fun in it too. In that sense, exploring the 'demand side' of cultural crossovers, expanding life-worlds and mediaculturalism more generally becomes necessary as a means of addressing the anxieties commonly expressed at the scale of community. Community, of course, forms the discursive point at which personal expression becomes subject to police action, either figuratively or actually. Cultural engagements at the community level, in turn, draw attention at the national scale, where everyday practices often become linked to political legitimacy, the requirements of citizenship and the gatekeeping of national institutions and narratives (McLaughlin et al. 2011). Nonetheless, alongside such continuing proclivities for sovereign normativity, transnational media streams have become well established as a common feature of everyday life across all social strata.

The interlacing of transnational communication of various kinds within the personal, local and national scales must also be approached from a global perspective. Here the maturation of a global media apparatus (most explicitly in the form of the World Wide Web) necessarily interacts with the rich cultural geography of our world. At this larger scale, earlier maps of a political 'world system' defined by a 'centre-periphery' power relationship are being redrawn to somehow account for the growing mobility of various forms of media content and communication flows across a more multi-polar terrain (Curtin 2003; Thussu 2007; Wallerstein 2004). As a consequence, researchers have been working steadily towards a new cultural geography that reflects the growth of transnational satellite broadcasting, the circulation of international media formats and the increasing importance of pan-regional publics (Chalaby 2005; Moran and Keane 2003; Turner and Tay 2009). This mode of engagement with transnational audiences tends to demarcate culture in the form of supra-national zones defined by mutual investments in particular forms of language, faith and custom. This 'area studies' approach to contemporary media has been well suited to the empirical description of the global media economy, since it is more easily adapted to the broad categorization of various 'territories' for media industries and products. There is also a strong geopolitical framing at this level, given the origins of international communication studies in the disciplines of political science and international relations during the 1970s (see Kraidy 2013: 1–8). Nonetheless, work done at this scale relies upon validation at the grassroots since, in essence, any coherent geography of media reception must seek explanations that can be demonstrated at the global, regional, national, local or, even, subjective scale.

Thoughts on the Floor

In the process of unpacking the title of this book in such substantive terms, I have sought to presage some of the central themes of the ensuing chapters as well as identify some of the academic challenges that impact upon what is, in all fairness, a somewhat grandiose undertaking. Taken as a whole, transnationalism scales up the central problematic of reception studies quite considerably. To tackle this, we must seek new ways to conceptualize the implicit connectivity between internal cognition, environmental conditions, patterns in communication flows, and social imaginaries of varying strengths and dispositions. To prepare the ground, at least, an extended exploration of different configurations of transnational audience formations seems warranted. This will naturally involve the juxtaposition of different scales, but also the uncovering of different registers through which we can interrogate the interactions between media flows and the cultural geography of a diverse world. My account will also remain attentive to the temporal dimension, which I will periodically allude to in terms of the evolution of both media technologies and academic thinking. The outlook of studies in transnational communication has itself changed profoundly from the Cold War period in which it began, through the high tide of decolonization, the millennial triumph of neoliberal globalization, and into the present contingencies of neo-pragmatism and the return of the Great Game.

At a practical level, the primary purpose of the book is to support readers who are setting out to research transnational audiences in a wide variety of settings. I have attempted to do this by collating and inter-relating the many factors that I see as being relevant to that task. Whether I have been successful, or not, will be determined by the extent to which the various discussions brought together here become pertinent to actual research projects and the data they collect. In that respect, transnational perspectives on mediation will really bear fruit as and when they allow us to calibrate a broad spectrum along which we can zoom in and out. If we can accommodate scale, and that is a big if, we can understand transnational relationships as occurring between both individuals and mass movements, and between both specific localities and broad regions. At this point, a more effective synthesis of research on a global scale becomes conceivable. At the very least, a transnational model of media reception should not be reduced to the comparison of one administrative zone with another, because this would simply reconstitute an *inter*national mode of enquiry. In considering the alternatives, our present theoretical understanding of transnational audiences draws upon a number of distinct explanations of human culture that describe the meeting points between reception studies and media geography. At this early stage, we have many of the pieces laid out around us and should now proceed to work on the larger puzzle.

Part 1

Imagined Worlds: National, International, Transnational

2   The Nationalization of Media Audiences

From the outset, we must question the privileged status of the national framework adopted by media studies. How did the media come to be so comprehensively nationalized? Given that any 'media history' needs to be aligned with a wider set of histories, it is also prudent to consider how the idea of the national itself developed over the period in question. In that respect, it is obviously significant that modern nationalism as we experience it today is scarcely much older than the mass media systems that concern us here. A firm birth date remains a matter of debate amongst historians, but for our purposes, it was the long nineteenth century that witnessed the great evolution of civic nationalism and its steady transformation into the cultural nationalism that prevailed across much of the world in the twentieth century. So, without making this too much of a history lesson, the key thing to bear in mind is that the rise of the mass media and the rise of nationalism occurred in parallel. This is why the most influential thinkers on nationalism have all tended to see the mass media as being absolutely central to the spread of nationalism and to the present form of the nation state. Conversely, for those scholars focusing on media history, it is widely accepted that the institutions of the nation state have played a vital role in the development of everyday media (for example, Winston 1998).

Cultural Nationalism in the World System

While we can identify a number of cogent geopolitical, technical and economic factors behind the linking of mass communication and national audiences, our basic conception of the role of culture is critically important. Thinking about culture on a national basis has become a predominant way of thinking about our own place in the world, and about the geography of humanity more broadly. Like most things that we take for granted, this is far from being a simple matter. Culture, as Raymond Williams (1983) famously said, is one of the most complicated words in the English language. It carries a whole host of meanings, and the present epoch of mass media and consumerism has massively expanded the usage of the term. We can talk blithely in everyday conversations about the glories of 'classical culture' and about our fondness for 'café culture', while complaining about the everyday psychosis of 'office culture' or, indeed, about the 'culture of complaint' that has taken hold in heavily mediated social systems. It is obvious, from the start, that these are hardly 'cultures' in the same fashion. Various forms of the expressive arts have maintained a strong claim over the term culture since the nineteenth century, but the notion of cultures of behaviour has become increasingly widespread since the 1960s. Above these competing and very modern usages of the word, the idea of national and ethnic cultures as overarching frameworks for determining the identities of just about everybody in the world holds sway.

In everyday usage, the word culture variously denotes artistic endeavours, social behaviours and environments, as well as linguistic, racial and religious identities. Consequently, classical culture, café culture and the culture of complaint are all components of an intrinsically French culture, to be distinguished from a transplanted American 'mall culture' or the equally vigorous whingeing of the nearby English. Thus, we tend to begin from the more or less explicit observation that human society is variable in forms of expression and behaviours across different regions and populations. These differences are recognized officially in the phrase 'cultural diversity', which encapsulates the notion that human differences operate at the level of language, spiritual belief systems, socializing rituals, kinship structures, moral regulation, cultural performance and formal political organization. With the important exception of the latter, these factors are all seen as contributing towards a sense of collective identity. Since social knowledge is seen to be both expressed and received through an overlapping set of culturally distinctive processes, there is a further implicit assumption that human difference in its present form is to a certain degree determined by the stability of cultural forms. This is why successive generations of English-speaking children are compelled to read Shakespeare and play football. Given that the vast majority of social communication now takes place via media technologies, the mass media are inevitably seen as having a profound effect upon the existing order of cultural diversity. We can, and probably should, think about cultural diversity in any number of ways. We could, for example, think about differences between generations, social classes and professions, or about preferences in politics, sexuality or consumption (all, arguably, matters of taste). Nonetheless, the distinctions of culture in our present world system are primarily made on the basis of ethnicity.

The precise meaning of the word ethnic, derived from the Greek *ethnikos*, is 'outsiders', although its contemporary use more typically denotes social groupings identified on linguistic, racial and/or religious grounds. Prior to the middle of the twentieth century, the word 'race' would have been more commonly used, but the hierarchy of racial supremacy fashioned in the colonial world was progressively discredited by the eclipse of European colonialism, the Jewish Holocaust and the American civil rights movements. With 'racism' publicly eschewed, the somewhat nebulous concept of ethnicity has taken its place, marking a shift from understanding human differences in terms of innate racial characteristics towards a system of differences based upon the cultural practices of distinct 'ethnicities'. In an age of nationalism, this anthropological scheme of human difference has had enormous political significance. One reason for this is the critical juncture that takes place with the acceptance of the principle of 'self-determination' as famously expounded by US president Woodrow Wilson in 1918. If all peoples have the fundamental right to choose their own government, and the definition of peoples is primarily made on the basis of ethnicity, then this implies that each and every ethnic group should have its own nation state. In all likelihood, this was hardly what Wilson had in mind (since he wasn't proposing self-government for African-Americans), but the inexorable combination of self-government and ethnic particularity has driven the worldwide phenomenon of *cultural* nationalism for most of the last century.

Without a specified cultural component (as in simply 'we, the people') the liberal ideal of nationalism merely implies that each and every citizen should have common rights and responsibilities, not that they should have a common culture or ethnicity. When compared to the autocratic monarchies and Empires of the eighteenth century, *liberal* nationalism can thus be seen as a democratic and inclusive alternative to aristocratic privilege and, typically, long-distance and self-interested government. By contrast, *cultural* nationalism further implies that citizenship is predicated upon common membership of a single ethnic group, which generates a political crisis in any territory where there is an ethnically diverse population. Over the past 150 years, this very modern 'crisis of culture' has given rise to new national federations, the dissolution of Empires, civil wars and mass migration. It has furnished statehood for numerous peoples of the world, bloody genocides for others, and various state-sponsored programmes of cultural re-education designed to achieve the assimilation of 'ethnic minorities'. Nonetheless, after all of this social engineering and much bloodshed, hardly any nation in the world has an ethnically homogeneous population in the twenty-first century. Consequently, governments devote a huge amount of resources to managing the 'problem' of ethnicity close to home, while loudly celebrating cultural diversity at the United Nations. Since both xenophobia and cosmopolitanism draw their legitimacy from matching ethnicity and culture it becomes as difficult to separate the two terms as it is to decouple them from the political process.

Precisely because cultural nationalism is the most widespread and influential political ideology of the modern world, any cultural analysis of nationalism faces a particular set of conceptual problems. National frameworks provide the systematic parameters for discussing culture, but contemporary nationalism in itself, from a historical perspective, is a phenomenon of culture. If we add the functional inseparability of media systems and contemporary culture, then it is far more practical to simply correlate culture, ethnicity, entertainment, communication and political rights than it is to try and untangle them. Nonetheless, if we want to understand transnational communication, then we have to denaturalize, and then interrogate, the implications of a cultural-nationalist world system for mass media and their audiences. For opposite reasons, the majority of strictly national media studies also tend to be prefaced with references to the work of renowned historians of nationalism such as Ernest Gellner (1983, 1998), Benedict Anderson (1991, 1998) and Anthony Smith (1988, 1998, 1999). Whilst there are important differences between the explanations they offer, all of their respective positions rest centrally upon the role they attribute to culture, and they also implicate the mass media as a prerequisite for the emergence of modern nation states. As such, the ways in which culture is defined in such theories become absolutely central to our understanding of the linkages between media and nation.

The Standardization of Cultures

Ernest Gellner (1983, 1998) takes a notably functional approach to the question of culture in modern societies. Essentially, Gellner sees cultural processes as serving the purpose of creating a 'common literacy' that underpins the rise of national systems. Looking back, Gellner notes that the cultures of the pre-industrial epoch in Europe were emphatically non-national in character. Prior to the nineteenth century, social hierarchies were rigid and constituted a huge cultural divide between rulers and ruled. The 'high culture' of the aristocracy was typically supra-national and provided a shared reference for elite groups, while the 'low cultures' of the masses were extremely local. Gellner thus contrasts pan-continental aristocratic high cultures with a large number of local peasant cultures, themselves far too small to constitute anything as big as a national space. He subsequently claims that the organizing principle for the role of culture changed radically with the advent of modern society. Modern industrial society requires large numbers of peasant low cultures to be re-located into urban centres. Consequently, the distinct dialects and idiosyncratic customs of regional cultures necessitated a higher degree of standardization in order to create the huge workforce needed to populate the new factories and workshops. Correspondingly, the project of industrial modernity rested upon an improved and standardized field of communication that was made possible by the adoption of an official script, vocabulary and grammar. This regularized state language was disseminated through the combination of print media and an increasingly inclusive (and thereby, monopolistic) system of education.

The administration of these standards had to take place at the state level, since only the machinery of state could provide the mechanism by which such a rapid standardization of language and culture could be achieved. This top-down process is at the root of all the modern institutions that constitute the nation state: schools and universities, the press, bureaucracy and industry alike. These new 'national' idioms were defined by clerical elites serving the commercial and political interests of the state, and then handed down to the population. Nonetheless, the creation of standardized national languages and universal systems of education was, and still is, in all cases dependent upon media technologies and massive investments in literacy. As Gellner notes:

> The capacity to either articulate or comprehend context-free messages is not an easy one to acquire. It requires schooling, prolonged schooling. And modern society, given that work is semantic in this manner, requires everyone to possess this skill. It is the first society in history in which literacy is near universal . . . And the communication must take place not merely in a 'high' (i.e. codified, script-linked, educationally transmitted) code, but in a definite code, say Mandarin Chinese or Oxford English. That is all. It is this which explains nationalism: the principle – so strange in the age of agrarian cultural diversity and of the 'ethnic' division of labour – that homogeneity of culture is the political bond, that mastery of (and one should add, acceptability in) a given high culture . . . is the precondition of political, economic and social citizenship. (Gellner 1998: 29)

However prosaic the motives may have been, the common instruction of all citizens quickly formed the basis for a larger scale of community and identity. Standard print languages thereby activated the connection between culture and political identity which had been dormant in pre-industrial society. Mass literacy induces a common culture on a larger scale, which extends and then solidifies a field of national discourse. In Europe, the political consequences were manifested in the displacement of the plural and stable hierarchies of old dynastic states by the more homogenized, mobile hierarchies of the nation state. The resulting reorientation of political geography saw the unification of the German and Italian speaking peoples into political nations and the disintegration of multilingual states such as Austria-Hungary. The rewards for Europe's standardized cultures can be seen in the transition from localized and low-technology markets to sophisticated and large-scale national industries. The penalty to be paid was an ongoing antipathy towards linguistic diversity within national populations, as regional cultures became subsumed in favour of the new national standard. We can see this clearly in the repression of regional dialects in Britain and France from the late eighteenth century onwards. For our present purposes, however, the larger point is that this very modern relationship between social organization and cultural identity was facilitated by media technologies in the service of economic necessity.

A simple explanation does not make it a simple matter. In the modern world, the disjuncture between the linguistic and political maps of the world is, if anything, heightened by the rise of the principle that they should be conjoined. Nonetheless, the importance of linguistic geography to media studies is quite obvious, since in order to engage any medium of communication it must operate in a language that we can understand. This is a basic functional necessity. Beyond that, the scale of mass media systems inevitably favours the functional supremacy of the larger languages over the smaller ones. As such, English, Spanish or Mandarin language media arise to serve, and then practically reinforce, the predominance of those languages. This, in turn, also prevents the emergence of a single global language. In both respects, the geography of language serves to determine the size and scope of political and media systems to an extent comparable to the way physical and economic geographies have favoured state imperatives in the making of media markets. Where there is a strong geographic and demographic concentration of a language system, there is a greater likelihood of a matching nation state and a language-specific media system that determines the extent of the public sphere and the national audience. Thus, if we watch Italian television, we can expect the content to focus upon the affairs of Italy and to offer entertainment which reflects Italian tastes, settings and social mores.

Imagined Communities

By contrast, Benedict Anderson (1991) has offered an equally influential theory of nationalism focused on the subjective consequences of mass literacy for the popular imagination. For Anderson too, the emergence of modern mass media was an essential component of the concurrent rise of modern nationalisms. However, Anderson's central proposition is that nationalism is not a state-driven process of economic standardization as

Gellner claims, but rather a popular political process that arises from new perceptions of shared social experience.

> I propose the following definition of the nation: it is an imagined political community – and imagined as both inherently limited and sovereign. It is imagined because the members of even the smallest nation will never know most of their fellow-members, meet them, or even hear of them, yet in the minds of each lives the image of their communion . . . The idea of a socio-logical organism moving calendrically through homogeneous, empty time is a precise analogue of the idea of the nation, which is also conceived as a solid community moving steadily down (or up) history. An American will never meet, or even know the names of more than a handful of his . . . fellow-Americans. He [*sic*] has no idea what they are up to at any one time. But he has complete confidence in their steady, anonymous, simultaneous activity. (Anderson 1991: 6/26)

Drawing on the Hegelian example of how reading the newspaper became the modern replacement for morning prayer, Anderson argues that the spread of print media, particularly newspapers, encouraged individuals to imagine themselves as forming part of new, larger and more abstracted social formations. A sense of 'fraternity' arises amongst readers precisely because 'each communicant is well aware that the ceremony he [*sic*] performs is being replicated simultaneously by thousands (or millions) of others of whose existence he is confident, yet of whose identity he has not the slightest notion' (1991: 35). From this perspective, the unifying power of nationalist discourse lies not in the functional needs of the state, but rather in the inherently social nature of storytelling and the abstracted, but powerful, bonds that it forges within its audience. The major effect of mass media systems, therefore, is to produce a radical shift in popular concep-tions of community. For unprecedented numbers of people, their scale of association becomes extended beyond the boundaries of those people they can physically converse with. Instead, the idea of community begins to include all those who shared in the consumption of the same printed word. Thus, the spread of 'print-capitalism . . . made it possible for rapidly grow-ing numbers of people to think about themselves, and to relate themselves to others, in profoundly new ways' (1991: 36).

Anderson saw the press as playing a central role in creating national readerships, in many cases before a corresponding nation state had come into being. Drawing upon his knowledge of Southeast Asia and Latin America, Anderson discusses how the popular ideal of nationalism took hold in these areas and mobilized populations in the pursuit of statehood and self-government. Thus, while Anderson also describes print technolo-gies as an industrial catalyst for the rise of nationalism, it is not the process of standardization but the scale of ideas introduced by the mass media that holds the greater significance. The concept of an 'imagined community' forged by popular sentiment and social communication encourages us to think of the nation as a contingent, dynamic and mediated event. As the rapid global diffusion of print-capitalism facilitated an increasingly universal imagination of modern forms of nationhood, its influence was compounded by parallel developments of the nation space. Cartography, the census and the building of museums all set territorial, demographic and cultural boundaries around newly imagined national spaces and displayed them for shared viewing and identification by an *audience* of literate citizens (Anderson 1991: 163–85). Extending this process, the proliferation of other forms of mass-media culture like radio and television sequentially strengthened the social bonds between performance, perception and political imagination (Anderson 1998).

The 'imagined community' as a nationalizing force driven by print-capitalism has two primary limitations: comprehension and persuasion. In terms of the former, the central role played by standardized print-language in creating national awareness is at once unifying and divisive. It is unifying because it brings together as fellow readers populations previously sundered by distance, dialect and/or foreign rule. It is divisive because the sheer diversity of spoken human language places limitations upon the reach of any standardizing print-language, and thus the communities which can be imagined through it. As such, linguistic geography proves once again to be a salient factor, but in this model there is also the scope of symbolic and emotive appeal to be considered. The persuasive appeal of an imagined community to any individual is predicated upon the inclusive or exclusive nature of representation. Each individual must be able to identify themselves as being spoken to, and as being one amongst like others. Therefore, the centralizing concepts around which a national imaginary is formulated might be (either singly or in combination) racial, dynastic, ideological, theological or geographic, but the particular discursive formation put forward in each case will of necessity set limits upon its persuasive power. After all, it is hard to create fraternal instincts from performances which exclude or deride people 'like' you. Some people get fuzzy patriotic feelings from reading the UK's *Daily Mail*, but many do not.

Ethnicity and Mythology

At variance with his contemporaries, the classical historian Anthony Smith has disputed the premise that the nation is 'recent and novel' and a 'product of modernisation and modernity' (Smith 2000: 47). For Smith, the phenomenon of nationalism has a longer term historical presence. In his view, national cultures are powerfully embedded within an 'ethno-cultural subconscious' found amongst any given population. Hence, the fundamental appeal of modern nationalisms emanates from the inherent desires of the people to assert their ethno-cultural particularity. From this perspective, the driving force behind the rise of cultural nationalism is the 'shared memories' buried in the subconscious of various ethnic groups, along with a necessary sense of attachment to a historic national territory. The definition of a normative nation for Smith is 'a named human population sharing an historic territory, common myths and historical memories, a mass, public culture, a common economy and common legal rights and duties for all members' (1999: 11). Smith explains the absence of nationalist movements in past historical periods by suggesting that 'ethno-nationalisms' have been latent rather than absent, and therefore simply awaiting an opportunity to assert themselves in the form of nation states. These pre-modern social imaginaries, dubbed 'ethnies' by Smith, have served to define the essential 'core' populations that create an 'authentic' national consciousness in the modern world.

Smith concedes that modernity has a powerful transformative effect upon pre-modern ethnies (which result in demands for autonomy and statehood) but nonetheless claims that modernity is not the ultimate creator of such desires. If there is no hegemonic ancient myth of cultural particularity and sacred homeland amongst the population, then there can be no viable nationalism, since 'what gives nationalism its power are the myths, memories, traditions and symbols of ethnic heritages and the ways in which a popular living past has been, and can be, rediscovered and reinterpreted' (Smith 1999: 9). In that respect, the key term in Smith's definition of nationalism is the 'shared historical memory' of the ethnie. In *Myths and Memories of the Nation*, he defines this 'essential element' of human identity as:

> a reflective consciousness of personal connection with the past . . . later generations carry shared memories . . . of the experiences of earlier generations of the same collectivity . . . defined, first of all by a collective belief in common origins and descent, however fictive . . . and thereafter by shared historical memories associated with a specific territory which they regard as their 'homeland'. On this basis arises a shared culture. (1999: 208)

Thus, myths of racial origin and sacred territory are the real basis for nations, which originate amongst the 'people' rather than the elites, and are enforced through 'oral traditions of the family, clan or community, and its religious specialists . . . sometimes overshadowed by canonical texts – epics, chronicles, hymns, prophecies, law-codes, treatises, songs and the like – as well as by various forms of art, crafts, architecture, music and dance' (1999: 208). Once more, cultural production in all forms is inextricably linked with social reproduction. In this instance, the primary function of culture is the assertion of ethnic particularity amongst members of a social group and the transmission of this identity from one generation to another. Thus, it is not functional integration, but rather symbolic association which motivates nationalist sentiments and thereby shapes our present state system. Ethnic symbolism predates modernity and the mass media, but reaches maturity when these forces allow it to extend its ambitions to the attainment of state-hood. Consequently, the a priori fact of cultural diversity makes a system of ethnically specific nations inevitable. Nationalism, as such, rests upon cultural identities that are ethnic in their formulation. Cultural practices enact performances of ethnic particularity as their primary function. From this perspective, we have to understand linkages between media and nation as being centred upon ethnic particularity, rather than linguistic standards or social imagination. Since Smith argues that ethnic consciousness emerges from the long sweep of history, any form of representation and its wider meanings will be shaped in the first place by the ethnicity of its producer and their audience. This formulation has critical implications for national media systems and for the state system, since 'true' nations must have an ethnic majority population with a common culture situated in an historic territory.

By Smith's own admission, this does not bode well for multicultural or colonial societies, of which there are many. In such instances, their claim to nationhood becomes predicated upon the use of state institutions to impose the ethnic consciousness of a dominant group. This might be, by his examples, English settlers in North America or the Javanese in Indonesia. However, such forms of cultural domination seem unlikely to overwrite deep historical memories of difference amongst the minority groups, and so the national space will remain partially undermined by the presence of 'outsiders' within the national space. Smith insists that ethnicities can accommodate processes of assimilation and exchange whilst remaining cohesive, and that they can be inclusive rather than simply exclusive. Yet the very premise of his theory seems to suggest that this must be a subordi-nate process compared to the overwhelming strength of ethnic particularity on which his ethno-symbolic approach to history is founded. We might also note that while Smith concentrates solely upon the 'symbolism' of ethnicity, the 'inherited' nature of his 'shared historical memories' carries genealogical and, therefore to some extent, racial overtones. In the present day, if we do accept this coupling of culture and nation, then we would naturally expect the United States or India to develop ethnically specific channels rather than national media forums. We could also anticipate pan-Arab and pan-Malay media audiences and, ultimately, nation states. At the very least, we have to remain attentive to the close connections between the concepts of culture and ethnicity that currently prevail, and their symbolic representation via media systems.

Reading from the Songsheet

When we consider the varying explanations of nationalism provided by historians, the central importance of the culture concept to the arrangement of the modern world is clearly evident. We are duly reminded, amongst the multitudinous studies of fleeting fashions in form and style, that cultural studies is a serious business after all. As we have seen, the 'big' explanations of nationalism all rest upon the role of culture and all propose, in various ways, that nationalisms require media technologies to achieve their goals. Indeed, paradoxically, they invest strongly in the very notion of 'powerful' media effects that has been contested so strongly by scholars in cultural studies. Beyond this commonality, the theories of nationalism discussed here place different degrees of emphasis upon economic, linguistic, idealistic and ethnic imperatives. They can also be differentiated in terms of where they see the motivations for nations arising, whether from the elites or the masses. History, then, can be read in a number of ways. The way we read it inevitably gives rise to a certain model of culture and subsequently a particular set of roles for media systems and, by extension, an equally distinctive set of audience formations.

Teach Your Children

Certain media, such as television, are highly dependent upon linguistic specificity, and thereby provide a useful case for Gellner's arguments. Taking the British example, the press, radio and television were all used heavily in the promotion of 'BBC English' (or 'received pronunciation') as a standard dialect until the 1970s. It was only at this point, as the extension of the political franchise took hold, that 'common' patterns of speech and regional differences began to be commonly heard in the media. In many respects, this democratization of the linguistic field only became permissible once print and broadcasting had already erased many of the differences between regional variants of English or, at least, made non-metropolitan citizens conversant in the favoured accent of the state. For speakers of other languages, there was longer to wait. It wasn't until 1982 that Welsh language television was introduced in Britain. As such, even within a relatively well-established and largely monolingual national space, language can remain a site of contest. Gellner's 'that is all' theory of nationalism would likely deny the culturally specific claims of any national aesthetics, but he would doubtless have identified that a group of language-specific media domains would be a logical outcome of modernity. A long-imminent breakthrough in translation software seems likely to break down some of the functional barriers between linguistic zones, but even in the present era of the Internet, a range of language standards remain necessary to ensure effective communication between distant writers and readers.

Gellner also clearly positions culture as a functional appendage of the economic base of modern societies, dispersed in a top-down fashion through literacy programmes. Accordingly, he would most likely have seen national media systems as a viable mechanism for transmitting knowledge and skills to the national population. By this reading, culture is largely a matter of mutual comprehension. Equally, if our need for it derives from our economic function, then the hours we spend online as a child are primarily intended to furnish our adult usefulness as a data retrieval clerk. Adding a layer to established codes, digital technologies have themselves given rise to their own language systems, including a veritable horde of descriptors, concepts and expressions that must be mastered, lol (Hale 2006; Baron 2008). In both respects, media systems address practical matters of literacy and their audiences can be conceived in largely instructional terms. That is, if they become articulate and economically productive, then their schooling has been successful. Certainly, there is some merit in Gellner's emphasis on media technologies as skills systems, an aspect rarely considered in audience research (at least, when it is conducted outside of the context of formal education). If we consider the massive public investments made over the past twenty years in digital literacy campaigns, along with their justification as a critical requirement for national populations needing to compete in a globalized knowledge economy, then Gellner's functionalism takes on a more contemporary edge.

You May Say I'm A Dreamer

Drawing from liberal nationalism in the colonial world, Benedict Anderson naturally looks beyond language for the determining factor in nationalism. His is a consciously proletarian model, where national cultures are popular in their origins. Nationalisms arise from the enlargement of social consciousness at the grassroots. Anderson's model of imagined community is media-centric, in that he claims it was the spread of mass communication that brought these new political affinities into being. In this model, mass media function as a powerful nation-builder. In a popular context, Anderson's particular emphasis on the constructed-ness of nationhood and the socializing force of audience participation gives far greater scope to what forms of nation can be imagined. While various elite groups may enjoy a high degree of control over the means of communication, the participatory and narrated nature of effective national imaginaries compels them to cajole and persuade, rather than simply instruct, the imagined communities in whose name they claim power. As the central interlocutor in all of these processes, media systems provide an essential site of dialogue, and hence a prerequisite, for any national imaginary. The broad equation of mutual sentiment with national symbolism thereby facilitates a critical engagement with the participatory and popular aspects of nationalism. As such, the imagined communities concept can be readily applied to disparate nationalisms arising from a wide range of political and social contexts. The larger point, perhaps, is that if the legitimacy of imagined communities is established through discursive relationships, then those communities are subject to negotiation. This opens up the tantalizing possibility of social change via collective mediation. Most likely that is why Anderson's concept of the imagined community has been particularly influential in media studies.

For text-based researchers, it is Anderson's broad notion of a collective symbolic imagination that justifies the reading of media texts as allegorical 'imaginative' renditions of national cultures or subcultures. Unravelling these narratives with the sophisticated toolkit of contemporary discourse analysis allows researchers to reveal the depth and complexity of the preferred readings encoded in national media content. These 'meanings' are implicitly taken to represent a collective popular imagination operating within the society in question, that is, the presumed audience. Suspicious of hypothetical spectators, audience researchers generally prefer to align specific media content with a sociologically recognizable 'community' sample whose collective 'imagination' can be read off a sample of qualitative commentaries or responses to media content. Under both paradigms, the majority of media studies using the 'imagined communities' model tend to emphasize the creative agency that flows from the active process of imagination amongst media consumers. Paradoxically, however, there is a strong tendency to present both the textual evidence and the sample responses from audiences as generalizable accounts from which we can infer coherent imagined communities at a larger scale (see Athique 2008a). As such, it may be worth noting that while Anderson suggests that mediation encourages us to perceive the presence of imagined others within a common social formation, he does not necessarily claim that individuals will imagine these abstractions in a singular and quantifiable fashion. Put more simply, we may all imagine a national community, but need not imagine it in the same way.

Time (Is On My Side)

Adopting a classicist outlook, Smith sees the spread of mass communication enabling historical genealogies to assert themselves. Thus, for him, all forms of culture are primarily ordained to transmit and maintain inherited ethnic specificities. Accordingly, Smith's ethno-symbolic approach positions culturally specific national media systems as a central mechanism for maintaining social cohesion through the perpetuation of traditions. The national media thereby stage a series of national performances that establish the primacy of a 'majority' ethnic mythology. If we look for evidence of this in terms of media content, we could turn again to the BBC and its particular investment in historical documentaries and more general heritage programming (including the interminable Victoriana of period dramas and the scrutiny of historical relics in the attic, on the high street and under the ground). In most other contexts, we can also identify a significant body of national media programming drawing upon the 'great and glorious history' of the nation in question and the achievements of its various forefathers. The promotion of classical arts on Indian state television, Hollywood's dramatization of the settlement of the 'Wild West', or Japan's re-working of the Samurai cult would all fit this mould. Across the board, regularized programming in support of religious events, folk festivals and artistic canons all serve to articulate traditional forms and outlooks. Taking a less historical line, we could also identify the evocations of sacred territory and the contest of ethnically marked bodies in international sports. Taking a less literal line, an anthropologist would look for the markers of ethnic specificity in forms of speech, social mannerisms, familial systems and moral values across all forms of content.

The linkages between media content and the putative centrality of indigenous ethnicity can often be tenuous, however, and much depends on how much we want to stretch or determine the nebulous meaning of ethnicity itself. Nonetheless, the central premise of Smith's argument is that people feel compelled to perform their ethnic specificity and that is what culture is for. Accordingly, we would expect to find ethnicity, not only as a predominant trope in media narratives, but also as a central concern of audience respondents and a recognizable feature of audience demand. The accompanying model of reception that is implied by Smith's claim is common to many national media analyses. It is characterized by an attempt to conjoin what I will define here as the 'reflective' and 'effective' capacities of media representation. The *reflective* capacity of media analysis asserts that media texts can somehow capture and represent the symbolic essence of the producing nation. After achieving this feat, media productions can be read as evidence of the visual, aural and narrative form of a nationally specific aesthetic. On this basis we come to believe that media productions demonstrate in some fashion the cultural identity, behaviours and beliefs of the society from which they originate. Conversely, the accompanying claims for an *effective* capacity of national media relate to the presumed power of the media as a socializing force with a degree of agency in developing national idioms. As an effective representation, media productions are taken to have a persuasive impact upon the cultural identity, behaviours and beliefs of their audiences. Thus, national representations do not merely capture the national essence, they also transmit it to the audience in a didactic fashion. Taking both aspects together, we are given to assume that the media not only captures who we are, but also reminds us who we are.

Reading National Audiences

If we employ the confluence of media, culture and nation as a starting point then our attention is naturally directed towards first identifying the essence of national belonging, often in ways that bear little relationship to the formal bureaucratic conditions of citizenship. Unsurprisingly, then, studies of national media formations tend to deploy a model of reception that emphasizes the ways in which national media content reinforces, or even creates, distinctly national audiences. Within that framework, there are many further questions to be asked of their mediated constituencies, especially in an era of mass consumption, big bureaucracies and electoral government. Contemporary states have a natural interest in the efficacy and range of national media systems as a socializing force. It is equally obvious that, in various ways, the development of national media 'brands' has been driven by large-scale economic competition between states and by the need for functional coherence and mass literacy in industrial societies. At a more fundamental level, the present state system predisposes close linkages between culture and nation as a requisite for our prevailing political ideology. Nationalism, having supplanted 'god and man' and 'king and country', offers us a doctrine of 'us and them'. Within the field of difference that this creates as an international system, distinctive national brands are generously employed to identify competitors as well as promote both products and influence.

While discussions of national media industries may have a comparative (and even outward) orientation, our approach to national audiences has been consistently parochial. The fundamental logics of cultural nationalism stipulate that audiences will, should and must congregate around commonalities of language, citizenship and ethnicity. If such a confluence is taken as the primary purpose of cultural interaction, it follows that people should be most interested in communications with their cultural compatriots and in representations of people most like themselves. As such, when addressing audiences at the national level, there is an obvious tendency to focus upon whether the majority ethnic culture is being threatened by foreign media imports or diluted by subcultures. Such concerns pair cultural nationalism with the effective role of media. At a more instrumental level, we also commonly seek to assess what forms of mediation are capturing the imagination of the nation at a given time, since national audiences are constituencies to be wooed by advertisers, media creators and politicians alike. However, we rarely question our underlying assumptions about the homogenizing concept of the national audience or the perceived links between culture, citizenship and place that it tends to imply. We instead proceed from a basic assumption of a common media culture amongst which national content enjoys 'resident' status. Any 'non-resident' model of media consumption therefore has to begin from audiences that fall outside of the normative viewing position established through national markets and nationalist ideologies.

Recommended Reading

Benedict Anderson (1991) *Imagined Communities: Reflections on the Origins and Spread of Nationalism*, London: Verso.

Stewart Anderson and Melissa Chakars (2014) *Modernization, Nation-building and Television History*, London and New York: Routledge.

Michael Billig (1995) *Banal Nationalism*, Thousand Oaks: Sage.

Ernest Gellner (1998) *Nationalism*, London: Phoenix.

Mette Hjort and Scott Mackenzie (eds) (2000) *Cinema and Nation*, London and New York: Routledge.

Sabina Mhihelj (2008) *Media Nations: Communicating Belonging and Exclusion in the Modern World*, Basingstoke: Palgrave Macmillan.

John Postill (2006) *Media and Nation-building: How the Iban Became Malaysian*, New York: Berghahn Books.

Anthony D. Smith (1999) *Myths and Memories of the Nation*, Oxford: Oxford University Press.

Graeme Turner (1994) *Making It National: Nationalism and Australian Popular Culture*, St Leonards: Allen and Unwin.

3 · Imperialism, Dependency and Soft Power

While historians tend to situate culture within a series of grand narratives of human development, we must also be attentive to the more particular histories of the moving image. In the accounts we have considered so far, the primary emphasis falls upon the parallel spread of print media and nationalism during the age of empires. It is equally significant that the subsequent development of audiovisual media systems has also taken place alongside a profound change in the political organization of our world. The United Nations, as the international order forged in the period after the Second World War, is a historically unique framework for managing human affairs. Its primary function is the establishment of a jurisdiction above the sovereignty of states, through which inter-state conflicts can be contained and issues of global concern can be addressed by collective instruments. The origins of the UN (and its failed precursor, the League of Nations) lie in a distinctly American critique of the imperialist system of the nineteenth century. In many respects, the broad enthusiasm of American citizens for shaping this kind of 'world government' in the post-war years seems almost antithetical to the contemporary politics of the United States. Nonetheless, the United Nations has been the most significant mechanism for addressing the obvious shortcomings of an earlier international system that relied merely upon pursuing a military balance between the largest powers. The vast majority of today's nations could not have existed prior to the institution of the UN, which seeks to provide a collective guarantee for the sovereign rights of all nation states. In this 'world of nations', a national media industry is not only an internal system of public address but also an essential component of international statehood. So, in defiance of their fiercely internal logics of belonging, contemporary nationalists can never be oblivious to the international dimension. Nations, after all, only make sense in comparison with other nations.

In this context, the questions typically being asked around media systems at the international level tend to revolve around whether a national brand is garnering market share, international goodwill or political influence. This tells us, immediately, that while the present system formalizes political sovereignty on cultural grounds, an attendant assumption of cultural autonomy does not necessarily follow. Prior to the institution of the United

Nations, the predominant culture within each of the most powerful empires had the greatest reach, regardless of the aesthetic value or social benefits of that culture per se. The United Nations system formally disavows the rule of the strongest over the weakest. Nonetheless, while all nations enjoy legal equality over matters of culture, they do not necessarily possess equal means for cultural production, nor do they possess equal range in terms of the bandwidth that each national culture comes to occupy within the world system. Thus, for much of the post-imperial period, the greatest economic and military powers have continued to exert the greatest cultural footprint. It therefore becomes defensible to claim that the form and function of imperialism endures at a cultural level. Given that modern culture has become synonymous with its mediation, and that the history of audio-visual media has been closely aligned with the so-called 'American century' (roughly, since 1917), it is the United States that has most frequently been identified with an 'imperial' dispersal of media content. The precise forms of debate on this issue have evolved over time, as various media systems have reached maturity and the geopolitical situation has continued to evolve. Consequently, any assessment of transnational media flows as agents of imperialism requires an explicitly historical narrative.

Imperial Disputes

Whether the phenomenon of 'cultural imperialism' is considered purposeful or simply inherent, the longstanding presence of American popular culture within other national spaces obviously runs counter to the doctrine of cultural nationalism upon which the present state system rests. To be fair from the outset, there are a number of other states with a significant presence in the cross-border media trade, and thereby a place within a broader field of cultural imperialism. It is also worth noting that the origins of the enduring bogey of 'Americanization' actually predate the United Nations by a number of years. It was not in the era of decolonization, but rather in the inter-imperial disputes of the early twentieth century that American popular culture was first charged with subversion at the international scale. The medium in question was film and the accusation was novel for its time. In the very early years of the cinema at the end of the nineteenth century, conceptions of the medium within a national framework simply did not exist. Driven by commercial aspirations, movie shows spread rapidly around the imperial world, carried first by an eclectic range of individual entrepreneurs and then by a smaller number of consolidating transnational companies. The significant French share of the early motion-picture industry in the United States at the beginning of the twentieth century did not provoke charges of cultural imperialism, nor lead to the erection of trade barriers, in polyglot America. Rather, it was the convulsion of Europe in the Great War of 1914–18 that proved to be the most significant factor in the rise of American movies to worldwide pre-eminence, leading to the re-birth of cinema as a source of national(ist) concern (Thompson 1985).

The 'perils' of transnational media influence became a substantive discourse during the 1920s, when calls emerged for economic protection for the ravaged European film industries (De Grazia 1998: 20). State intervention in the movie market was promoted as a matter of restoring national pride, and, equally, as a way of restoring European industries to their 'rightful' share of international markets. As such, the debates of the 1920s centred firmly on competing imperial interests and international prestige. Tellingly, neither the British nor the French perceived any contradiction between patriotic protectionism at home and perpetuating the export of their own cultural artefacts to their colonial subjects. In that respect, it would certainly be difficult to reconcile the Empire Films resolution adopted by the British Imperial Conference of 1926 with the later framing of national media as a valiant self-defence against American cultural influence (Barnouw and Krishnaswamy 1980; Jaikumar 2006; Skinner 2001). The British Film Institute started life, after all, as the Empire Film Institute. Aside from the inevitable imperial competition between the major economic powers of the day, another contributing factor to the rise of anti-Hollywood rhetoric in Europe between the wars was governmental concern about the 'social influence' of the new medium, both on the lower social orders at home and on imperial subjects abroad (Jarvie 2000: 79–81). Views on the cinema as a potential site for sedition reflected a growing fear of the masses, set against the swift rise of labour movements in Europe and of anti-colonial nationalisms in Asia.

The origins of what would become the 'cultural imperialism' debate therefore display some particular readings of culture and its audience. For the European establishment, culture was substantially a matter of prestige (and thus, of implied superiority). Along with their scientific and technical achievements, the worldwide projection of a sophisticated high culture was absolutely central to their international status as advanced civilizations. In that sense, cultural 'superiority' was a prerequisite for ruling the 'less refined' masses at home as well as claiming the right to tutor the 'less advanced' peoples of the world. This two-faced 'civilizing mission' thereby provided political justification for their continuing military and economic occupation of large parts of the world. American popular culture appeared to threaten the foundations of this 'white elitism' precisely because it eschewed high culture in favour of a more visceral, low-brow mode of entertainment. For Europe's educated elite, the prevailing perception of the new audiences that had arisen with the cinema hall was that they were largely illiterate, emotive and easily influenced. Because movies were accessible without any formal education, they obviously circumvented the checks and balances instilled by systems of rational learning. Following the precepts of modern disciplines such as psychology and sociology, the impact of audio-visual stimuli on the masses was therefore assumed to include enormous behavioural 'effects'. Since this was widely believed to be the case for the majority of the domestic population, the impact upon the 'less developed' mindset of Europe's non-white subjects was taken to be even greater. Across the board, therefore, the majority of the world's population were regarded as simplistic, childlike and easily swayed by flashing lights.

The Second World War between 1939 and 1945 demolished European movie production along with everything else. In the years that followed, the major European states were forced to reinvent themselves as simple nation states rather than imperial powers. In that era of austerity for Europeans, the popularity of cinema as a social institution reached its peak. The Hollywood majors, backed by the US government, were aggressive in securing their hegemony in Western European markets. They also vigorously pursued market dominance in Asia, where the Europeans were being simultaneously compelled to relinquish their colonial presence. In counterpoint, the success of 'neo-realist' filmmakers (originally in Italy) and the growth of *auteurist* cinema across continental Europe laid the aesthetic foundations for a network of nationally defined art cinemas that would culminate in the 'New Wave' movements of the 1960s. The rise of European film criticism thereby contributed rhetorically to discourses of national reconstruction and nationally specific mass cultures, often in a fashion that was explicitly critical of rising American imports. At the same time, the role of cinema itself was changing rapidly with the implementation of television broadcast systems in both Europe and America. For most of Europe, the sheer cost of broadcasting infrastructure and the geographic range of TV transmitters favoured a national level and state-funded approach. In the United States, by contrast, a plural commercial model was driven both by geographical scale and the private sector. On both sides of the Atlantic, the growth of mass consumerism and the resulting explosion in the market for popular culture provided the impetus for sustained academic research into the social effects of television broadcast. Very much dominated by 'media effects' models, this was the historical context in which audience studies came of age.

Cultures of Decolonization

Elsewhere in the world, even greater changes were taking hold. Indeed, the collapse of European imperialism in Asia and Africa between 1947 and 1994 can be seen as the major geopolitical event of the twentieth century. This drawn-out process was not merely the result of war fatigue, but also the long anticipated outcome of local nationalist movements that had pursued independence from the beginning of the century. The political map of the world was recast as the inhabitants of India, Indonesia and Indo-China achieved statehood between 1947 and 1954. A parallel process occurred in North Africa and the Middle East, and the rest of Africa would subsequently follow in the great wave of 'decolonization' that created the 'Third World'. For the most part, these 'new' countries inherited underdeveloped economies and narrow state institutions, and only very rarely did they possess the luxury of anything like a media industry. As fledgling nation states, they would nonetheless pursue the goal of realizing national media systems. This was typically seen both as a crucial component of a modern state and as a necessary vehicle for postcolonial governments to communicate with their citizens. Beyond its purely functional purpose, the shaping of a postcolonial public sphere had powerful cultural connotations. In most cases, the cause of an 'indigenous' culture had been mobilized in driving out rulers from an alien culture. At the same time, however, the leaders of the great anticolonial movements were themselves mostly graduates of colonial systems of education that framed the world from the perspective of the European colonizers. This dichotomy was perceived keenly by the radical Afro-French thinker and Algerian revolutionary, Franz Fanon, who argued that the politicians and intellectuals of the new nations had been infected by the logics of the imperial power, and were thus intrinsically separated from the vast bulk of the populations they sought to rule (Fanon 1967).

For Fanon, the recovery of a 'native' subjectivity was critical, since without such a shift there could be no meaningful liberation. Fanon's prescient critique of a 'neocolonial' class of leaders adopting the role of their former masters would be keenly felt throughout the postcolonial world. It also highlighted the residual power of a cultural influence that had been constructed over several centuries. Looking forward, Fanon's call for a 'decolonization of the mind' and a 'native awakening' constituted a sweeping rejection of the purported cultural superiority of the Western world. His plaintive call to restore cultural authenticity on the basis of folk traditions drawn from the peasantry would prove seductive, but putting it into practice was no simple matter. The majority of postcolonial states had been constructed with little regard to the cultural identity of their inhabitants. As such, they were commonly home to several different cultures, and the question of whose culture should be elevated to the centre of national life was difficult and frequently dangerous. Indeed, attempts to 'revive' various indigenous cultures as the core of postcolonial states have commonly led to repetitions of the tragedies that shook Europe earlier in the century. From the five rivers of the Punjab to the marshes of Mesopotamia and the jungles of the Congo, the cultural nationalisms of the Third World would also prove to be bloody affairs. Echoing the thoughts of Chairman Mao, the elevation of peasant cultures suggested by Fanon would frequently see the old elites of Asia swept away, with the decolonization of the mind taking a particularly violent turn in the cultural revolutions that followed. In that sense, Fanon's repositioning of revolutionary Marxism on racial lines was readily combined with a cultural militancy that manifested the extremes of both left and right.

Nonetheless, the fundamental premise of Fanon's argument was widely accepted: that the cultural legacy of imperialism was deep and enduring and that it must be confronted. Otherwise, the internalization of an ongoing inferiority complex would guarantee continued subservience under a new flag. Following Fanon, the Palestinian intellectual Edward Said would later describe in great detail how the 'Orient' had been symbolically constructed as the 'other' to European civilization. This image had been formalized in a panoply of representations carried in print and on screen. This 'orientalism' not only underpinned the self-image of white racism, it also diffused a distorted vision of the non-Western world that was subsequently internalized by the colonized subjects themselves (Said 1978). At the heart of Fanon's righteous anger and Said's careful deconstruction lies their identification of culture as an essential constituent of human dignity. Similarly, they both seek to illustrate the various ways in which culture is utterly intertwined with an ongoing geopolitical struggle, one in which the cultures of Africa and Asia had long been trammelled by the boots of imperialism. These were concerns that brought together many nations of the 'developing world', from parliamentary India to the Arab monarchies and revolutionary Cuba. In this framing, cultural autonomy becomes more than a matter of prestige, serving instead as a necessary precondition for economic and political independence. Thus, the cultural politics of the anti-colonial movements were heavily invested in the recovery of 'native' cultures that had been suppressed or denigrated by colonial rule. The lingering presence of the colonial culture, in its broadest sense, was seen as an active component within the broader process of domination.

In that respect, thinkers like Fanon and Said fully accepted the strongest notions of pervasive media influence. Western dominance of the media trade was described as a key component of imperial domination in the field of international communication. Under the terms of this critique, the premise of media effects is powerfully extended by the recognition of a long-term and all-encompassing process of foreign influence as an historical fact. Following Marx, the form and content of colonial culture was taken to represent a coherent ideology that guided the imperial system and made its operation possible. Where foreigners ruled, their ideas ruled, and vice versa. Imperialism was thereby defined as a pervasive and systemic form of global domination, entrenched by many centuries of formal and informal subjugation. For this reason, the mass media, whose provenance was Western, were as politically suspect as they were practically essential to modernization and 'development'. Since imperial ideas were internalized as much by the dominated as they were by their masters, colonial audiences were seen as having been acculturated to view themselves through the eyes of foreigners. For their part, Western representations of non-Western subjects were seen to systematically denigrate entire cultures, thereby encouraging those colonized audiences to become disconnected from their own cultural identity. Fanon and Said argued that this process was continuing after the end of formal imperialism, constituting a well-established cognitive disease that required shock treatment. These conclusions motivated a broader call for Third World publics to resist, subvert and ultimately take control of the machinery of representation. In that sense, this rejection of Western culture, of which the United States sought to position itself as the inheritor state, presaged the cultural conflicts that would inspire the 'clash of civilizations' described by Samuel Huntingdon in the 1990s (Huntingdon 1996).

Cultural Imperialism as a World System

The radical phase of anti-colonial struggle in Asia and Africa was reasonably lengthy, and did not reach its full conclusion until the end of South Africa's apartheid regime in 1994. During the 1970s and 1980s, the gulf between developing and developed nations remained wide. Indeed, for much of that time it appeared to be increasing rather than decreasing. The majority of colonial states had won their political independence, but remained economically dependent upon the rich Western countries that had formed the heart of the imperial system. As such, the pace of development rested not so much on the actions of national governments, but rather on the patronage of the former colonial powers or a close relationship to the paramount economy of the United States. The influence of the West, via its leadership of world bodies such as the IMF, its dominance of global education, its international news networks and its worldwide cultural presence, was obvious. As such, the question of cultural imperialism was debated at length, both in academic circles and at the United Nations. UNESCO, as the component of the United Nations charged with matters of education, culture and communication, saw a massive expansion in its membership as new nations came into being. Consequently, UNESCO became more and more critical of the obvious domination of global communications by leading Western nations (the United States in particular, but also the UK and France) (Tomlinson 1991: 70–5). This led to the call for a 'New World Information and Communications Order' and the McBride Report in 1980, as well as later provisions to protect the 'cultural diversity' of the world (Sparks 2007).

The impetus for these resolutions stemmed from a need to counter the structural hegemony of Western media companies as well as the influence of the 'homogeneous global culture' their products purportedly promoted. These 'culture wars' between the developed and developing nations reflected the wider imbalances that characterized what American sociologist Immanuel Wallerstein (1974) called the 'world system'. Although the United Nations formally recognized a patchwork of sovereign nations, Wallerstein described the underlying international order as a single economic system through which a 'core' of rich developed nations extracted resources from the poorer 'peripheral' nations. Given their greater wealth and technological advantage, the core states effectively determined the pathways taken to development by the poorer states. Their motivation in 'leading' the developing world in this way was both paternalistic and intrinsically self-interested. According to Wallerstein, behind the high rhetoric of international co-operation, the relationship between core and periphery continued to be a relationship of exploitation. In essence, then, this was an imperial operation that had less to do with reducing poverty than it had to do with sustaining capitalism. The capitalist model of development promoted by the West, and by the United States in particular, ultimately served to perpetuate the 'dependency' of poorer states upon the richer ones. For this reason, the emerging Third World was being forcibly integrated into global capitalism at a considerable disadvantage. Thus, the new world system of the United Nations operated in a similar fashion to the old imperial system, but this time around domination was conducted indirectly and from a distance.

Paying attention to media flows specifically, the American Mass Communications scholar Herbert Schiller (1969) defined cultural imperialism as an ideological process that was essential to the operation of capitalism as a system of global domination. In a modernizing world, the everyday conduct of cultural imperialism necessarily required the domination of the airwaves. Hence, the success of cultural imperialism relied upon the successful pursuit of media imperialism (that is, establishing a dominant position within the global media apparatus). Evidence for these twin processes could be inferred from the structural domination of 'international' media channels and outlets by Western concerns, from the commercial dominance of Western media producers in the market for content, and from the unparalleled global presence of Western popular culture. In the late twentieth century, the major culprit in the conduct of media imperialism was (allegedly) the United States, whose movies and television shows constituted the vast majority of transnational media flows. Schiller described a global media system where transnational flows are dominated by multinational corporations (MNCs) with an obvious stake in the promotion of capitalist values. Drawing their core support from the rich capitalist countries, the MNCs supplied transnational media exports that effectively dominated the airwaves in developing societies. Given the context in which this material was being produced, the MNCs exported media content that either explicitly or implicitly promoted consumerism and competition as its core values. Schiller thus identified a global media apparatus that was intended to reinforce the power and prestige of capital, to promote consumption as a central ambition in human life, and to link the two within an overarching view of modernity and development.

From this perspective, the central role of advertising in the global media system reflects a broader subjugation of culture to capitalist aims and ambitions. According to Schiller, the United States serves as the hub of this programme, with the form of its own popular culture being absolutely determined by its role within the capitalist system. The overarching thesis of Schiller's argument was that American culture is synonymous with capitalism and, even as formal imperialism was withering away, its underlying motives of capitalist domination were continuing unabated in the cultural domain. During the 1970s, these views became particularly resonant with the Latin American experience, where the forceful presence of US corporations and American foreign policy was paralleled by the dominance of US imports in media programming. It was argued that Latin America, as a whole, had been forced into a pattern of 'dependency' upon the United States and its interests in the region (Cardosso and Faletto 1971). One aspect of this phenomenon was 'cultural dependency', where the role of arts, education and entertainment were all determined by a blueprint established in North America (Salinas and Paldan 1979; Straubhaar 1991). The fact that US media companies had long established themselves as the leading producers for Latin American markets supported the view that their structural dominance of media systems in the Western hemisphere constituted 'media imperialism'. Hegemony in technology and ownership was naturally complemented by a predominance of US programming and local derivatives that aped its genres, topics and perspectives, thereby providing evidence of 'cultural imperialism'. Such a situation implied, to all intents and purposes, that for audiences in the developing world, 'the media are American' (Tunstall 1977).

Like the Afro-Asian critiques of European cultural domination, the Latin American cultural dependency theorists mobilized an equation of culture with ideological influence. In that sense, they had a shared understanding of transnational media flows being inscribed with the power relations inherent to the world system. For Latin American critics, however, the mobilization of an indigenous cultural nationalism was complicated by their shared experience of Iberian colonialism, their very mixed populations and the much earlier establishment of their political independence. The borders of South America are not defined on a cultural basis, its countries share a common imported religion and their own internal hierarchies between European, African and American populations typically preclude the kind of primordialism suggested by Fanon. In many respects, they actually share a great deal of their historical experience with the United States itself, and this affinity itself compounds the problem of dependency. As such, the target of their criticism was primarily the role of US culture in perpetuating political and economic subjugation. In essence, it was international capitalism rather than Caucasian culture that was being contested. By contrast, the earlier European reaction to American cultural imports, which continued well into this period, was characterized by a more obviously conservative reaction to popular culture in general. Here it was populism, as exemplified by US media production, which provoked resistance. Conversely, the various critics of cultural imperialism had relatively little to say regarding the clunky but consistent efforts of the Soviet Union to conduct its own cultural diplomacy around the globe. In that light, despite their significant differences, all of these debates were very firmly located in the historical and geopolitical conditions of decolonization and the Cold War.

New Orders for the New Century

It is obvious that the terms of the cultural imperialism debate were fundamentally recast by the emergence of the 'New World Order' that followed the collapse of the Soviet Union in 1991. From that point, a substantial political bloc devoted to the critique of capitalism no longer existed. Equally, the completion of the long road to decolonization in Asia and Africa by this time also served to dissipate the mobilization of the 'Third World' as a coherent political voice. Thus, the end of the century saw the United States returned to a position of international paramountcy that it had not enjoyed since the early 1960s. The subsequent proclamation of a 'New American Century', however, has since proved to be short lived. Intransigent military conflicts and the steady transfer of economic power towards Asia have sapped the basis of a late imperial revival in the twenty-first century. Nonetheless, in the media sphere specifically, there were two major developments at the close of the twentieth century that had enormous impact upon our understanding of media within the world system. First of all, the rapid growth of satellite television practically superseded the cherished regulatory authority of nation states over broadcast content, heralding an era of transnational television. The second, and even more radical, phenomenon was the rapid take off of the World Wide Web during the latter half of the 1990s. As a truly global system using the backbone of the Internet, the Web created the first integrated global media environment. Thus, the fleeting era of the 'New World Order' became the setting for the great transnational shift in media systems that I will discuss in more detail in the following chapter.

As political, economic and technological realities have continued to evolve in the first two decades of this century, the American share of broadcast content has visibly declined throughout the world. The basic reason for this is that most of the major states around the world have themselves become increasingly prolific producers of media content. In 1991, transnational media corporations were carrying images of American military success into every corner of the world, clearly supporting the dominance of Western players in the production of global narratives. By the 2000s, however, the 'CNN moment' had passed and satellite technology was becoming more significant as an enabler for the diversification of the news environment. Credible alternatives to American and British sources arose in the form of Al Jazeera, ZEE, TV Globo and other transnational networks (Thussu 2007). Brazil, India, Japan and China have all become substantial media producers and are cementing their position as media exporters within their own regions. European states, despite their failure to compete with Hollywood in the international movie market, have successfully established themselves as significant competitors in the international television trade. All in all, by the turn of the century, the global media environment had changed substantially enough for Jeremy Tunstall (2007) to revisit his earlier work and conclude, instead, that 'the media *were* American'. In public perception also, the wider re-emergence of a more multi-polar world narrative has done much to detract from the urgency that had previously driven debates on cultural imperialism.

In some ways, this reassessment is quite contradictory, since the growth of transnational flows theoretically implies a greater volume of imperialist 'effects'. Arguably, the fact that American hegemony in the audiovisual trade is being diluted by the actions of half a dozen other 'media powers' suggests a rebalancing of cultural imperialism, rather than signifying its demise. As a point of comparison, the development of the World Wide Web since 1993 displays some broad parallels with the trajectory taken by television. During the first decade of the Internet boom, the vast majority of the available content was in the English language, the major service providers were all based in the West, and the bulk of users tended to be white, educated English-speakers. Given the dominance of American software and hardware companies over the larger domain of information technology, there was sufficient cause to be concerned about the rapid formalization of another US-centric media system. Even in the United States itself, the far greater levels of Internet access and online representation by educated, white, male citizens in comparison to their opposites quickly raised the spectre of a 'digital divide' between the Internet enabled and the excluded (Hoffman and Novak 1998). This differential was also systematically replicated at the global scale, with the take up of the Web in developed Western nations far outstripping the non-white states of the erstwhile developing world. In that respect, it seemed logical to assume that a technological disparity between different regions would stem from, and then subsequently reinforce, the existing divisions between the developed and developing worlds (Norris 2000).

Digital Sovereignty

The digital divide became a more pressing concern than disparities in broadcasting, because the Internet combines entertainment with telecommunications and information processing. Consequently, the Internet represents a revolutionary logistical system, as much as a content delivery vehicle. As a network system, the value of any web platform or portal increases exponentially with the number of participants. Because much of the 'production' of content on the World Wide Web rests with the audience, it is proportionate access to the system itself that is typically seen to provide the litmus test for inclusion in the information age (Ragnedda and Muschert 2013). In theory, the gains made by individual citizens scale up to macroeconomic advantages due to increases in the reach and efficiency of networked communication (e.g., Tapscott 1995; Peitz and Waldfogel 2012). For both reasons, governments and non-government organizations across the world have deployed substantial resources in promoting Internet take up in all corners of the world. Although the drive towards a Global Information Infrastructure (GII) was initiated by the United States, the dangers of being left behind in the sweeping digitization of the global economy prompted priority investment during the 1990s from those developed and developing nations that could afford it (Malaysia's 'cyber-corridor' being a good example). Nonetheless, embracing the commercial potentials of the medium inevitably entailed facilitating access to large volumes of unvetted foreign content. The purported 'neutrality' of the World Wide Web thereby threatened the earlier role of those individual states as gatekeepers for media content.

It is not surprising, then, that most countries have instituted laws criminalizing particular kinds of immoral and/or seditious material sourced from the Internet. If anything, the individuated access of content via the World Wide Web appears to have been more threatening to culturally conservative or authoritarian states than the mass address of satellite broadcasters. A number of Gulf States, for example, continue to raise objections to the open architecture of the medium. Going further, the People's Republic of China deployed an overarching mechanism in 2003, known as 'great firewall of China', by which Internet content accessed in China is filtered with reference to government restrictions that cover political as much as cultural and moral domains (Zhang and Zheng 2009). The infrastructure that provides the gateways for the World Wide Web in China has also been put very firmly under state control. Effectively, the People's Republic of China has been able to use its growing economic and political influence to determine the creation of a national space on the global Internet. This distinctively sovereign zone is now the largest single user base for the World Wide Web. While we should recognize that such restrictions were an established feature of earlier broadcast systems, they have proved highly controversial in relation to the Internet. In a large part, this is due to the founding principles of open and uncensored access upon which the World Wide Web was established. In international forums, China has consistently been rated negatively in terms of providing the levels of 'Internet Freedom' that have been increasingly taken as a proxy measure of social and political freedom (MacKinnon 2012).

Essentially, we can see those debates as encapsulating an inevitable collision between a particularly strong commitment to state sovereignty and a radical experiment in extending a distinctively American conception of free speech to a global communication system. An initiative of this kind, and its governance by a series of non-governmental actors, obviously disrupts the prevailing notion that political sovereignty is closely linked to an exclusive domain of legislation. At the practical level, the allocation of legal jurisdiction over a global media apparatus that is not meaningfully located in any one country raises numerous and substantial challenges for law enforcement and revenue collection agencies all around the world (Kohl 2007). The legislation that has subsequently emerged in response has itself caused a number of controversies, particularly the Digital Millennium Copyright Act by which the United States claims the right to prosecute violations of US law on the Internet regardless of where the crime allegedly took place (Stokes 2014). This assertion of supra-national jurisdiction could easily be construed as a claim for imperial privileges, although enforcement is another matter entirely. The Megaupload case, involving a US attempt to extradite the New Zealand resident owners of a file-sharing company based (but not accessible) in Hong Kong provides a useful example of the complexities of sovereignty in the digital era (Leslie 2014).

The simultaneous revelations around the overt use of the Internet as a global surveillance system by the National Security Agency (US) and GCHQ (UK) has highlighted the ways in which certain nation states are able to coerce information technology providers and take effective control of the World Wide Web (Greenwald 2014). The claims being made regarding the reach of digital surveillance have highlighted the ease with which state actors can conduct global surveillance by such means, without being restricted by the illegality of those activities in the territories where information is being gathered. The activities of the NSA, as disclosed in documents released by the whistleblower Edward Snowden, have provoked renewed debate around the merits of an international jurisdiction for the World Wide Web. In many respects, the Snowden case provides the inverse scenario to the prior usage of the Internet by the Wikileaks portal to widely distribute confidential data obtained illegally from the United States government to a worldwide public (Beckett and Bell 2012). The illegality of both 'leaks' was firmly established by the raft of digital property and national security instruments enacted in the 2000s and, consequently, the key protagonists have become fugitives living under the diplomatic protection of foreign states for lengthy periods. For our purposes, however, what the Snowden affair brings into sharp focus is the disproportionate power that a small number of countries can wield over the operation of a supposedly 'neutral' Internet. The predominance of US-based software companies, and the status of the regulatory bodies and operating standards governing the Internet, bring into question whether we should consider the present 'global' configuration of the Internet as a demonstrative case of 'media imperialism'.

Hardwired and Software Power

Global access to the Internet ensures that the medium is available to actors across the world, from states to corporations to civil society groups and individuals. Nonetheless, the 'bird's-eye' view of its operation is only available to a relatively small technical elite, who tend to operate from, and for, traditional sites of media power. Prior to the Snowden revelations, both Russia and China were loudly accused by the United States of orchestrating digital violations of data and information in other sovereign states, but it has become increasingly apparent that geopolitical struggles between the major world powers have infused every level of our information architecture. Consequently, the imperatives for achieving 'cyber-security' are leading to an exponential growth in technical and legal defences within the system. They become necessary because of the new media capabilities that enable those seeking to make use of the interactive features of the network system to access or reconfigure data. The usage of the Internet for such purposes by international criminal networks has been widely touted, but the more pervasive rise of commercial espionage and 'information warfare' between states is also an undeniable reality of the World Wide Web (Healey 2013). Due to their technical complexity, the conduct of generalized surveillance, 'information warfare' and 'cyber security' is, in large part, controlled by state actors. Accordingly, such activities inevitably reflect the geopolitical tensions of the present period. It is immediately evident that the growing compulsion for systematic global surveillance has been fuelled by the strategic dilemmas that characterize the 'war on terror' instituted following the September 11 attacks on the United States in 2001.

For the historically minded, there is also a much longer back story in which competitive intelligence gathering has always been a driver in media systems development (Standage 1999; Williams 1974). In this context, a contemporary critique of media imperialism has to be concerned with the balance of power in the world system, but it also has to be about the use of such power. Where any state or corporation has a disproportionate concentration of capacity within the global network, there will be attendant concerns around undue influence in world affairs. This would apply equally to the media assets of nation states and to the market share of multinational media corporations. At the same time, using that excess capacity to disseminate medical or agricultural knowledge of universal value is quantitatively different from using that capacity to subvert or degrade the sovereignty of others. Ultimately, the final proof of 'media imperialism' rests upon an aggressive intent, and this would not necessarily restrict its conduct to the biggest players. Perhaps most critically, we should recognize that the motivations for asserting a hegemonic position over digital systems are fundamentally different from those associated with achieving control of the airwaves in the preceding broadcast media environment. The most compelling measure of contemporary media imperialism is probably not who monopolizes the choice of available content, but rather who has secured the greatest capacity to control the data harvest.

At the level of content, the diffuse nature, distributed access and vast scope of the Internet clearly make it much more difficult to control 'the story' in this new environment. Interactivity effectively ensures that the vast bulk of content originates from the 'grassroots', that is, from audiences rather than from the traditional 'mouthpieces'. This is obviously significant if we want to consider the more nuanced problematics of 'cultural imperialism' in the twenty-first century. This is not to say that the geopolitical dimension is no longer relevant. The US diplomat, Joseph Nye, continues to argue that there are cultural great powers, as much as there are military and economic powers (Nye 2008, 2011). As an expressive, functional and commercial vehicle, the World Wide Web reflects the obvious overlaps between the three domains, as in the case of China and the United States, but it also demonstrates the disparate reach of individual countries in particular fields. Nye has noted how cultural influence, or what he calls the 'soft power', of countries like the UK and India both exceeds and complements their military and financial leverage (or 'hard power'). Outstanding artists, scientists and sportspeople are major contributors to the creation of a favourable impression amongst other national populations, as are authoritative media outlets, world-class universities and credible democratic standards. When these achievements can be communicated effectively at the international level, the aggregation of soft power becomes persuasive in nature (Nye 2005). By fostering the external perception of a country as a benign influence in the world, soft power can create a receptive environment for international initiatives.

Nye contrasts the costly and morally complex projections of military posture and economic control with the long-term influence of such soft-power instruments, thereby arguing for a much more positive reading of 'cultural imperialism'. He attempts to circumvent the 'intrusion of foreign ideas' thesis by suggesting that transnational communication is almost always preferable to the other available instruments of foreign policy. Hard power, however implicit in its usage, is essentially a coercive tool in international relations and creates enduring resentments. Looking back to the Cold War, we can see that the scientific achievements of both the United States and the Soviet Union in the Space Race generated substantial prestige for both superpowers, while their respective military interventions in Vietnam and Afghanistan clearly damaged their international standing. For Nye, in the day-to-day discussions that sustain the international order, national media brands such as the BBC play a vital role in establishing and projecting soft power and enabling consensus. By the same measure, Hollywood cinema can be seen as an effective ambassador for the American way of life, but also for the spread of democracy during the twentieth century. This, in turn, helped to promote a consensus-based approach to international relations and a conducive environment for growth and development around the world. Following this logic, we might assume that the relative decline of American cultural imperialism since 2001 implies an increase in the use of the more costly and damaging instruments of hard power. Arguably, this is bad both for the United States and for the rest of the world.

Reading Imperial Audiences

When we step outside of the specific domain of foreign-policy formulation in which Nye works, both the continuing reach and the decline of American cultural imperialism (as such) raise complex questions around the popular reception of transnational communication. The 'digital divide' of infrastructure constraints has narrowed substantially over the past decade, and the World Wide Web today is not a predominantly Anglo-Saxon medium to the extent it once was. Increasingly, the digital domain has developed a multi-vocal, multilingual and multi-polar field of content. This is not to say that the system is culturally neutral, since in any network system population counts for a great deal of the value that is generated. More users implies more bandwidth, and thus greater imperatives for commercial development in the predominant world languages. That is why the cultural and linguistic geography of the digital domain is unlikely to correspond with the United Nations principle of equal sovereignty between polities of different size. Larger countries in terms of population, such as China and India, possess a greater capacity for projecting their cultures at a global scale. This may be why both of these formerly strident critics of 'cultural imperialism' have become ardent investors in the notion (and practice) of 'soft power'. Leaving the emerging powers aside, it remains the case that media systems still constitute the primary source of Western visibility in other parts of the world. Those media exports continue to be simultaneously popular and regarded as symptoms or agents of cultural aggression.]

Whether or not we accept the competing conceptual frameworks of 'soft power' or 'cultural imperialism', it has become abundantly obvious that as the development process advances everywhere, it necessarily becomes more and more difficult to 'shield' general populations from transnational influence. If cultural imperialism is to be put to the test in a meaningful way, then we require a rigorous method for assessing the longitudinal impact of media imports on the behaviours and worldview of the receiving population. This is no easy task given the more or less ubiquitous presence of transnational media content around the world. Similarly, cultural influence must be broad ranging by its very nature, and would be very hard to capture in any single media transfer (and thus any conceivable study). Within a more limited range, taking my distinction between a foreign cultural presence and a conscious 'imperialist' intent to exert influence by cultural means, it is probably feasible for researchers to examine the reception of planned projections of soft power via media exports. That is: 'are popular perceptions of country X improving in country Y as a result of media campaign Z'. Such campaigns or content streams are, however, only a very small component of transnational communication as a whole. In the majority of cases, the reception of transnational media flows is not readily reducible to a barometer of inter-state relations. Nonetheless, in each and every case, any substantive study into transnational audiences must consider the prevailing geopolitical relationships that determine both the form and the reception of transnational media flows.

Recommended Reading

Oliver Boyd-Barrett (2014) *Media Imperialism*, Thousand Oaks: Sage.

Franz Fanon (2001) *The Wretched of the Earth*, London: Penguin Classics.

Bernd Hamm and Russell Smandych (2005) *Cultural Imperialism: Essays on the Political Economy of Communication*, Peterborough: Broadview.

Joshua Kirlantzick (2007) *Charm Offensive: How China's Soft Power is Transforming the World*, New Haven: Yale University Press.

Pippa Norris and Ronald Inglehart (2009) *Cosmopolitan Communication: Cultural Diversity in a Globalized World*, Cambridge: Cambridge University Press.

Joseph Nye (2004) *Soft Power: The Means to Success in World Politics*, New York: Public Affairs.

Edward Said (1993) *Culture and Imperialism*, London: Chatto and Windus.

Herbert Schiller (2000) *Living in the Number One Country: Reflections from a Critic of American Empire*, New York: Seven Stories Press.

Daya Thussu (2013) *Communicating Soft Power: Buddha to Bollywood*, New York: Palgrave Macmillan.

John Tomlinson (1991) *Cultural Imperialism: A Critical Introduction*, London: Continuum.

4   Millennial Globalization and the Transnational Shift

When we consider the continuities between debates on media imperialism and soft power, it is obvious that national and international configurations of cultural geography will shape most approaches to media audiences. Nonetheless, it is also fair to say that the naturalization of both national and international frames was powerfully challenged by the far-reaching reconfiguration of technology, economy and politics that took place at the turn of this century. In debates surrounding the era of 'globalization', the media were commonly cited as both an obvious symptom and a fundamental catalyst for the inexorable shift to a transnational world. Both the scope and the speed of change at the end of millennium encouraged a wide range of commentators to declare a new global age that was destined to eclipse the national habits, institutions and markets that had become entrenched during the twentieth century. In an outpouring of euphoric 'newness', the simultaneous shift into what Mark Poster called the 'second media age' and what Francis Fukuyama called the 'end of history' was embraced by a host of neoliberals, neoconservatives and futurists (Poster 1995; Fukuyama 1992; Gates 1995). Accordingly, this emergent world order was, with equal vigour, denounced by an opposing host of fundamentalists, nationalists and socialists as well as more considered sceptics of varying persuasions (see Baumann 1998; Hopkins 2002; Robins and Webster 1999; Sklair 1995; Stiglitz 2003). Both the embracers and the denouncers of this new 'runaway world' largely concurred that the primary symptoms of rapid social change could be read off the increasing presence of supra-national forces in our daily lives (Giddens 2002).

Media technologies, therefore, constitute an essential component in the practical and symbolic manifestations of global acceleration. Arguably, their centrality rests upon their relative position within a matrix of what could be considered the prevailing consensus of sociological analysis:

a) the transformative potential of new media technologies,
b) the re-ordering of capital markets (and thus power) due to the implementation of such technologies,
c) developments in patterns of human activity (including employment and migration), and

d) shifts in the modes of cultural 'belonging' which can be conceived of within such a powerfully re-territorialized human sphere.

This now familiar matrix serves to signify globalization as a set of concrete processes, rather than a vague sense of 'one-ness'. It remains contestable, however, whether we can see such an expansive phenomenon emerging out of any single causal origin. Hence, we should be wary of reading the matrix from a) to d). Not one of these various components (or actors, if you like) is likely to be a singular determinant that can explain all of the others. Rather, it is better to understand them as operating within an overlapping matrix of social change. Despite the 'radical' newness with which it is associated, we can also see right away that the globalization process is taken to rest upon the same linkages between communications technologies and cultural identity that were previously seen to underpin a thoroughly nationalized world. Similarly, the attendant 'effects' of media in the cultural domain are seen as readily, if not instantly, translating into far-reaching political change. As such, globalization theory rests upon a familiar model of 'powerful media'. It follows, then, that some portion of these far-reaching changes can be attributed to the rollout of digital technologies and the particular qualities of the 'new media'. For the sake of precision, it is worth recalling what was actually new about it: the deployment of a system of social communication that is at once both global and interactive.

The historical moment is significant here. In 1991, the year in which the first World Wide Web browser was released, the communist system in the Soviet Union collapsed spectacularly and the Cold War came to a close. Television, as Anthony Giddens notes, had already played a key role in the opening up of Eastern Europe in 1989, and Western popular music, as Joseph Nye recalls, had done much to promote democratic freedoms behind the iron curtain (Giddens 2002; Nye 2004). In the decade that followed, light-speed exchanges of vast volumes of capital and information across the world via the Internet, driven in large part by computer algorithms, subsequently came to define a post-communist world. The same media infrastructure facilitated the dispersal of cultural forms to every corner of the globe. Interactivity gave private citizens the means to communicate with their counterparts around the world. In its application, this combination of live data processing and universal telephony clearly had the potential to supersede the ideological barriers and the national parameters of earlier media systems. These potentials were taken to imply the fulfilment of a singular global culture characterized by connectivity, accumulation and consumption (Featherstone 1990). Transnational media systems therefore provided the functional means for global integration while also serving to powerfully express the spirit of the times.

The Second Media Age

As of now, we live in an era where the 'New Media' of the 1990s are no longer new. Largely shorn of their utopian credentials amidst a tidal wave of targeted advertising and mass surveillance, digital communications now infuse our daily lives as a mature system firmly located in the mundane and precise actions of commerce and governance. Nonetheless, it remains significant that the heady era of 'New Media' arose in parallel with the era of 'high' globalization from 1991 to 2007, to which it contributed in important ways. Leaving the geopolitical context aside, the prevailing doctrines of technological futurism (essentially science fiction as a serious business) predisposed a central role for media systems in any functional globalization (as a socio-spatial expansion). It was the Canadian scholar, Harold Innis (1951, 1952), who first popularized the notion that the technical infrastructures and communicative forms of mass media are fundamentally space-binding and time-binding. That is, they work to standardize spatial perception, negate distance and re-regulate the human experience of time within their sphere of operation. The infrastructure of machineries designed by humanity to overcome the tyranny of distance includes tangible systems of transport such as shipping, aircraft and high-speed motorized land vehicles, but just as significantly it also includes mechanized carriers of information such as recorded works, telephony, broadcasting and digital information exchanges. Following Innis in the late 1960s, Marshall McLuhan (1964) famously postulated that the mass media effectively represented technological extensions of the human sensory system, the existence of which fundamentally altered the scale of human consciousness.

McLuhan (1962, 1968) posited the notion that the advent of the electronic media had brought into being a 'global village', where each and every part of the world would become interconnected by 'information highways' of mass communication. For McLuhan, living in this densely connected global society, and experiencing it through new mediums like television, would alter the emotional state of human societies. McLuhan's particular emphasis on the psychological and behavioural effects of media technologies in themselves (over and above their content) was consistent with a modernist conception of mechanized progress. Developed with television in mind, these ideas were applied extensively to the 'remediation' that took place with the rollout of distributed computing and network technologies during the 1990s (see Bolter and Grusin 2000). For some, the primary interest was charting the new sensory experience of using the Internet, since materials in a range of audiovisual formats became accessible in an 'interactive' digital state where their sequence of occurrence (via hyperlinks) and their form (the data itself) could be readily altered by the user (Negroponte 1995). Equally central to the 'user experience' is the fact that the World Wide Web is not simply a medium of reception (for reading), but also a system for communication between individuals. Thus, if we follow McLuhan's logic, this combination of interpersonal communication with mass broadcasting must inevitably give rise to new patterns of subjectivity and sociability.

Accordingly, the influential urban sociologist Manuel Castells was prompted to claim that the impact of information network technologies upon human societies was so great that we needed to think of economic relations, nation states and communities as themselves taking on the forms of networks. In his highly influential three-volume study of the 'network society', published between 1996 and 1999, Castells' thick description of globalization drew explicitly upon computing terminologies in order to propound an era of entirely new (or, perhaps, entirely renewed) social relationships, between individuals, between groups, between humans and machines and between citizens and states. Ultimately, Castells concluded that a fundamental re-territorialization of human relations was taking place with the advent of a 'global network society'. The technological backbone for this shift, the Internet, was seen as being intrinsically different from earlier 'mass media' technologies due to its individualized interface and its decentred structure (see Cavanagh 2007; Fuchs 2008). The term 'network' itself provided us with a well-established metaphor correlating technological and social structures. If society is to be described as a network then it must be seen as being structured by dense interconnections between many different points, or nodes. In Castells' model, the nodes in the global network society are the real or virtual places where information flows converge. If we take up such a technologically determined vision of globalization as a whole, then we can understand transnational media exchanges as representing such 'flows'. In visualizing those flows, the geography of global media becomes akin to the destinations map found in the pages of in-flight magazines.

Transnational media flows can therefore be read as symptomatic of a global media apparatus superseding the patchwork of national systems that preceded it. In much the same way as Gellner (1998) saw national systems as extending the functional interdependence of human societies, the advent of a global media system produces an escalation of scale to encompass the entire planet. This explains Castells' proposition that the global network society is not merely a pattern of transnational interactions, but a singular global culture in its own right. Having said that, the cultural geography of the world must still be accounted for. For McLuhan (1964), writing at a time when the distinctions between developed and developing societies were much stronger than they are today, the 'global village' could be divided up in terms of traditional oral cultures and rational print cultures. He therefore suggested that the interactive and discursive nature of electronic systems threatened the rationalized, literary and individualized mindset of 'hot' European societies, whilst exacerbating the tribal emotions of 'cool' primitive societies. These are obviously highly problematic concepts, but one point of note is McLuhan's observation that the new sense of the proximity between cultures that came with electronic media was likely to 'raise temperatures' and would lead not to a brotherhood of man, but to irrational exuberance and war (McLuhan and Fiore 1968). Two decades into the second media age, the constancy of crises and conflicts is readily apparent. What was McLuhan's solution? – to regulate the emotive temperature of different societies by deploying an appropriate mix of media.

Networked Audiences

If technology is taken to have such powerful transformative effects, it inevitably requires a reconsideration of audience structures. With the global network replacing the local crowd as our primary conception of the public, our conceptualization of the media audience becomes at once radically individuated and densely interconnected. Proceeding from the formal qualities of digital technologies, we naturally perceive the audience as being comprised of various device operators who are simultaneously interacting with malleable content and with each other. In this context, we can no longer assume the physical co-presence of audience members, nor their simultaneous activity in a common moment of time. While older media forms were seen to suggest a sociable but 'passive' mode of reception, the networked audience is inherently an 'active' proposition. However, we should note that this 'active' mode primarily relates to the need to operate the system itself as opposed to the tendency to think about the meaning of its content. As such, the active audience becomes a functional category in this context, rather than a critical one. Nonetheless, the increased degree of personalized control over the programming 'flow' being accessed certainly undermines any assumption of a common media experience based around the content of the medium. Consequently, the patterns of interactivity formed around digital platforms are qualitatively different from the mass reception of broadcast television or film exhibition. The contemporary media environment is more akin to a 'many-to-many' combination of telephone conversations, manipulated photography and hypertext magazines.

Having said that, we cannot simply pare our interest in media reception down to the level of an individual 'caller' or 'reader', since it is the interconnectivity and interactivity between individuals that underpins the network effect, thereby making it a profoundly social process. As with all network technology, the communicative capacity of a digital media system increases as the number of participants grows. Thus, the World Wide Web derives its present value precisely from the potentials for soliciting content from some 2 billion people, which is a far greater number of participants than it encompassed when Castells was proposing a global network society. With this achievement in scale, the rapid rise of social networking sites in recent years provides a useful contemporary example of his earlier vision of a new world where power is vested in social networks (Castells 1996). In our maturing network society, audience membership is no longer recreational or optional. In a very practical sense, both individual agency and civic participation have become inherently mediatized, and therefore require competencies for managing information, fostering connections and controlling the direction of communications. It is via such purposeful 'interactivity' that the social world unfolds in the densely mediated public domain. For McLuhan, it would be the remaking of the sensory environment that would ultimately define the behavioural effects of remediation. For Castells, it was not so much the sense of 'closeness' derived from the global media apparatus as its growing functional necessity in everyday life that demonstrated the transformative effects of network technology.

Amidst the 'space of flows' described by Castells, the simultaneous actions of physical dispersal and electronic connectivity operate across a global terrain. Castells goes to some lengths to emphasize that this is a universal system. In that respect, the World Wide Web software represents a radical proposition for media studies not only because of its new many-to-many configurations but also because the Internet gives it instantaneous global reach. The distinctiveness of the system thereby rests upon the combination of these two constitutive features: interactivity and universality. Castells' global network society was itself conceived at a time when the Internet was an overwhelmingly English-language medium dominated by American software companies (Norris 2000). Today, things are quite different, with Mandarin, Japanese and other languages functioning as distinct linguistic spaces within the framework of the World Wide Web. Equally, following trends towards universal surveillance that were encapsulated in the Snowden affair, calls for nationally specific 'sovereign' networks are becoming more commonplace. As such, the 'universal' transnational ambit of the

World Wide Web may not be guaranteed by technological possibility alone, but for now at least the sheer volume of transnational communication is unprecedented and still growing. In that sense, the new media environment has necessitated a shift towards researching 'virtual' audiences, since it is beyond our practical capacity to research a single global audience. Instead, this vast and dispersed public tends to be accessed by sampling the inputs they make into the hypertext system. This is likely why most approaches to the networked audience tend to posit a universal 'user' whose material conditions remain literally off screen.

Surfing the World Wide Market

While Castells describes globalization as a set of processes enabled in the first place by new technology, much of his analysis turns upon the subsequent transformation of the economic sphere. In a more interconnected world, instantaneous communications speed up the actions of international trade to unprecedented levels. Thus, the most obvious economic manifestations of transnationalism are the increasing speed, frequency and volition of international transactions. Since the Asian currency crisis of 1997, we have become painfully aware of the enormous power of computerized financial flows seeking profit in their rapid movements between different currencies, commodities and markets (Soros 2002; Das 2004). The role of the media within this opaque field of transactions is highly complex. This is precisely because media technologies are, at one level, enabling technologies for much of this activity. Further, it is the provision of communicative efficiency which enables new organizational structures and processes that allow for more complex relations of production and exchange at a global scale. It is no accident, therefore, that the era of multimedia is also the era of the multinational corporation. Integrated media technologies are essential for the operation of international business organizations. At another level, however, media content must also be counted as a tradeable commodity in its own right. In that respect, the age of globalization has seen rapid growth in the trading of intangible goods such as information, entertainment and services over and above trade in tangible, physical goods (Coyle 1999; Leadbeater 2000).

In the commercial domain, the aesthetics of the digital environment have been characterized by the predominance of popular culture modelled on the earlier mediums of print, television and computer games. Thus, having proclaimed the era of 'new media', a large number of 'old media' concerns have made extensive use of the system for delivering entertainment, providing information and communication services and promoting home shopping. In that sense, Castells reminds us not only of the enormous economic power of the information technology companies that determine the media infrastructure, but also of the significance of the businesses that provide media content. Within that domain, as Castells usefully notes, 'the advertising industry is the economic foundation of the media business' (1997: 257). In recent years, the exponential growth of digital advertising revenues and user-tracking technologies has transformed the ways in which new media networks operate, bringing the era of 'Web 2.0' into being (O'Reilly 2005). This draws our attention to a fundamental feature of media economics: the integrated nature of media commodities. The sale of media products such as videos or music is predicated upon the conjoined purchase of the necessary media hardware and subscriptions for media access. Beyond that, the attention of the audience created around media content represents value to advertisers who can then sell those 'eyeballs' to their clients. The present era of social media produces further revenues from 'scraping' information regarding the authors and viewers of media content. The central point of this is that the media audience itself is not simply a group of consumers but an intrinsic component of the overall package of commodities that make up the media economy.

This integrated commodity form means that the audience is every bit as much part of the product as the content they are paying to access. The existence of a vast international advertising business therefore draws our attention to the fact that academic debates on issues such as cultural identity, national citizenship or technological effects are always offset by a far larger, if no less complicated, commercial interest in media audiences. For producers of media content and providers of media services, audiences are markets first and foremost. An audience seen in this way can therefore be conceived of in terms of an interdependency between media producers, gatekeepers and consumers which attributes agency, albeit unequally, to all these actors. Although such a model encourages some questioning of why consuming-agents make their viewing choices, the terms of the enquiry will always attribute more weight to the decisive act of consumption than to any production of meanings. As such, the most commonly researched questions regarding media audiences are about what they have recently bought and what they might want to buy next. In this context, the advent of a global network society indicates the emergence of densely connected transnational markets available for exploitation via its worldwide infrastructure. Initially, of course, there has to be (and has been) a series of gold rushes in building and selling the technical infrastructure and the necessary software, but as the market matures the production of suitable content and services becomes essential to its continuation. It is at this point that serious thought has to be given to the forms of content that are most suited to the series of global networked markets described by Castells, whether these are culturally blind homogeneous products, aggregated niche aesthetics or distinctive content from one market re-purposed to 'cross over' to another.

Narrowcasting the Global

The interlacing of markets as a primary impetus for the global network society can be seen as symptomatic of the increasing power of multinational corporations in respect to national regulators. While the expansion of capitalism and its vested interests provided the prevailing weather for the recent phase of globalization, Castells saw the rise of transnational media corporations as being particularly significant. This is because they combined a commercial interest in market expansion with a supra-national hegemony over the bandwidth required for everyday social communication. As such, little of effect could be said or done without access to global media networks. During the high tide of national broadcast systems, national governments had very considerable regulatory powers over media ownership, content and access. However, this capacity to frame public debate dissipated very quickly with the coming of the second media age, leaving both democratic and autocratic regimes at the mercy of transnational media businesses. According to Castells, 'the change was technology-driven. The diversification of communication modes, the link up of all media in a digital hypertext, opening the way for interactive media, and the inability to control satellites beaming across borders or computer-mediated communicated over the 'phone line, blew up the traditional lines of regulatory defense' (1997: 255). Thus, the breaching of national boundaries by media transmission was a direct threat to the nation state as an arbiter of public discussion and social mores. For their part, the increasingly powerful multinational corporations that became predominant at the expense of national media operators tended to display a very firm and obvious commitment to a global network society, a system that itself threatened to make national polities increasingly irrelevant.

The technological revolution recorded by Castells was also accompanied by an acceleration of mergers and acquisitions that created gigantic media companies with interests spread across all forms of content and all parts of the globe. The simultaneous outcomes of a newfound passion for the privatization of state interests, reducing anti-competition regulations and the recasting of the technological field of communication all fed into this process. With regulations being dropped or rendered obsolete, the larger media businesses rapidly transformed themselves into supra-national forces of autonomous political power. Their power was, and is, as much political as commercial because flows of information necessarily constitute the major channels for social communication and cultural expression in a network society. This simple fact makes media access a prerequisite for any kind of contemporary politics. Access to global media 'airtime' becomes essential for holding power or achieving social change (and this is true for all players, including governments, insurgents and civil society movements). This is why Castells highlights the ubiquitous mediating power of the global communication networks that now structure the world system: 'The critical matter is that, without an active presence in the media, political proposals or candidates do not stand a chance of gathering broad support . . . [and therefore] . . . politics is fundamentally framed, in its substance, organization, process, and leadership, by the inherent logic of the media system, particularly by the new electronic media (1997: 317). As such, it is for political as much as technical and commercial reasons that the media operate as the central structure of the global network society described by Castells.

In delving into the politics of the era, however, Castells also noted a splintering effect that counterposed the aggregation of media businesses into ever larger formations. The personalized media flows arising from hypertext content and the channel multiplication that came with the digitization of television were not merely spilling over national boundaries but also fragmenting the concept of the mass audience. Whereas as few as three television networks had previously captured 90 per cent of the American public with a general mix of programming, the new media environment was splintering the audience across hundreds of specialist channels and thousands of different web portals. The era of broadcasting was giving way to an era of 'narrowcasting' where media consumers were being redirected into various forms of niche programming. Thus, the increasing reach of social communication across time and space was juxtaposed by the dissolution of the 'general public' into various micro-domains, or what Todd Gitlin (1998) has called 'public sphericles'. As audiences begin to aggregate more exclusively around particular interests, content providers seek to capture those audiences by producing niche material. For those wedded to the concept of media balance and an inclusive frame, this tribalization of audiences threatened to replace real debate with innumerable echo-chambers of the like-minded (Reese et al. 2007). Nonetheless, the mutually reinforcing dynamics of narrowcasting and niche audiences has established itself as a distinctive feature of the network society, with the rise of targeted advertising in the past decade reflecting the reality of this newly disparate audience.

Modernity at Large

In many respects we can see the transnational shift marked by the advent of Castells' global network society as a step change in long-running processes of technological development, economic competition and mass politics. In that sense, there are important continuities in the identification of primary causes, even where the particular affordances of digital media technologies serve to reorient the functional structure of economic and political power. Most likely, this is why Ella Shohat and Robert Stam (1996) were keen to emphasize the continuity between theories of globalization and earlier theories of modernization, seeing both as rooted in the diffusionist model of the 'imperial imaginary' of the colonial world. Although Castells regards the 'power of identity' as a substantial force in creating constituencies within the global network society, it is striking that the role of culture per se tends to remain reactive to technological and economic forces. Thus Castells sees ethnicity as only constituting a significant factor when it is attached to a particular political programme. In his contemporary exposition of the 'cultural dimensions of globalization', however, the émigré anthropologist Arjun Appadurai takes an opposite tack that sees ethnicity as the central organizing principle of a transnational world order. Equally, Appadurai explicitly rejects the proposition that globalization represents a continuation of long-running imperialist tendencies, and argues with some force that modernity is no longer confined to the centre-periphery model of transmission. Indeed, Appadurai proposes that in the contemporary imagination modernity has become 'decisively at large' (1996: 3).

Appadurai presents 'a theory of rupture that takes media and migration as its two major, and interconnected, diacritics and explores their joint effect on the *work of the imagination* as a constitutive feature of modern subjectivity' (1996: 3), going as far as to suggest that a 'mobile and unforeseeable relationship between mass-mediated events and migratory audiences defines the core of the link between globalization and the modern' (1996: 4). Appadurai identifies important disjunctures within the global flows identified by Castells, particularly between culture, politics and economics. Accordingly, Appadurai argued that the effect of these various flows was to construct a series of quite different global landscapes, each one interacting with the other but arising from its own logics. These 'five dimensions of global flows [can] be termed a) *ethnoscapes*, b) *mediascapes*, c) *technoscapes*, d) *financescapes* and e) *ideoscapes* . . . These landscapes are the building blocks of what (extending Benedict Anderson) I would like to call *imagined worlds*' (1996: 33). By this proposition, Appadurai expands Anderson's notion of 'imagined community' beyond the confines of its original purpose – that is, explaining the emergence of national imaginaries – to the new business of mapping global imaginaries. Reversing the polarity of Castells' account of globalization, Appadurai places his primary emphasis on culture, understood as an interface of ethnicity and media flows. Following this perspective, his attention then shifts to the emergence of complex transnational 'imagined worlds' inhabited by dispersed ethnic communities.

The theory is once again media-centric, since Appadurai points to the role played by transnational media currents in shaping and sustaining equally transnational audiences. They do so by addressing 'deterritorialized' ethnic subjectivities (which he describes as 'diasporic public spheres') that are 'diverse amongst themselves' yet constitute 'the crucibles of a postnational political order. The engines of their discourse are mass media (both interactive and expressive) and the movement of refugees, activists, students and laborers' (Appadurai 1996: 22). Such a position is indicative of Stuart Hall's earlier proposition that transnational migrant communities, or diasporas, 'are at the leading edge of what is destined to become the truly representative "late-modern" experience' (Hall 1993: 362). This centralizing of migrant subjects within the discursive construction of the cultural dimensions of globalization was subsequently underlined by Stuart Cunningham and John Sinclair, who suggested that, 'to the extent globalization presents more and more people with the experience of difference and displacement, the diasporic experience becomes not so much a metaphor as the archetype for the kind of cultural adaptiveness which our era demands' (2000: 15). As such, the position taken by Appadurai has enjoyed widespread authority in the discussion of media and globalization. Clearly, the role played by the diaspora of human beings in shaping currents within the worldwide diaspora of media content necessarily forms an important component of transnational media consumption. The 'work of the imagination' which is so central to Appadurai's notion of 'modernity at large' also reflects the continuing influence of Anderson's notion of an 'imagined community' when it comes to understanding the relationship between media reception and political identity.

Mediascapes

In keeping with the broader sweep of globalization theory, Appadurai puts the electronic visual media at the heart of contemporary social change. He identifies transnational media practices in particular as constituting a catalyst for and primary evidence of a changing world. Appadurai's focus upon transnational media exchanges is also significant in that he seeks to discard rather than nuance the centre-periphery models of modernization which dominated earlier debates on media and cultural imperialism.

> The crucial point is that the United States is no longer the puppeteer of a world system of images but is only one node of a complex transnational construction of imaginary landscapes. The world we live in today is characterized by a new role for the imagination in social life. To grasp this new role, we need to bring together the old idea of images, especially mechanically produced images (in the Frankfurt School sense); the idea of the imagined community (in Anderson's sense); and the French idea of the imaginary (*imaginaire*) as a constructed landscape of collective aspirations, which is no more and no less real than the collective representations of Emile Durkheim, now mediated through the complex prism of modern media. The image, the imagined, the imaginary – these are all terms that direct us to something critical and new in global cultural processes: the imagination as a social practice . . . The imagination is now central to all forms of agency, is itself a social fact, and is the key component of the new global order. (Appadurai 1996: 31)

Appadurai is emphatic that the 'cultural imperialism' thesis should be discarded as a totalizing explanation. Even where media dispersal is conceived of and undertaken with 'soft power' in mind, the effects on the ground are far from certain. Furthermore, the inherent portability of media products that allows for the 'media outreach' ambitions of dominant states also facilitates the widespread dispersal of alternative products. As digital technologies simultaneously lowered production costs and offered limitless and costless global distribution, the previous structural bias towards the developed world was effectively negated. Thus, in a globalized world interlinked by digital systems, transnational media flows simply cannot be explained through any of the unidirectional models of dissemination constructed by the mass communications theories of the mid-twentieth century. Thus, Appadurai's notion of the mediascape seeks to describe the emergence of a multi-polar world, where transnational media flows span borders in all directions. To be fair, even in the United States, Hollywood has never been the *only* source of media products. Indeed, the bulk of the world's media industries, however discursively orientated they might be towards a national public, have fairly consistent histories of exporting products to audiences outside of the 'national' domain. The growing visibility of 'contra-flows' from the East and South also has a number of precedents, but the expansion of this activity during the 2000s has provoked extensive commentary from media scholars (see, for example, Thussu 2007). For Appadurai, this expanding matrix of overlapping information flows was directed less towards a new global cosmopolitanism and more towards the shifting human terrain of the ethnoscape. That is, the growth of transnational media currents was closely identified with a human population on the move.

It is critically important that Appadurai's 'global ethnoscape' is an imagined world defined by ethnic particularity. This ethnocentricity explains his assertion 'that we regard as cultural only those differences that either express, or set the groundwork for, the mobilization of group identities' and that therefore 'we restrict the term culture as a marked term to the subset of these differences that has been mobilized to articulate the boundary of difference' (1996: 13). If we do so, then we will naturally expect migrants to extend the mediascape of their 'indigenous' culture when they relocate to other countries. This social imaginary is then sustained by media flows from the homeland, and by the newfound capacity to maintain this distant cultural environment within the new physical location. According to Appadurai, the audiences emerging from the new diversity of media flows would be distinguished by their adherence to their own globalized ethnic culture. The ethnoscape concept therefore suggests a mosaic of ethnic cultures sustained by easy mobility and media connectivity. This cultural geography is no longer contained within the political geography of nation states, but instead manifests as a dense patchwork of transnational public spheres. By this model, the Indian mediascape expands to include communities in New York and Sydney, while the mainstream American media encompass Anglo-Saxon audiences in Australia and Britain but not, perhaps, the entire population of the polyglot United States. For Appadurai, transnational global ethnicities were destined to replace national citizenries as the primary cultural and political unit. In that respect, Appadurai's reading of the cultural dimensions of globalization was remarkably similar to Anthony Smith's ethnic model of national cultures, albeit radically mobilized by air travel and satellite television.

Transnational Agents

One of the common features amongst the predominant explanations of globalization was their adherence to a discourse of powerful media influence, conjoined with a strong technological determinism that positioned information technologies in particular as a, if not the, primary driver for the great transnational shift of the 1990s. In that respect, it can be argued that both Castells and Appadurai were essentially casting globalization as a series of media effects. Having said that, the influence of 'active audience' theory also makes itself felt in both narratives. This is noteworthy, since the notion of critically aware, and therefore 'active', audiences had emerged from two decades of intellectual opposition to the idea of all-powerful media on which much globalization theory rests. In addressing the consequent question of agency for the masses, Castells allows media audiences to move from the 'passive' mode primarily through the actions of grassroots politics. That is, he sees resistance to the interests of a global ruling elite emerging via a growing host of social movements that now compete for bandwidth in a global media system that serves as a battleground of ideas. Agency is available therefore to those who are sufficiently organized to develop an effective media platform and get their message across.

Appadurai, by contrast, goes much further in that he sees media consumption alone as representing a site of agency for consumers. Consumers are naturally quite different from social movements, in that they are individuals rather than party organizations but also because their engagement with the media tends to be personal rather than political in a broader sense. Appadurai also opens up some space for the role of gratification, or pleasure, something which is conspicuously absent from most academic studies of media audiences. As he puts it:

> it is wrong to assume that the electronic media are the opium of the masses. This view, which is only beginning to be corrected, is based upon the notion that the mechanical arts of reproduction largely reprimed ordinary people for industrial work. It is far too simple. There is growing evidence that the consumption of the mass media throughout the world often provokes resistance, irony, selectivity, and in general, *agency* . . . this is not to suggest that consumers are free agents, living happily in a world of safe malls, free lunches, and quick fixes . . . Nevertheless, where there is consumption there is pleasure, and where there is pleasure there is agency. (1996: 7)

In particular, Appadurai emphasizes the role of media consumption in fostering a more active social imagination, the capacity of which is transformed by the expansion of the media system to the global scale. This explains his assertion that imagined worlds are a recent phenomenon for most people, since: 'it is only in the past two decades or so that media and migration have become so massively globalized, that is to say, active across large and irregular transnational terrains' (1996: 9). The agency that Appadurai identifies amongst media consumers is derived from a process of empowerment triggered by the expansion of media access and control over content. By his reading, agency is itself an 'effect' of media systems. The specific outcome of this effect during the 1990s being that: 'the imagination has broken out of the special expressive space of art, myth, and ritual and has now become a part of the quotidian mental work of ordinary people in many societies' (1996: 5). Because media consumers are considered to be increasingly aware of a whole series of 'imagined worlds', their reception of media content is likely to be influenced by an increased scale of reference and a more critical awareness of their place in those worlds. This has obvious implications for their choice of content, their reading of materials, the messages they author, and for their social imagination in general. As such, the notion that individuals are active agents in processes of mediation due to their own 'mental maps' of the world becomes critically important to the study of transnational media flows.

Reading Transnational Audiences

Looking back, we can see that the period of 'high globalization' from 1991 to 2007 was generally regarded as an era dominated by media power. It was also a period of far-reaching technological remediation, as digital systems replaced analogue ones. Given the prevailing tendency to see new technologies as an overarching explanation for social change, all of the major theories of globalization gave central importance to the advent of digital satellite broadcasting and the public Internet. While the interests of different thinkers focused variously upon politics, economics or culture, the new media environment was consistently identified as a major constituent of the sudden shift towards a transnational world order. In the anticipated new world system, the tidy alignment of markets, cultures and media systems within sovereign states was expected to give way in favour of a single integrated global market, a multicultural society and a universal media apparatus. As Castells puts it: 'The globalization/localization of media and electronic communication is tantamount to the de-nationalization and de-statization of information, the two trends being inseparable for the time being' (1997: 259). Taken as a whole, globalization theory provides us with a vision of technologically interactive, physically transnational, but culturally ethnic, niche audiences taking over from technologically passive, nationally defined, but culturally homogeneous, mass audiences. Its prevailing ideas around media reception are technologically determined, but necessarily complicated by the increasingly interactive nature of the system. Its prevailing ideas around culture are ethnically determined, but complicated by the constancy of cultural exchange and the inevitable diversity of all human societies.

For researchers, the functional contribution of media systems to globalization can be empirically identified at a number of levels. Examining a logistical role for media technologies that favours international relationships provides one set of evidence for *globalization through media*. Identifying a growing volume of international trade in media content points to the ongo-ing *globalization of media markets*. Finally, assessing the internationalization of capital ownership in the media business provides evidence of an emerging *global media apparatus*. At the conceptual level, we can plainly see how the overarching idea of globalization picks up various strands of functionalist, traditionalist and liberal thought on nationalism and adapts them for a new technological and geopolitical setting. The substantive claim, that transna-tional communication represents a fundamental break with the nation-state system, is far-reaching and is yet to be established in truth. Certainly, the global media market was becoming more integrated throughout this phase of high globalization, with this scale increase being matched by increasing content diversity and the rise of narrowcasting. This directs us towards a lesser claim of globalization theory: that old national publics are giving way in favour of transnational constituencies centred upon specific inter-ests (which might be political or ethnic depending upon which theorist you choose to follow). This proposition is more amenable to meaningful research. In a practical sense, the task of giving substance to, or falsifying, either claim falls to audience researchers.

Recommended Reading

Arjun Appadurai (1996) *Modernity At Large: The Cultural Dimensions of Globalisation*, Minneapolis: University of Minnesota Press.

Nestor Garcia Canclini (2014) *Imagined Globalization*, Durham, NC: Duke University Press.

Manuel Castells (1996) *The Information Age: Economy, Society and Culture, Vol. I: The Rise of the Network Society*, Cambridge, MA and Oxford: Blackwell.

Manuel Castells (1997) *The Information Age: Economy, Society and Culture, Vol. II: The Power of Identity*, Cambridge, MA and Oxford: Blackwell.

Manuel Castells (1998) *The Information Age: Economy, Society and Culture, Vol. III: The End of Millennium*, Cambridge, MA and Oxford: Blackwell.

Jean K. Chalaby (2005) *Transnational Television Worldwide: Towards a New Media Order*, New York: I. B. Tauris.

Nick Couldry (2012) *Media, Society, World*, Cambridge: Polity.

Nataa Durovicova and Kathleen Newman (eds) (2009) *World Cinemas: Transnational Perspectives*, Abingdon and New York: Routledge.

Shani Orgad (2012) *Media Representation and the Global Imagination*, Cambridge: Polity.

Daya Thussu (2007) *Media on the Move: Global Flow and Contra Flow*, London: Routledge.

Steven Vertovec (2009) *Transnationalism*, London and New York: Routledge.

Part 2

Media Flows:
Diasporas, Crossovers, Proximities

5   Mobility, Migration and Diasporic Audiences

At its heart, the era of high globalization was conceived around three forms of movement: of money, people and media content. Increases in the mobility of all three phenomena have been understood as mutually reinforcing the globalization process, and it is this recognition that marks the decisive transnational shift in media studies that took place at the turn of the century. Earlier concerns, of course, remain, and the role of mediation in national and international affairs continues to receive substantial scrutiny. Indeed, the strategic aims of researchers concerned with social communication at those scales have perhaps not changed so considerably. What has changed, however, is that we cannot readily conceive of the world in terms of an array of self-contained national cultures, aesthetics and media systems. The interpenetration and interdependence of national domains has become what Appadurai (2013) would call an everyday social fact. In seeking a primary cause for this recasting of our social imagination, the underlying technological determinism that informs media studies in general has naturally predisposed an emphasis upon the symbiotic embrace of globalization and digitization. More broadly, however, the equally normalized divisions across the humanities and social sciences between disciplines concerned with culture, economics and politics have also come into question. As such, the sociology of audiences has been evolving within an intellectual environment that might best be described as an era of reconsideration. This process remains ongoing, not least because the inherent complexity of a global media apparatus is bound to increase exponentially.

In this context it has made sense, practically speaking, to deal with exemplary accounts of transnational media reception rather than seek to encapsulate the totality of such exchanges. Audience studies, by their very nature, require a constituency. As such, the strong correlation of media flows and human movements in globalization theory provides us with an obvious starting point: the migrant media audience. Accordingly, a sizeable body of literature concerning 'migrant communities' has emerged from the Western academies over the past twenty years. Against the wider backdrop of globalization, choosing a migrant population as a test case for transnational reception makes obvious sense, both conceptually and practically. There is scarcely any urban location in the world today where you would not find a recently resettled community. The relative accessibility of migrant populations is augmented by their typical concentration and, unlike broad national audiences, migrant populations tend to be amenable to the small-scale qualitative studies that have become predominant in audience research. A more integrated and more personalized global media system also guarantees that transnational mediation is going to be a critical component of contemporary migrant experience. In media studies, therefore, a substantive programme of social research has evaluated migrant communities across the developed world through descriptions of their cultural practices, social behaviours and attitudes (Julian 2003; Karim 2003; Chapman 2004 et al.). Subsequently, our prevailing knowledge of migrant cultures has often been extrapolated either from their patterns of media usage or from their subjective responses to significant media content.

Multiculturalism and Diasporas

The expanding literature on media and migration is also an obvious reflection of the particular concerns of developed Western countries, where the reverse tides of post-imperial migration and the changing political landscape following the Cold War have made migration a central concern of social policy and, indeed, of politics in general. For several decades now, the project of 'multiculturalism' in Western nations has sought, more or less explicitly, to harness the positive potential of a more culturally diverse society in an era of global economic connectivity while simultaneously managing the potentials for what is seen as an undesirable dilution of the existing (and increasingly state-regulated) 'national' culture. The particularities of multicultural policy have naturally varied according to different geographic, demographic and historical contingencies, but across the board multiculturalism can be best defined as an internal reorganization of nationalist narratives in order to accommodate greater social (but primarily ethno-cultural) diversity. Amongst the proponents of multiculturalism, there have been continuing debates over the relative merits of assimilation or co-operative diversity as the ultimate goal of official programmes. This debate has been usefully captured in the (admittedly superficial) contrast between the 'melting pot' of the United States and the 'mosaic' of Canadian society. In the former case, migrants are encouraged to assimilate themselves over time to the common culture of their new home. In the latter, the various communities that make up the nation are encouraged to preserve their different identities within a contract of mutual coexistence.

Nonetheless, in the world of 'us and them' shaped by cultural nationalism since the nineteenth century, migration inevitably provokes a crisis of assimilation. If a shared culture is taken to be the primary bond of nationhood, then cultural differences must logically introduce fissures into the national polity. This, in turn, explains the acute sensitivity of developed countries to all aspects of behaviour by migrants from other cultures. Despite their typical operation within the personal domain, the cultural practices of migrant communities have therefore tended to become a matter of official scrutiny. That is why countries such as France have intense debates and even laws about what is acceptable to be worn on someone's head. In this wider context, the identification of ongoing transnational media exchanges with the country of origin are frequently regarded as a failure in the interaction (or contract) between citizens and the national media of the 'host' nation. When this occurs on a large scale, a profusion of transnational migrant cultures is taken to suggest a 'fragmentation' of the national public sphere. Multiculturalism consequently provides a set of official remedies to this perceived threat. In the media, one of its biggest achievements has been the appearance on screen of media staff from racial minorities who nonetheless perform within the 'right accent' of the dominant culture. This intervention becomes important, since it has been widely recognized that 'foreign cultures' tend to be associated with unflattering stereotypes that are pejoratively applied to migrants, both consciously and unconsciously. Thus, programmes of affirmative action undertaken by mainstream media providers are intended to naturalize migrant groups in the eyes of the majority, as well as encouraging migrant citizens to believe in the benefits of assimilation and the promise of 'equal opportunity' within their new home.

It is also worth noting that the rise of migration as a central concern of social and cultural policy has been coterminous with the arrival of visible populations of brown and black people in countries where the population had previously been overwhelmingly white. That is not to say that multiculturalism has not come to play an important role in other societies where racial and cultural diversity is an official matter (the Asian states of Malaysia and Singapore are good examples). Nonetheless, the growing importance of 'cultural minorities' within media studies, and the social sciences in general, is a reminder of the extent to which global academic agendas continue to be guided by the contemporary concerns of the 'white' countries. In Britain, the influential Jamaican-born scholar Stuart Hall made a powerful case during the 1980s for increasing the recognition, representation and inclusion of non-white Britons in the mainstream media. Along with other colleagues in cultural studies, Hall (1978) was able to demonstrate empirically how negative representations of racial minorities fed into racism, discrimination and social tension. Hall also discussed the ways in which a growing number of second-generation black Britons were forging a unique cultural identity based upon the creative negotiation of cultural differences within the United Kingdom (Hall 1988). By the 1990s, this process could be widely seen in the works of novelists, musicians, filmmakers and other artists. Thus, the cultural contributions of migrant communities would be given official endorsement in the pursuit of a multicultural Britain.

The highlighting of cosmopolitan, cross-cultural currents in the performing arts encouraged scholars from a wide range of disciplines to position 'diaspora' as a defining condition within a globalized world. Diaspora, like ethnicity, is a term which originates from the Greek language. Until the 1990s, it was generally deployed in order to describe a condition of permanent exile based upon the ancient Jewish experience of forced deportation and statelessness. In service of multiculturalism, however, the term has been broadly extended to include any and all forms of ethnically defined expatriate community (see Axel 2002). Thus, 'diasporas' are now defined as émigré communities living outside their 'ancestral homeland' (and most often spread across multiple states). The early consolidation of the idea of a 'diasporic subject' in literary studies fed into broader theorizations of a 'diasporic condition' (Cohen 2001). From a sociological perspective, 'diasporic communities' are typically considered to be 'minority' populations in their adopted places of residence but, taken together, they are also seen to represent new global formations based upon shared ethnicity rather than proximate habitation. It is precisely this new understanding of diaspora that informs Arjun Appadurai's claim that the consumption by migrants of media artefacts addressing their own ethnic specificity was providing the catalyst for the imagining of 'diasporic public spheres' (1996). Thus, in the broader context of a globalization defined by the mobility of media, capital and human beings, the notion of diaspora inevitably suggests the existence of 'diasporic audiences'.

Diasporic Audiences

In attempting to define the nature of these audiences, it is helpful to first distinguish them from the related notion of the 'minority audience'. To start with, in any media system based upon mass broadcasting, there is an obvious inclination to focus upon the most common denominator. In that respect, media industries founded upon popular appeal are much like nationalism itself. Nonetheless, this common denominator approach tends to favour a majoritarian address that is not only 'middle of the road' in aesthetics and outlook, but is also visibly skewed towards the largest identifiable demographic. We could conceive of a 'majority audience' in a number of ways, say by identifying a generational, gendered or classed-based distinction between majority and minority publics. That is why many 'youth' trends in popular culture are treated as subcultures that operate outside of the mainstream. Commonly, however, the pervasive logic of cultural nationalism tends to favour an ethno-cultural distinction between majority and minority populations. Thus, the word 'minority' becomes associated with racial or cultural difference. However, this itself does not necessarily imply a migrant population. In Australia, the co-location of television programming for indigenous Australians with that intended for Asian and European immigrants and metropolitan intellectuals (on the publicly funded SBS network) is a useful example of conscious minority-audience provision. But the functional cohabitation of minority and migrant audiences within this platform does not make them the same thing.

A more specific category of migrant audiences might allow us to conceive of a section of the public that is concerned with this common experience as an aspect of their lives. However, notwithstanding the generally crude instructional materials produced by immigration departments, there is little evidence that migration alone implicates a particular viewing culture or audience. Further, in a world where people are increasingly on the move, the likelihood of a common idiom amongst migrants cannot be taken for granted. Australia, once again, is a good example, with its migration policy having shifted from a heavily British bias prior to the 1970s to becoming one of the most ethnically diverse countries in the world by the twenty-first century. In this setting, the ethnic identity of migrants (with its powerful links to language, birthplace and social rituals) becomes a more cogent way of identifying niche audiences within a multicultural society. This is where we can adequately identify a 'diasporic audience' as being a social body defined: 1) in specifically ethnic terms, 2) arising from a process of immigration, and 3) taken to be served by a particularized stream of media content. Of course, in the Australian context, this definition would apply to virtually the entire population, but in practice the 'mainstream' media lays claim to a broad Anglo-Saxon identity. Thus, while there may be a reasonably good case for the study of the ways in which British expatriates use media to maintain their cultural identity, this generally isn't the 'diasporic audience' that anyone is interested in. This reflects the implicit fourth defining component: that a diasporic audience must be a minority culture.

This definition appears to be broadly supported in the framing of studies within the field (Carstons 2003; Julian 2003; Panagakos 2003; Karim

2003; Chapman 2004). As one of the few people to attempt a formal definition, the Australian cultural policy expert Stuart Cunningham has described diasporic audiences as ethnic minorities that support narrowcast media environments. He defines these media environments as 'public sphericules', that is: they are 'ethno-specific global mediatized communities' which 'display in microcosm elements we would expect to find in the public sphere' (2001: 134). In making this case, Cunningham introduces a social and political context broader than media consumption alone, and he also stipulates that diasporic audiences must be connected transnationally to others who share their ethnicity. So, in effect, Cunningham introduces a fifth component: that a diasporic audience be connected to similar formations in other countries. Mediation must, of course, be instrumental in maintaining any such linkage. From the perspective of their host nations, diasporic cultures continue to be minority positions and are thereby 'social fragments that do not have critical mass' (Cunningham 2001: 134). Nonetheless, since the diasporic media audience is globally connected, it simultaneously represents a larger transnational domain where 'Sophisticated cosmopolitanism and successful international business dealing sit alongside long-distance nationalism' (Cunningham 2002: 273). This global networking is taken to imply that diasporic audiences remain oriented 'toward those they see as their kind in other nations and (often still) in their nation of origin, even while they face the challenges of negotiating a place for themselves in the host culture' (Cunningham and Sinclair 2000: 12).

Floating Lives

One of the early, and influential, studies of a diasporic audience was carried out by the British sociologist Marie Gillespie (1995). Using a combination of household ethnography and reception studies of particular texts, Gillespie explored the social and cultural attitudes of British Asian families in London's Southall district. Gillespie's findings indicated the complexities facing a younger British-born generation who were attempting to accommodate the requirements of, and differences between, two cultures. The study described patriarchal structures where the older generation sought to perpetuate Indian (more accurately, Punjabi) traditions within their new home. For their part, the younger generation was keen to embrace some of the freedoms of British life, while remaining wary of its (apparently) lower moral standards. As part of the study, families were brought together regularly for the viewing of Hindi feature films and episodes of the televised rendition of the sacred Hindu epic, *Mahabharata*. Questions about

Indian culture and identity were posed around these texts, while questions about Western culture were posed around the class-exploitation soap opera *EastEnders* and Peter Brooks' secularized, multi-racial dramatization of the *Mahabharata*. Broadly speaking, the responses reinforced the popular view of Indian families as being religious, intensely patriarchal and conservative. Conversely, mainstream British culture tended to be positioned in terms of secularism, female empowerment, social breakdown and moral decay. Arguably, the choice of texts in the reception study somewhat predisposed the perpetuation of what are mutually stereotypical views. Nonetheless, the role of television watching among Indian families as a means of keeping their bearings in polyglot London was usefully explored, and there were numerous insights into the dynamics of Southall's diverse South Asian community.

A further comprehensive study of diasporic audiences was funded by the Australian Research Council between 1996 and 1998. This programme, led by Stuart Cunningham, John Sinclair and Gay Hawkins was subsequently published as a book, *Floating Lives: The Media and Asian Diasporas*, in 2000. Whereas Gillespie's study had focused upon one particular community, *Floating Lives* engaged a team of researchers who explored media use amongst a range of migrant populations in Australia, including Chinese, Indian, Thai and Vietnamese communities in Brisbane, Canberra, Melbourne and Sydney. Intended to underpin policy development for multicultural media provision in Australia's diverse society, this study provided a comprehensive framing of the history and composition of each social group alongside a detailed examination of the patterns of media usage found amongst these communities. In order to access communities assumed to be somewhat inscrutable to outsiders, and to avoid the artificiality of a reception study, a number of suitable ethnic researchers were recruited to conduct interviews and gather other materials within each group. As a consequence, a rich body of material was collected that cast light upon the particularities that determined the role of popular culture in each community. A series of recommendations were made for extending the scope and availability of culturally specific content via Australian outlets, as well as involving migrant communities more deeply in planning media provision. In many respects, these arguments ran counter to the turning of the tide in terms of promoting multiculturalism in Australia, but the study remains highly valuable for the insights it provides into community media environments.

In the late 1990s, playback formats like VHS played a major role in extending the reach of ethnic media across the world (see Athique 2008b). Cable television, too, was poised to transform the availability of ethnically specific media content in Australia. The potentials of the Internet were already apparent in theory, although the available bandwidth was not sufficient at that stage for carrying video content. Accordingly, the *Floating Lives* research uncovers an ad hoc domain where a network of grocery stores serves as a distribution system for (often pirated) film and television from Asia. The enthusiasm amongst migrant communities for producing their own media content was also made apparent in the study. This was particularly true of the Vietnamese community, which primarily consists of refugees from the erstwhile republic of Vietnam and hence tended to reject official media imports from unified communist Vietnam (Cunningham and Sinclair 2000: 91–135). In that sense, this community was a true diaspora of exile in the older sense of the term, and its homespun media productions consciously evoked a homeland lost in both space and time. The pursuit of this 'exilic' nostalgia through media productions has parallels with Hamid Naficy's (1993) account of the American community of Iranian exiles. By contrast, in Australia, the relatively small and recently arrived Thai community was vigorous in the pursuit of the very latest media content from the kingdom. The Indian community appears once again as primarily religious in its motivations, although recruiting participants through religious organizations may have played a part in this. The community is also cast as diverse and divided, with obvious tensions between the twice-displaced Indo-Fijian community and more recent, and generally professional, arrivals from the subcontinent itself. The most sophisticated networks of community media are found amongst Australia's cosmopolitan Chinese community, drawing upon its longstanding trade connections across Northeast and Southeast Asia.

One of the great strengths of the *Floating Lives* research is its close attention to the structural configuration of media use amongst migrant communities. In that respect, what is striking when we look back at this work now is the exponential growth in the availability of media content for migrant communities. In the late 1990s, cable television and videocassettes were making 'minority' content available to communities who had previously faced great difficulty in sourcing any culturally specific material. Twenty years later, we can readily assume the instant availability of such content to more or less anyone in more or less any location. As such, the imperatives for publicly funded provision laid out in *Floating Lives* may well have receded in a context where the World Wide Web and satellite systems allow communities to make their own media provisions with relative ease. Nonetheless, the detailed framing of the composition and conditions of each of the communities within the study serves to demonstrate the critical importance of providing context around audience research. What the study doesn't do is present the same level of rich ethnographic responses that characterize Gillespie's work. Conversely, however, the *Floating Lives* work is much more focused upon the dynamics of community media in its own right, while Gillespie's interest in media use is largely intended as a convenient window into the assimilation of a migrant community. This dual purpose has proved to be a continuing characteristic of our approach to diasporic audiences.

Digital Diasporas

Over the past decade, the media revolution described in globalization theory has advanced quite considerably. Massive investments in telecommunications infrastructure have provided the higher bandwidth capacities that have allowed the World Wide Web to become an effective video delivery platform. This vast network upgrade has been augmented by the revolution in wireless and mobile technologies which have, in turn, leapfrogged infrastructure bottlenecks and vastly extended media access throughout the developing world. The manifold combinations of telephony and digital processing that characterize network technologies have not only remediated established media formats like video and print. They have also provided the basis for new platforms such as Skype, Facebook and Twitter. These are tools specifically conceived for a global network society, and their almost universal range has profound implications for our understanding of transnational mediation. This is a point to which I will return, but for now it is sufficient to say that the media ecology has evolved substantively in recent years and this is naturally reflected in more contemporary accounts of diasporic media audiences. First of all, it is obvious that the fusion of personal communication and mass entertainment has negated what was previously a profound technological and conceptual division of labour. Secondly, the elaborate chains of long-distance distribution associated with physical media formats have been steadily giving way to Internet-based digital streaming and roaming access via mobile devices. Thirdly, the interactive and instantaneous qualities of a mature network system have seen live, real-time interaction across national spaces become far more accessible.

All of these factors make 'perpetual contact' across national boundaries accessible to contemporary migrants (Katz and Aakhus 2002). In this environment, it is logical that the attention of audience researchers has tended to move away from video cultures and towards a range of Internet platforms. As a consequence, there has been a concomitant shift in emphasis from performance cultures to patterns of social interaction. Nonetheless, while the massive growth in access to transnational communications in technical terms may have superseded some of the earlier policy considerations surrounding media provision for migrant populations, there has also been some consistency in the underlying concerns that inform research in this area. Indeed, some of the anxieties that provoke concern around the cultural practices of migrant communities have been greatly exacerbated by the dark side of globalization: terrorism, militarism and economic instability. At the present time, a gathering backlash of xenophobia across the world is targeting migration in particular, but it also manifests itself more generally in parochial populism, militarism and a distaste for international business. Despite their exemplary status as multinational businesses par excellence, global media networks have proved to be surprisingly enthusiastic in promoting the return of these sentiments. In that sense, both the light and dark sides of McLuhan's prophecies of the electronic age appear to be bearing fruit.

> The world after September 11, 2001, is a scary place. Many, already feeling powerless due to globalization, now feel even more vulnerable to factors beyond their control. From social, political, economic, and psychological points of view, current events and media reports lead us to fear 'other' perhaps as never before. The result in some circles is a creeping xenophobia and general anxiety about the unknown. Two logical targets for this fear and insecurity are immigration, especially diasporas – immigrants who still feel a connection to their country of origin, and information technology (IT). Much has been written about them to inspire fear, including their links to terrorism. (Brinkerhoff 2009: 1)

National security concerns thereby provide a powerful framing for Jennifer Brinkerhoff's study of Internet usage amongst migrant communities in the United States. *Digital Diasporas: Identity and Transnational Engagement* (2009) analyses a range of web portals that cater to, and promote, the engagement of émigré communities with their distant homeland. In examining the discussion and interaction taking place on these websites, Brinkerhoff seeks to understand the personal, cultural and wider political significance of diasporic organizations. A total of nine web portals are examined, which variously serve communities of Afghans, Somalis, Tibetans, Nepalis and Egyptian Christians. All of these portals are committed to an active engagement with the politics or economic development of the countries from which the migrants have come. Brinkerhoff thus adds a further two components in her own definition of the diasporic audience: it must be actively engaged with the politics of the 'homeland', and it must constitute a formal organization. This conventionally political framing of diasporic media use forms the basis of the distinction that Brinkerhoff stipulates between diasporas and migrants more generally. Her disciplinary interest in international relations somewhat guides this approach, but it also has some resonance with official approaches to diasporic communities (e.g., Singhvi 2001). Benedict Anderson (once again) had previously commented on the 'long-distance nationalism' of migrant communities exerting a political influence on the states from which they came, albeit in largely negative terms (Anderson 1994). For her part, Brinkerhoff was determined to counter growing concerns in the United States about 'cyber-jihad' and the 'enemy within' with a more positive account of the valuable contributions being made by diasporic organizations to development, reconstruction and diplomacy.

In examining the interactions between community members in these online forums, Brinkerhoff is able to explore the complex reorientations of identity required by migration. She identifies a strong emotive identification with ethnicity and homeland that provides a stable anchor for individuals. Despite an obvious commitment to cultural maintenance, the influence of liberal American values is also apparent amongst community members, who then transpose these ideas and their experiences back into debates about the future of their various nations of origin. Although their personal rewards are primarily emotive, these forums are instrumental in mobilizing cogent economic and political contributions to improving the situations 'back home'. Consequently, Brinkerhoff goes on to make a series of clear policy recommendations. First and foremost: that the US government should resist its inclinations to restrict diasporic websites or intrude upon the privacy of their participants. More broadly, Brinkerhoff goes on to recommend a greater role for diasporic organizations in international relations and increased official support from both 'host' and 'homeland' governments. Thus, Brinkerhoff's treatment is explicitly political in a formal sense, and much could be said about the particular choices of communities, the nature of the organizations involved, and the ideological framing of the study, all of which serve to shape conclusions amenable to US foreign policy. For our purposes, what is arguably most striking (and possibly ironic given Brinkerhoff's stricture on privacy) is the methodological issue. That is, rather than relying upon face-to-face interviews, attending community events or analysing cultural performances, Brinkerhoff was able to ascertain the nature of community interaction by harvesting commentary from the websites themselves. The advent of this form of 'virtual ethnography' has rapidly become a standard practice, and this itself is hugely significant for contemporary audience studies (Kozinets 2010).

Polymedia

A useful counterpoint to the explicit geopolitical framing of Brinkerhoff's study is Mirca Madianou and Daniel Miller's (2012) recent research into the use of contemporary media for sustaining transnational family relations. Here, the emphasis shifts from formal cultural organizations to extended family networks, and from political debates to intimate and interpersonal communication. This was a research programme that set out to explore the ways in which Filipino migrants in London maintain their connections to children who remain in the Philippines. The unique conditions of the Filipino diaspora prove to be particularly significant to this case. The government of the Philippines has long promoted labour export as a means of securing a considerable inflow of capital via remittances from Filipino seamen, construction workers, domestic maids, child carers and nurses. These schemes have established niches for Filipino labour across the world. Although such stays overseas are often lengthy, they do not generally constitute permanent migration, and therefore the proportion of migrants leaving families behind is very high. Since the role of women in this labour economy is significant, there are many Filipinas who spend long periods separated from their children. The importance of extended families in the Philippines supports this dynamic, with relatives playing a key role in caring for children across the wider family, and adults in turn having extensive obligations beyond the nuclear family unit. Given the difficult economic circumstances for many Filipino families and the central importance of securing a relatively expensive education for their children, the pull of offshore labour contracts is very strong (see Parrenas 2006).

In London, the Filipino diaspora is primarily visible through the nursing staff recruited for Britain's National Health Service and in the new service class that has arisen amongst London's professional property-owning classes. As such, this is a markedly feminine diaspora and, given the matriarchal sensibilities of British society, the long-term separation of these women from their children is markedly anomalous to prevailing discourses of parenthood. As such, a major component of the study was intended to interrogate the mother-child dynamics in these transnational families. This was done through extensive interviews with Filipino mothers in London, as well as with their children and relatives in the Philippines. Connectivity between these family members from one side of the world to the other is necessarily dependent upon media technologies and, consequently, a large part of the study examines the role of various media platforms in framing long-distance interactions. The study examines the use of older media forms such as letters, cassettes and telephone calls, but the major focus falls upon the widespread usage of Internet communications such as email, Skype and instant messaging. Madianou and Miller identify a substantial number of options readily available for maintaining regularized contact with distant family members, but also emphasize that the particular affordances of each medium shape the ways in which such communication takes place. In that sense, their study leans heavily upon 'medium theory' in detailing the ways in which interpersonal communication is shaped by the technologies in use (2012: 103–23). At the same time, the study is also sensitive to the anthropological dimension, that is, to the ways in which Filipino cultural practices and social norms exert an equally critical influence upon the content, conduct and timing of communication.

In presenting the stories of these transnational families, Madianou and Miller are able to explore a set of mediated relationships which are sometimes fraught and destabilized, but just as often also liberating and empowering. The women in the study are not cast as exploited labour from the Third World, but rather as educated and aspirational women who have made informed decisions about their relocation. These respondents tended to exude a positive view of life in the UK, and several of them were electing to stay for extended periods or even permanently. At the same time, they also made considerable efforts to maintain extensive and regularized communicative and economic relations with their families back home. As opposed to many studies that frame diasporic media use primarily as a matter of cultural survival stemming from permanent disorientation and a longing to return home, this case study uncovers a more complex field of strategic decisions made by individuals seeking to maximize the potential of living a transnational life. The conscious politics of British multiculturalism come less into play here, due to the metropolitan setting, the relative neutrality of the UK-Philippines relationship, and the absence of a second-generation community. Consequently, a more individualized focus gives us an entirely different framework for understanding media and migration. The particular mediums in use here are also critically important. Most early studies of migrant communities were primarily concerned about the cultural differences revealed in their reception of mainstream national media content, or with the role of ethnic media in sustaining cultural identity in an alien setting. Madianou and Miller, by contrast, are overwhelmingly concerned with the new prevalence of interpersonal communication at the transnational scale. This therefore reflects an important switch in emphasis from the symbolic to the functional registers of mediation.

As a consequence of their study, Madianou and Miller advance a theory of 'polymedia' that emphasizes the strategic choices made by media users when engaging a whole series of options made available by different combinations of digital devices and telephony. This 'rich' field of communication choices for migrants reflects an inherent characteristic of the era of 'social media' in which we presently live. The rapid extension of these capabilities, and their attendant literacies, into developing societies such as the Philippines marks a very significant shift in the global media ecology. For migrants, it transforms an experience that was long associated with profound disconnection from family and a cultural absence that caused ongoing distress. In its place, we are beginning to see a world in which families interact regularly across the global space, and ethnically specific media and information are instantly available worldwide. This, of course, prompts us to consider diasporic audiences in an entirely different light. The shift from community organizations to individualized transnationalism is also evocative of the intense personalization of media platforms that has become prevalent in the era of 'polymedia'. Thus, Madianou and Miller's treatment of migration is redolent of a broader shift in the field of mediation more generally, where moral decisions come to rest with the user rather than the broadcaster or policy maker (2012: 138). How far does this go? Certainly, if minority media practices no longer require a communal presence, then this has profound implications for the ways in which we seek to aggregate such practices under the heading of 'audiences'.

The Call for Hybridity

What becomes immediately evident through the literature on diasporic audiences is the extent to which the cultural practices of migrant communities become over-determined by the wider geopolitical concerns of state actors. The explicit question of where these people belong is always accompanied by the implicit question of who they belong to. Given the powerful linkages between ethnicity, cultural practice and communal identity expressed in most definitions of diaspora, their place within a world system determined by cultural nationalism inevitably positions their media usage as an inherently political affair. In the multicultural polities examined in the studies covered here, there is evidence of a continuing desire to organize ethnic minorities into recognizable communities with the appropriate organizations and 'notables' with whom the respective authorities can communicate at a policy level. This is largely a hangover of the old colonial system on home turf, and while there are benefits for ethnic lobbies within this system, their domain of everyday culture inevitably becomes subject to governance and intervention. To be fair, some countries (such as France)

are more fervently assimilationist in their approach to migrant populations, while other major economies such as Germany or Japan simply do
not naturalize 'ethnic' outsiders. This does not, of course, make the cultural milieu of migrant communities in those countries any more or less
diasporic. Nonetheless, the heavy hand of state interests in many academic
approaches to media reception amongst migrant communities does much
to undermine Appadurai's (1996) prediction that nation states and national
publics are being subsumed by ethnic cultures flowing back and forth across
the surface of the world.

The global mosaic of the ethnoscape cannot so easily escape its own investment in the present state system. Indeed, it is precisely the mutual adherence to the precepts of cultural nationalism in both diaspora theory and the
modern nation state that make such an outcome highly unlikely. In practice,
what Appadurai's theory of culture under globalization seeks to achieve is
a reterritorializing of nationalist models of culture onto biological rather
than physical terrain. An alternative reading of the cultural significance of
diasporic communities, propounded forcefully by Stuart Hall, argues instead
for the inherent hybridity forged from literacy in multiple cultures (Hall
1990, 1993; Hall et al. 1996). Contrary to ethnic essentialism, Hall saw the
maintenance by migrants of ethno-cultural connections with 'homelands' as
being subject to a continual evolution, as everyday practices and identities
are inspired by complex sets of shifting social referents in their immediate
environment. Taking this line, Rajinder Dudrah believes that diasporic social
conditions 'can be considered as taking up the interplay of migrant people,
their successive settled generations, and their ideas in terms of a triadic relationship. This relationship can be thought of as working between the place of
origin, place of settlement, and a diasporic consciousness that shifts between
the two' (Dudrah 2002a: 20). As a critical intervention in cultural politics,
the 'hybridity' approach positions migrant subjects as more than simply passive markers of ethnic territory, championing them instead as cosmopolitan
innovators capable of crossing cultural divides and making culture anew.

In considering migrant audiences as 'hybridities' rather than 'minorities', our attention is directed towards processes of cultural fusion and the
instances of code-switching that arise when people inhabit and interpret
multiple cultures. At the same time, the term deploys not only cultural but
also biological inferences. In that sense, it further strengthens the linkages
between race and culture that characterize research into diasporic audiences
more generally. This has inevitable, and quite considerable, political implications, as Marwan Kraidy (2005) has noted in his extensive appraisal of the
pursuit of hybridity within the academy. Evolving from its origins in anti-
colonial theory and a radical critique of racism in Britain, Kraidy saw the

subsequent trajectory of debates around hybridity in the United States shift towards the celebration of a 'global multiculturalism' curated by the West. By taking up hybridity simply as a descriptive category of 'Westernized' ethnicities, 'glocalized' cultures and of mixed-race populations, the concept was shorn of the political potentials that might have arisen from the empowerment of non-white subjects (Kraidy 2002). Nonetheless, within the academy itself, hybridity was a 'hot topic' during the 'multicultural' 1990s. It was commonly deployed as a referent to the border zones within the perennially unstable categories of race and culture. As such, hybridity became a catchphrase for ethnic cosmopolitanism as well as a rationale for focusing upon the border zones (or 'interstices') at the expense of the cultural thickenings that marked the centres.

For Kraidy, the 'progressive' credentials of the hybridity paradigm must lie in the political, as opposed to the categorical, dimension of such work. The origins of the concept in the politics of discrimination should be recognized. Thus, hybridity must be considered as 'a space where intercultural and international communication practices are continuously negotiated in interactions of differential power' (Kraidy 2002: 317). The radical potentials of such enquiry should not be co-opted by a mainstream 'multiculturalism' that simply incorporates ethnicities by eating their food and showing them off on television. Indeed, by replacing a critique of structural relations with the grant of symbolic legitimacy, 'ethnic social justice' becomes reducible to the corporate multiculturalism of Disney features. By the logics of neoliberalism more broadly, a progressive agenda for race easily becomes synonymous with the establishment of brown brands as 'consumer empowerment'. In the other direction, calls to mobilize hybridity as a platform for a continuing anti-colonialism among migrants who have, in the majority, willingly joined the populace of the erstwhile imperial states has its own problems. Certainly, many states have been keen to suborn their émigré populations as ethnic lobby groups for their own interests, without much care for their hybrid sensibilities and, sometimes, for quite racist reasons. International politics is an uncaring business, especially for those in the border zones. At heart, then, the political arguments around hybridity represent a face-off between ethnic instrumentalism of various kinds and a genuine aspiration towards multiplicity in the personal and political.

Communalism in Practice

Reflecting on the studies considered in this chapter, we can see the predominance of communal identities and ethnic sociability in the work of both Stuart Cunningham and Jennifer Brinkerhoff. We can see the complexities of cultural negotiation and individual agency more clearly in the work of Marie Gillespie, Mirca Madianou and Daniel Miller. There is a methodological issue here, in that research conducted through community organizations tends towards communal generalizations, whereas more individualized or family-centred studies tend to draw out less homogeneous positions. Either way, the media consumption of diasporic communities, whilst taken to be exemplary of contemporary global modernity, is figured as a heavyweight concern: 'a struggle for survival, identity and assertion' (Cunningham 2001: 136). We can also see, then, that the 'burden of representation' placed upon ethnic minorities is overlaid with an equal burden of reception that inherently politicizes their media habits. Nonetheless, despite an obvious tendency to triangulate ethnicity, culture and audience, we must always remember that ethnically specific media typically make up a relatively small component of the media diet in migrant populations. More often than not, these people will be engaging with the mainstream media of the nation in which they reside. When they do this, of course, they become figured as 'minority audiences' rather than diasporic ones. Furthermore, they will also be engaging with wider transnational flows that address neither their ethnicity nor their national situation. So, in that sense, diasporic audiences are not closed social formations, which is not to deny the imaginative appeal of ethnic solidarity across national boundaries.

Within the academy, the established paradigm for examining diasporic audiences is based upon an underlying notion of 'mediatized ethnic minorities' whose cultural consumption is assumed to be a mechanism for ethno-cultural maintenance and communal representation. Following these precepts, the diasporic media audience tends to be considered as either: 1) overwhelmingly concerned with the maintenance of an ethnic culture, or 2) beset by the challenges of combining different cultural streams. This body of work therefore rests upon an explicitly ethno-cultural understanding of society, and naturally tends to position migrant media habits within the established logics of cultural nationalism. Because there is often an official interest in these kind of studies, the interests of both 'home' and 'host' states tend to be present in the framing of the research. The cultural politics involved are necessarily complex and, in light of domestic ethnocentrism and wider geopolitical situations, such studies can often be fraught with dangers for both researchers and their subjects. There are also significant methodological issues that commonly arise, not least because the media usage of a sample of migrants is often taken as a convenient 'identity window' for qualitative researchers and policy makers to extrapolate the worldview of an entire population. Although ethnicities are typically large, sample groups are invariably small (given the need for in-depth qualitative approaches to the complex research questions in play). Such studies are prescriptive, in that members of this audience are required to speak for, and only through, their ethnicity. Racial profiling inevitably places a particular characterization upon their responses, even where there is much variation in habits and responses.

There is some cause, then, to be wary of the ethnic microcosms inferred by Appadurai and Cunningham. In an era of resurgent ethno-nationalism this is a politically dangerous approach for obvious reasons, but it is also an empirically suspect claim. Taking a wider view, it is becoming evident that audiences everywhere are increasingly engaging with a pluralized media environment that favours transnational flows and niche content. This would include not only minority but also 'majority' citizens. In a putative 'global' media environment such behaviour constitutes a relatively logical pattern of consumption. Any model for transnational media reception must therefore deal more explicitly with the 'channel-multiplication' that is inherent to globalization, and a tidy mosaic of ethnic audiences with their own media channels cannot fulfil this obligation as readily as Appadurai suggests. In that respect, the function of media content in policing the boundaries of ethnic difference is likely to prove no more tenable than the notion that culture smoothly demarcates the geographical and bureaucratic borders of a nation state. Civilizational discourses aside, it is important to remember that media consumption remains primarily a matter of entertainment and interpersonal relationships, and must therefore be understood as a source of gratification at some level. The role of pleasure in the media choices being made by 'ethnic' communities should not be made entirely subservient to explanations which portray ethnic media use as a statement of (either heroic or threatening) social and cultural identification (see Banaji 2006).

Reading Diasporic Audiences

It is largely axiomatic for studies of diasporic audiences to match ethnically specific media content and respondents, and this kind of a priori positioning tends to perpetuate perceptions of migrant communities as ethnocultural ghettoes. In practice, diasporic audiences consume a lot of media in which they have no ethnic investment. At the theoretical level, to demand a tidy anthropological schema from cultural representation, or a new political order, is to miss the point of popular culture. Indeed, Brinkerhoff's further assertion that diasporas must be formally organized and politically engaged in the politics of their homeland would narrow the focus even more. For audience researchers, this would constitute an unwarranted shift from analysing the phenomena of transnational mediation itself in order to privilege the use of media in exilic politics. Such marginal activities are better considered as being a small subset within diasporic media flows, the volume of which is overwhelmingly dominated by interpersonal communication between families and friends, and by the broader dispersal of commerce and entertainment. The continuing significance of diasporic audiences to transnational media flows is at once obvious, but they can (and have) been overstated as an archetypal case. Appadurai, for example, argued that the world was becoming transnational 'in a specifically diasporic sense'. With the benefit of hindsight, I believe that much greater care should be taken to distinguish between the diaspora of ethnic populations and the global dispersal of media products. Certainly, we should not privilege the overlaps between the two at the expense of other phenomena emerging from the mobility of media. Diasporic modes of reception are, more properly, particularized occurrences within a more diverse media ecology.

Recommended Reading

Andoni Alonso and Pedro Oiarzabal (eds) (2010) *Diasporas in the New Media Age: Identity, Politics, and Community*, Reno: University of Nevada Press.

Olga G. Bailey, Myria Georgiou and Ramaswami Harindranath (2007) *Transnational Lives and the Media: Re-Imagining Diasporas*, Houndmills: Palgrave Macmillan.

Jennifer Brinkerhoff (2009) *Digital Diasporas: Identity and Transnational Engagement*, Cambridge: Cambridge University Press.

Stuart Cunningham and John Sinclair (2000) *Floating Lives: Media and Asian Diasporas*, St. Lucia: University of Queensland Press.

Leopoldina Fortunati, Raul Pertierra and Jane Vincent (eds) (2013) *Migration, Diaspora and Information Technology in Global Societies*, New York: Routledge.

Marwan Kraidy (2005) *Hybridity, or the Cultural Logic of Globalization*, Philadelphia: Temple University Press.

Mirca Madianou and Daniel Miller (2012) *Migration and New Media: Transnational Families and Poly-Media*, London: Routledge.

Wanning Sun (2006) *Media and the Chinese Diaspora: Community, Communications and Commerce*, London and New York: Routledge.

6   Mediaculturalism, Universalism and the Exotic

As a particular manifestation of transnationalism, the study of diasporic audiences often adheres to the notion that when people move across the world they will seek to remain within the same cultural configuration. That is, at some level these are considered to be transnational, but not cross-cultural, flows. Those who have focused more upon the 'hybridity' or dual-culture arguments do not necessarily concur with the more mono-cultural definitions of diaspora. Instead, they tend to position cross-cultural migrants as possessors of what is essentially 'dual citizenship' in cultural terms, a capacity that makes them the natural interlocutors between cultures. When we go beyond a genealogical reading of transnational culture entirely, we must seek to account for the longstanding trade in cultural products between countries that clearly have little or nothing to do with migration as such. It is widely recognized, of course, that media businesses have tended to be global operations throughout their history. Indeed, a relatively short period of terrestrial television broadcasting during the late twentieth century is the closest we have come to nationally contained systems, and even then this tended to spill across borders (as well as broadcasting significant volumes of imported content). By extending these qualities, satellite television is an explicitly transnational business, and movies, music and publishing have always been so. Contemporary information technology, for technical as much as commercial reasons, is inherently global in scope. Nonetheless, despite the long pedigree and considerable cash value of media exports, the transnational trade in cultural goods has long been one of the most complex issues facing globalization enthusiasts at consecutive rounds of trade negotiations. Cultural specificity and cultural diversity have powerful links to nationalist sentiments and have long been championed in the fight against cultural imperialism.

At the same time, however, foreign media content has been consistently popular with audiences. Indeed, where it has been restricted, a black market for such goods has quickly come into being. However enthusiastic consumers may be, most academic commentary on media imports is essentially defensive, if not downright negative (see Jarvie 2000). National media industries complain about competition from foreign producers but, at the same time, the vast majority of them vigorously pursue their own media exports. As such, the importance of offshore markets is widely understood at a commercial level, even where a taste for such content runs counter to media and social theory in general. A liking for foreign content directly challenges nationalist conceptions of what culture is all about. This is why media imports can, and often do, come under attack from social and religious conservatives concerned about their social influence. At the same time, because this material has tended to be commercial in nature, and a large volume of it has come from the United States, it has also tended to be opposed by commentators with artistic or socialist persuasions. So, essentially, nobody likes it but everybody loves it. As with all transnational mediation, there are geopolitical forces in play, and we have already explored some of the broad ideological concerns in theories of media and cultural imperialism. In everyday practice, however, the cross-cultural trade in media content is more commonly structured by commercial motivations, in terms of both threats and opportunities. What is almost never discussed in any great detail is the basis upon which we can conceive of the 'crossover' audience for media exports. This conceptual gap will be our focus in this chapter, taking our lead from two major media streams that operate in multiple cross-cultural configurations.

Doing Dallas

The first stream, suitably enough, is the longstanding predominance of American television exports discussed in chapter 3. The cultural imperialism thesis formalized in response to this hegemony rested upon the proposition that such content had an overt ideological influence on its viewers. Without this proposition, the balancing of global media markets is merely an economic matter comparable to many other sectors. Nonetheless, because these concerns were very much centred upon cultural influence, the hightide of American predominance during the 1970s and 1980s naturally suggested the need for substantial reception studies by which the proposition of 'Americanization' as a media effect could be tested. The problem, as John Tomlinson has noted, was that the cultural imperialism thesis required prohibitively large-scale and comparative evidence on a global scale (1991: 55). Such evidence could only come from audience research. Since cultural identity and media reception are complex subjective processes, however, they tend to require detailed qualitative approaches that do not easily extrapolate to a global scale. Similarly, in a world structured by cultural diversity and affinity in any number of ways, the numbers of variables involved in establishing cultural imperialism *in toto* would have to be accounted for on a vast case-by-case basis. At the time when the threat of Americanization was being most keenly felt, and with the available research methods, any authoritative study would have required the deployment of practically every media specialist and anthropologist in the world. As such, any definitive answer to the question of cultural imperialism would have involved something like a 'Manhattan project' for cultural studies.

This is not to say that, prior to the rise of 'big data', no useful work could be conceived of in terms of exploring the reception of imported television. Nonetheless, the contours of the international media trade before the turn of the century did mean that the ubiquitous global presence of American film and television generally provided the most accessible basis for research into cross-cultural reception. One of the most significant moments in the 'internationalization' of audience research during the heyday of terrestrial television was the work conceived around the popularity of the American television drama, *Dallas*. This was essentially a soap opera centred upon the melodramas unfolding within a fabulously rich Texan oil family. The series was carried by broadcasters around the world, and the near fatal shooting of the family patriarch 'J. R. Ewing' became a significant enough 'television event' to receive coverage on national news broadcasts. Despite this incredible popularity, the show was also seen to encapsulate everything that was disliked about American popular culture. That is, it was capitalist, sexist, ostentatious, low-brow and emotively cheap. Addressing this conundrum of overwhelming popularity and stringent critique, cultural studies scholar Ien Ang set out to explore audience responses to the serial in the Netherlands. In part, her motivation was to test whether her own enjoyment of the show, and her conscious dislike of its underlying ideology, resonated with the experience of others. At another level, this work was part of the broader push in cultural studies to take popular culture seriously, and to overturn the academic disdain for it that was still prevalent at that time.

Another important strand in Ang's work was to interrogate the obvious contradictions marked by the simultaneous popularity and snobbish disparagement of American popular culture in European countries. Using written responses from viewers as the primary data, Ang's *Watching Dallas* (1985) attempts to draw out the complex ways in which emotional pleasure and ideological offence can be taken simultaneously from a text. The broadly critical position taken by these viewers towards everything that *Dallas* appeared to represent was not substantively altered by the simple fact they enjoyed it so much. Indeed, rather than revealing any process of Americanization, Ang felt that her respondents had if anything internalized, and tended to reproduce, the domestic critiques of both popular and American culture. Nonetheless, the emotional exploitations of this overblown melodrama were simply too enjoyable to give up in the name of 'cultural correctness'. The undeniable popularity of the *Dallas* format would lead to many subsequent imitations around the world, but at the peak of its popularity it also provided a unique opportunity for a comparative study of cross-cultural reception. This was taken up by the Israeli mass communication experts, Tamar Liebes and Elihu Katz (1984, 1988, 1993). To begin with, they arranged screenings of *Dallas* to small groups of viewers from differing ethnicities living in Israel's complex multi-ethnic and multi-faith society. These respondents were grouped together on the basis of ethnic identity and then questioned about their understanding of the show, its narrative and its cultural significance. Liebes and Katz were thus able to explore how the particular cultural identities of the various groups led to differing interpretations of the text.

The Ethnic Comparative

Liebes and Katz's study from 1984 to 1990 implemented a variant of the reception model promoted by British cultural studies (primarily Brunsdon and Morley's *Nationwide* studies (1978; Morley 1980)). In this case, it was ethnicity rather than class that provided the variable amongst audience samples, with the central text being a transnational import rather than a hegemonic national text. Broadly, there were two major, and contradictory, findings. First of all, there was more or less universal agreement on the central concerns of the show itself and its appeal to the general public. These centred on the dynamics of kinship, on moral dilemmas for family members and on the pressures raised by familial conflict and financial success. These 'universal' themes were taken to have greater significance than the American 'accent' of the show per se. Conversely, however, the 'translation' of the central meanings of *Dallas* to suit the sensibilities of each ethnic group was also a major finding of the study. For example: Arab viewers tended to describe the show in terms of the tensions within a patriarchal family structure, Russian immigrants tended to describe it in more sociological terms, and Kibbutzniks tended to apply a more Freudian frame of analysis to the narrative. On this basis, the central claim of the research was that the international popularity of the text rested upon its capacity to engage themes of universal human concern, but that the meanings ultimately derived from watching the show were primarily determined by the moral frameworks specific to each ethnic group.

Because they took the various readings of *Dallas* to be ethnically specific, Liebes and Katz conducted an analysis that sought to categorize the nature of these readings in terms of cultural values. Arabs and Moroccan Jews were seen as being more concerned with moral values than dramatic conceits. Equally, these groups were perceived to read the text more literally, to take its message more seriously, and to conceive of the programme from a largely patriarchal perspective. In direct contrast, the Kibbutzniks (mostly European immigrants) and the Americans were seen to comprehend the text in ways that were more ironic, critical and playful, and they demonstrated a greater capacity to identify with the characters at a more personal level. The odd group out was the Russian immigrants, who tended to perceive the text as an ideological whole and to assess the characters as ideal types operating within the primacy of social structures. We could, perhaps, assume the influence of a Marxist teaching in these responses, given the Soviet origins of these immigrants. As the research was subsequently extended to include respondents in the United States, it was found that American viewers tended to read the text in a similar fashion to Ashkenazi Jews in Israel. They were less likely to see *Dallas* as a commentary on American culture. As a point of distinctiveness they were the only group in which the oil business was seen to be a significant reference point.

There are obvious strengths and weaknesses in the conception and execution of the Liebes and Katz studies. In the first place, the sample groups are necessarily small but readily taken to indicate the cultural viewpoint of an entire population. Secondly, the 'lab' viewing of the text, the narrative comprehension exercise, and the ethnically specific focus group structure constitute obviously artificial conditions of reception. In the analysis, there is an unreflexive tendency to make massive generalizations about ethnic identities that go well beyond the literal content of the responses provided by the viewers who took part. The correlation between Sephardic Jews and Arabs and the self-identification of mostly Eastern European Jews with Anglo-Americans are powerful structuring discourses within Israeli society that could and should have been dealt with more critically. The former, at least, is both ubiquitous and highly controversial. These are extant discourses that do not simply emerge from the research findings, but are instead superimposed by the researchers themselves in the study design. The anomalous responses of the Russians provide some indication of their indeterminate place within Israeli cultural politics as they began to arrive in the late 1980s and early 1990s. Since then, they may have swapped Marx for Freud and learned to take life less seriously, but in this study they are captured in a less assimilated state. In light of all this, it is somewhat problematic to take multicultural Israel as a microcosm for comparative transnational reception. Rather, the representative positioning of the ethnic groups is specific to the politics of the country itself, if none the less revealing and valuable in that regard.

Liebes and Katz's underlying premise of the ethnic specificity of reception is a mainstream view, notwithstanding the obvious need to situate such categorizations more clearly within the wider social and political structures in which they are being read. In that qualified sense, the specificity of reception is usefully validated by the particularities of the Israeli study itself. When taken in tandem with the more Eurocentric concerns of Ang's study, the potentials for comparative studies of reception are readily apparent. Much has, of course, changed since the days of the *Dallas* studies. The shift of economic and technical capacity towards Asia, the much lower costs of media production after digitization, and the far greater profusion of overlapping and competing media sources make it more difficult to achieve the worldwide prevalence enjoyed by *Dallas*. Even the high-end television serials produced by HBO do not have quite the same impact that the much cheaper *Dallas* once had. The lasting influence of the show can be seen in Brazilian telenovelas and Hindi soaps, but whether this provides evidence of Americanization per se is doubtful. More significant for our present concerns is the fact that new media technologies have made larger comparative audience studies a more practical proposition for researchers. As such, there have been some significant initiatives in global audience research in recent years, based in large part around the Hollywood blockbusters that continue to operate as the archetypal global texts (e.g., Barker and Mathijs 2007).

Transnational Cinema

As we switch our attention towards cinema, there is also a useful opportunity to think of cross-cultural communication beyond the narrow confines of the 'Americanization' debates. Cinema, has of course, been dominated in financial terms by Hollywood to an even greater extent than has global television. At the same time, there have always been significant film industries in Europe and Asia that serve export audiences as well as domestic ones. Hong Kong cinema has long served a broad regional market as well as benefiting from the 'cult' status achieved by its martial arts action features around the world (Pugsley 2013; Srinivas 2003; Yau 2001). Japanese filmmakers have long received international recognition for art cinema, and many Japanese productions have inspired Hollywood directly (from *Seven Samurai* to *The Ring*). French art film has had a steady export market for intellectual audiences in the English-speaking world, as well as having a double life as a soft-porn product in Asia (at least, it did in the pre-Internet era). Indian films, commonly pirated, have found export markets from Japan to Morocco. British cinema survives primarily as a supplier of period dramas and other kitsch to the US market. As such, while Hollywood remains the financial juggernaut, the 'film world' is at least multi-polar. Of course, we should also recognize that Hollywood itself is an inherently transnational business that has always pursued global markets and global talent. The equation of Hollywood and American culture is commonplace, but not without its problems. Nonetheless, for much of the twentieth century, there was a widespread, and quite remarkable, consensus concerning the practice of positioning the cinemas of the world as primarily national, indigenous institutions neatly arranged in a hub-and-spoke relationship with an 'international' Hollywood industry.

Hollywood is, without a doubt, the quintessential transnational media industry. In recent years, however, the popularity of the 'transnational cinema' concept has been more commonly associated with 'hybrid' cultural products appearing on the reworked menu of 'world cinema' (Chaudhuri 2005). As such, when we talk of transnational cinema, we are encouraged to think in categorical terms, for example of Franco-Australian co-productions shot by German directors. We are also commonly directed towards films dealing explicitly with the 'fourth world' of immigrant cultures in various locations or directed by personnel of mixed or diasporic cultural backgrounds. Essentially, transnational cinema is a loose term used to denote any film where the diegesis falls outside of the strict 'resident' conditions imposed by the long dominant 'national' theories of cinema. So, in that sense, transnational cinema is an emergent discourse, by which I mean that it is neither a radically new proposition nor one which can be easily contained within the ways of thinking that went before. While there may be much to celebrate in the 'cultural fusion' referenced by the term, we must somehow account for the audience that arises for these films. They are clearly not intended solely for the gratification of a small, matched and similarly hybrid audience, since the returns are unlikely to be adequate. Rather, they are intended for the consumption of some 'other' audiences. This leaves us with a conceptual difficulty, since it is a well-established paradigm that film audiences are overwhelmingly directed towards the reassurances of their own national cinema, augmented only (and massively) by their love of universal Hollywood films.

It would seem reasonable, then, to ask where this new hybrid 'transnational' style fits into the cultural order of 'world cinema'. That is a question, however, I would prefer to leave to others. For the purposes of understanding transnational audiences for feature films, such contrived examples are hardly likely to address the broader questions in any depth. Those who speculate in the cultural industries generally do so on the basis of their interpretation of a known market conceptualized in the form of an audience.

It is the capacity for imagining large numbers of plausible – but fictitious and essentially unknowable – consumers upon which commercial success depends. Thus, the more pressing questions are why, and under what conditions, Americans become predisposed to watch French films, Germans become amenable to Australian films, or Turks develop a liking for Indian films. In that sense, the problem is that the edifice of world cinema is based upon non-resident viewing conditions that, theoretically at least, it disavows. A distinguishing feature of academic treatments of 'national cinemas' has been their consistent tendency to assert various 'reflective' and 'effective' attributes of feature films as essential components of national identity (Hayward 1993; Gittings 2002; Hake 2002). What they offer to 'non-domestic' viewers has always been rather less clear, which is highly problematic given that many of these national producers are aggressive exporters. The negative framing of transnational media reception, more broadly, is entirely discordant with the celebratory aspects of the international film festival circuit that forms the high table of 'world cinema'. It also has very little relationship to the political economy of the cinema, which is rarely national in any of its operations. These are factors that draw our attention to the shortcomings of the theoretical introspection of national cinema studies within an overtly international world system.

The Culture Vultures

In order to identify some of the major configurations of transnational audiences for non-Hollywood cinema, I will draw upon the most high-profile case of recent years, that being the 'Bollywood' phenomenon. The term itself is fairly recent, given the 100-year history of cinema production in the Indian subcontinent. Nonetheless, 'Bollywood' somehow captures a moment when one of the more substantive 'other' commercial industries begins to consciously seek a global expansion of its audiences. In actuality, the heightened international profile of Indian cinema only became possible because it had already established considerable export territories over many decades prior to the moment in which it became fashionable in Western markets. As such, Indian films had a global presence long before they were given global significance. This belated recognition came when they began to enjoy commercial success in Anglo-Saxon countries, and not insignificantly, at a time when those countries were seeking to court India for various commercial and geopolitical reasons. For their part, the embrace of the transnational paradigm by Indian producers was primarily a response to economic liberalization during the late 1990s. As export and currency controls were loosened, there was a newfound awareness of the commercial potentials of export activity for an industry whose global footprint largely stemmed from the circulation of pirated films in the developing world (Athique 2008b). Looking to a new horizon, both the importance of 'hard' currency returns and the legacy of colonialism directed new export ambitions towards the Western hemisphere.

Given the origins of Indian cinema in the colonial period, the notion of a 'Western viewer' was itself as old as the study of Indian cinema. Since the days of Satyajit Ray and the Indian Film Society movements in the 1950s there had been a consistent comparison between an Indian audience, typified by illiteracy and an enthusiasm for escapist fare, and an occidental viewer acculturated to a diet of realism rather than fantasy, drama rather than melodrama, and psychological motivation over musical excess (see Vasudevan 2000). Of course, aside from the music, this realist model of Western audiences rather contradicted the popular fare consumed in European, North American and Australasian cinema halls. It did, perhaps, suit the kind of audiences addressed by art-house cinemas and film festivals, which in Anglophone countries have traditionally been the environment for the screening of foreign-language films. Prior to the 1990s the only Indian films to reach any significant Western audiences were art films operating in this niche market, described by Jigna Desai as:

> based on positioning 'foreign' films as ethnographic documents of 'other' (national) cultures and therefore as representatives of national cinemas. In particular, foreign Third World films that can be read as portraying the other through cultural difference (i.e., gender and sexual experiences or nativist renderings of rural village life). (Desai 2004: 39)

The art-house audience in the West represents a collection of consumers with various degrees of investment in an ethno-cultural scheme of 'world cinema'. This coalition of interests might include those with an academic or professional interest either in cinema or in the 'producing culture'. It also encompasses viewers whose consumption of foreign films represents a mixture of auto-didacticism and aesthetic pleasure-seeking gaining them a measure of cosmopolitan cultural capital. As much as exposure to foreign popular culture is generally taken to be bad for 'the masses', the suitably positioned consumption of 'quality' foreign produce by suitably educated viewers is taken to be a hallmark, even a requirement, of good taste. No self-respecting cineaste can be seen as being ignorant of an international pantheon of renowned directors. That is why art-house outlets co-locate a Third World 'exotic' with European *auteur* cinema and with the alternative or independent sector of the host nation's local film culture. It is significant that, for a long time, the art-house audience was the normative taste culture addressed by academic film studies. However, the turn towards the audience under the influence of cultural studies has been accompanied by a parallel shift towards the products of popular cinema as forming the object of study. Together these conjoined developments have had the curious effect of making the art-house crowd one of the least researched media audiences of all. There is scarcely any research on the art-house and film festival audiences that many of us frequent. This is a classic case, perhaps, of 'not seeing the wood for the trees'.

As far as we do understand it, the art-house audience is an intellectual niche arising from culturally literate and/or cosmopolitan members of the majority population who are willing to extend their consumption of media cultures (and media *as* culture). The idea that a cultural identity can be encapsulated in a film is maintained, but it is assumed that under the right conditions, and with the right education and objective distance, this can be accessed by a well-placed foreigner. 'Mediaculturalism' is thus the visual equivalent of an overseas holiday or learning to enjoy foreign foods. More prosaically, it has been noted that the art-house audience tends to include a large proportion of film professionals, students and academics (Lewis 1990). With the distraction of more recent generations into the pleasures of digital culture, however, this is also an obviously ageing audience. For producers, the art-house audience is the constituency frequenting the 'world cinema' menu offered by multiplex cinemas, film festivals, playback outlets and the various 'arts' channels available through cable television (Athique 2008c; Desai 2004; Huffer 2013). In general terms, then, we could say the art-house audience congregates ritually around the cultural conventions of 'quality cinema', a branding that is formally shaped by directors, distributors, exhibitors and critics. This taste culture has been established over the longer term by maintaining a strong distinction between popular and bourgeois taste cultures. Consequently, a significant portion of the art-house audience appears to consider itself as being literate and semi-expert in the medium.

Crossing Over

It was during the 2000s that Indian films of a very different kind began to appear outside of this sophisticated ghetto. Part of the reason for this was that migrant audiences resident in the West, inhabiting the same metropoles as the art-house audiences, had given *popular* Indian cinema a commercially viable presence in the new context of multiplex exhibition

(Kerrigan and Ozbilgin 2002: 200). A further factor at play in the sudden 'buzz' surrounding 'Bollywood' in the West was the success of a number of Indian-themed films produced by directors of Indian origin working within various Western film industries (see Desai 2004). The success of these films with niche (largely middlebrow) audiences encouraged the staging of various events designed to promote 'regular' Indian films amongst a more 'mainstream' audience. For example, the British Film Institute (BFI) organized an extensive showcase of Indian cinema, *ImagineAsia*, as part of a nationwide *Indian Summer* festival which also included the use of Bollywood themes in department store merchandise, visual art exhibitions and theatrical productions. This celebration of Indian popular culture under the rubric of 'multiculturalism' was consciously designed to provide a context for the consumption of Indian cultural products by the UK's majority white population. The BFI's *ImagineAsia* festival of Indian cinema was thereby considered a success primarily since it drew almost a third of its audience from outside of Britain's South Asian population (White and Rughani 2003). Similar experiments were also undertaken in North America and Australia, with the Indian film Industry collaborating to take its own Bollywood spectacular on an annualized world tour. This is the broader context within which 'crossover' became a buzz word in the Indian film industries (Kumar 2011; Khorana 2013).

The term 'crossover' naturally demands critical attention because, as Desai has observed, its use appears to be synonymous with the quest for white audiences for 'ethnic' media artefacts (2004: 66). The crossing described by the term is unidirectional in two registers: 'niche to mainstream' and 'ethnic to universal'. Crossing over from a niche audience to a larger 'mainstream' audience promises greater exposure and profits. Crossing over from an 'ethnic' audience to a 'universal' one also primarily indicates a market expansion, in this case, one that requires cultural barriers to be overcome. The term has not been widely used to describe the cross-cultural consumption of mainstream media by niche or ethnic audiences or to describe minority-to-minority media exchanges. Within the context of multiculturalism, a crossover event is defined by the success of media content originating in one ethnic culture with a majority audience located in the dominant culture. This is because, whilst the logic of multiculturalism challenges the idea of a culturally homogeneous national audience, it continues to assume 'that there are certain audiences that are commensurate with communities and demographic populations' (Desai 2004: 66). As such, crossover success rested upon Indian films 'appealing to white demographic markets', and thus becoming 'integrated into capitalist expansion through the logic and rhetoric of multiculturalism' (Desai 2004: 66). Multiculturalism is far from being a rhetorical project, however, since it also constructs and naturalizes a commercial market with both internal and external aspects. Within the host nation the acquisition, possession and display of products of foreign cultural provenance garners cultural capital. This activity is supported by a range of industries in the exporting nation that supply music, textiles, movies, literature, furniture and food.

Within this framework, the re-branding of commercial Indian films in the West as postmodern pop art, as exemplified by the trope of Bollywood, is very much part of the continuing cycle of 'post-sixties' orientalism. The recent Bollywood fad can thus be seen as the latest manifestation of India's status as one of the most leading nations in the erstwhile Third World that benefits from having its cultural produce 'appropriated' in Western markets. India is one of the heavyweights for multicultural products: from rustic tribal jewellery, oriental fabrics, sixties-style spiritualism, ethno-cultural and adventure tourism, 'new age' music, exotic foodstuffs, ethnographic texts and 'new literatures'. Indian films have joined this considerable bankroll as another source of foreign exchange earnings and another form of cultural currency in the ongoing encounter between India and its highly significant 'Western Other'. As such, the machinery of Western appropriation clearly functions with the support of equally significant machinery in the Indian economy which works to sell various versions of 'India' abroad. It is also worth pointing out that the promise of an off-the-peg experience of exotic authenticity is one of the primary strategies employed in the marketing of multiculturalism. In its visual manifestation, we can call it mediacultural-ism. This is, in each and almost every case, a fallacy convenient to all of those involved. As such, the recent dusting-off of Indian popular cinema and its new life as the camp, glamorous and low-context 'Bollywood' is typical, rather than atypical, of marketing Asian cultures in the West. To successfully 'crossover' into Western markets, an Asian film must have an appeal that goes beyond the 'resident' audience with which it has been tra-ditionally associated.

In order to capture a sufficient proportion of the foreign 'mainstream' (as opposed to the art-house) it must have some universal accessibility. At the same time, up against the hegemonic universality of Hollywood cinema, a crossover film must also have some cultural or locational specificity that translates into brand value. Hong Kong cinema achieved this with the mar-tial arts film, and Indian cinema has recently sought to break through with souped-up versions of its trademark musical melodramas. Nonetheless, notwithstanding the odd one-off success, a crossover audience is natu-rally unstable as a target market. Without any longstanding experience of Western consumers, Indian producers have to rely upon their intuition in conceiving projects that might appeal to this broad exotic constituency. At the same time, the pursuit of specifically 'crossover' projects constitutes an obvious risk. Media production revolves, after all, around supplying known audiences. Who would give up an audience of hundreds of millions in the subcontinent in the vague hope of a few thousand punters in London or New York? As such, what the crossover paradigm actually entails is shaping products that can extend the existing audience by combining different audience demographics. Thus, it is a combination of old and new (or home and away) audiences that is being pursued. When Hollywood does it, we call it dumping, but this is what underpins the ambitions of Asian producers as much as any drive for international recognition or predilection for code-switching. This draws our attention to a critical aspect of crossover audiences being part of a larger whole, and returns us to Liebes and Katz's question: how do people engaging with foreign content rationalize their own participation in cross-cultural consumption? To answer this, we need to go beyond tracing the relocation of the film itself in order to establish how the action of social imagination links viewers to other places.

Parallel Modernities

It is evident that both the universal presence of American television and the crossover ambitions of Indian film producers are powerfully structured by an enduring East-West binary. Similarly, the cosmopolitan art-house audience is undeniably afflicted by a variant of what Edward Said famously described as 'orientalism'. Where the newfound interest in the transnational ambit of Indian cinema is perhaps most useful, then, is in furnishing us with a rare opportunity to examine media exchanges that operate outside of the East-West encounter. It is generally well known that India's popular melodramas have sustained consistent audiences in Asia and North Africa over many decades. Pendakur and Subramanyam, for example, noted many years ago that 'African people and people from the Middle East are full of praise for the melodramatic elements of the feature film, the song numbers, the costumes and the "beautiful ladies"' (1996: 81). It is striking, therefore, that in contrast to the laborious efforts undertaken to secure crossover audiences in the West, these non-Western audiences have scarcely been given any thought at all by producers. Certainly, for academics, there are some compelling examples of cross-cultural exchange taking place here that would benefit from the insights of audience research. One good example of this potential is the unique work on the indigenous interpretation of Indian films in Nigeria undertaken by the anthropologist Brian Larkin, in which he also describes the emergence of local cultural forms modelled on their themes of familial loyalty and romantic desire (Larkin 2008).

Larkin recounts how he was initially intrigued by the dominant position of Indian films in the exhibition circuits of northern Nigeria, where 'Indian films are shown five nights a week at the cinemas (compared with one night for Hollywood films and one night for Chinese films)' (Larkin 1997: 1). Looking into the operation of the trade, Larkin was able to discover that the distribution of Indian films in Nigeria had been pioneered by independent Lebanese distributors in the 1950s. Since then, the majority of Indian films have been imported into Nigeria through a 'grey market', leaving them absent from official film import figures, despite being 'unofficially' the 'all-time favourite' of audiences (1997: 4). Given that other sources of transnational cinema are also available in the marketplace, Larkin was keen to understand why Indian films in particular had come to occupy such a hegemonic position in the popular culture of this West African state. As a result of his ethnographic research, Larkin concluded that the negotiation of modernity expressed in Indian films, emanating as it does from another non-Western perspective, was particularly resonant with the experiences of Nigerian audiences:

> Indian film has been a popular form of entertainment in urban West Africa for well over forty years and commands viewers because it engages with real desires and conflicts in African societies . . . Indian films are popular because they provide a parallel modernity, a way of imaginatively engaging with the changing social basis of contemporary life that is an alternative to the pervasive influence of a secular West. Through spectacle and fantasy, romance and sexuality, Indian films provide arenas to consider what it means to be modern and what is the place of Hausa society within that modernity. For northern Nigerians . . . Indian films are just one part of the heterogeneity of everyday life. (Larkin 1997: 16)

This engagement with the presence of a foreign, but non-Western, modernity is a process scarcely accounted for in the usual discourses of 'cultural imperialism' that equate cross-cultural flows with Westernization, capitalism and raw geopolitical power. India has a little bit of all three, but it certainly does not have the means to monopolize the marketplace and ram its films down anyone's throat. At the same time, an Indo-African flow clearly operates outside of the long-distance ethnic nationalism emphasized in diaspora theory. Larkin is prompted, therefore, to describe the processes of translation and appropriation which surround Indian films in Nigeria as examples of the 'ability of the media to create parallel modernities' (1997: 2).

> I use the term 'parallel modernities' to refer to the coexistence in space and
> time of multiple economic, religious and cultural flows that are often sub-
> sumed within the term 'modernity' . . . the experience of parallel moderni-
> ties is not necessarily linked with the needs of relocated populations . . . My
> concern, by contrast, is with an Indian film-watching Hausa populace who
> are not involved in nostalgic imaginings of a partly invented native land but
> who participate in the imagined realities of other cultures as part of their
> daily lives. (Larkin 1997: 2)

In making this statement, Larkin highlights the overwhelmingly 'non-
resident' conditions of Nigeria's media environment, where Nigerian
audiences are accustomed to a reasonably diverse diet of imported content.
Conversely, by Larkin's account, the pan-Indian commercial film is itself
a genre designed for cross-cultural appeal within a multicultural India. It
is a common denominator, a hybrid-universal narrative, and this mode of
address underpins its overseas appeal. Reading against the grain of cultural
theory in general, Larkin insists that ethnic particularity is far from being
an insurmountable barrier between Indian films and non-Indian audiences,
observing that: 'Despite the cultural gap between the Hindu Indian audience to which the filmic text is being addressed and the Muslim Hausa one
watching in northern Nigeria, what is remarkable is how well the main
messages of the films are communicated' (1997: 5). In that sense, an insider
knowledge of Indian cultures proves to be no more essential to the enjoyment of the Bollywood melodrama than an informed view of the United
States is to the enjoyment of *Dallas*. Nonetheless, the 'non-Western' provenance of these films does carry its own symbolic register, and this certainly
forms part of their appeal. Indeed, Pam Nilan (2003) has made precisely
this claim regarding the popularity of Indian films in Indonesia. Thus, in a
world of multiple transnational flows, the meaning of Indian films (as with
anything else) is inevitably constructed relative to the other choices available
to viewers.

There must, however, be a qualitative difference between the contextu-
alization of Indian films by distant Nigerians and the framings employed
by Asian audiences. Indonesia has centuries-old connections to India, and
a long tradition of cultural imports including both classical and modern
forms. Thus, in that longstanding 'parallel' encounter there is an important
continuity of inter-Asian dialogues. By contrast, the cult success of South
Indian film star Rajinikanth in Japan in the late 1990s was scarcely less exotic
than Hindi melodramas in their Western 'crossover' drive (Rajadhyaksha
2003; Srinivas 2013). At the other extreme, for audiences in neighbouring
South Asian states like Nepal and Pakistan, Indian films are very much the
resident media culture (Athique 2008d; Burch 2002). This close familiarity,

however, means that Indian popular culture cannot be so easily perceived as a neutral alternative to Western modernity. Rather, the acute cultural and political tensions within the region cast their own shadow over the making of meanings. Rahimullah Yusufzai's (2001) observation that Pakistani audiences love Hindi films as their own, including the fervently anti-Pakistan ones, provides a useful correlation with the schizophrenic European reception of *Dallas* described by Ien Ang. The broader point here is that while all these non-Western transnational exchanges could be considered as 'parallel' flows, the extant cultural geography means that they cannot all be 'parallel' in the same way. Some parallels, simply, are closer than others, and this presages the notion of cultural proximity that will draw our attention in the next chapter. For now, we can happily footnote Brian Larkin's research with the observation that the Bollywood-influenced video-film culture of Nigeria has since flourished to the extent that 'Nollywood' is itself now a significant media exporter in sub-Saharan Africa (Krings and Okome 2013).

Reading Crossover Audiences

It is striking that all of the studies referenced here find sufficient cause to assert that the cross-cultural appeal of transnational media flows rests upon their capacity to capture universal sentiments and motifs. This immediately brings to mind Vladimir Propp's (1984) century-old observation that there are really only a dozen different narratives at play in all the ethnic folk traditions of the world. As such, an on-screen villain is always readily recognizable as such, whether the role is being played by Gary Oldman or Anupam Kher. This simple fact serves as a reminder that human culture is about commonality as well as difference. What is relevant in theoretical terms is that neither national settings nor ethnic literacy are prerequisites for narrative comprehension or emotional gratification. This ease of translation is obviously antipathetic to the insistence of ethnic specificity that underpins the centrality we have given to diasporic audiences in globalization theory. This is not to say, however, that all of this 'universal' content is not ethnically marked in important ways. The provenance of media content is symbolically important and has a demonstrable bearing on how it is accommodated within the worldview of audiences. Equally, the studies considered here serve to demonstrate that the reception of 'non-resident' content is always inflected by the ethno-cultural domains inhabited by its various consumers. That is, the reception of 'universal' texts is subject to the cultural accents, social conditions and widely perceived geocultural relationships that predominate in the location where reception takes place. There can be no archetypal crossover audiences, since we can reasonably expect each and every crossover exchange to constitute a distinctive pairing of cultures, via which universalism is translated.

For analytical purposes, the crossover audience escapes the naturalized equation of cultural consumption and ethnic identity. Thus, if this is an imagined community, then it only exists in an entirely circumstantial sense. Nonetheless, the idiomatic reading of texts within such specific conditions of reception offers unique insights into the global scope of social imagination. To make the most of this opportunity, we should approach crossover audiences (of various kinds) as a grouping of patrons engaged in an outward-looking or exploratory activity, namely, mediaculturalism. A sociological enquiry into crossover audiences therefore needs to pursue a theoretical explanation that does not revolve entirely around *who* they are, but rather illustrates *when*, *where* and *under what conditions* the crossover audience is constituted. We can then consider the terms by which participants become amenable to cross-cultural narratives, and better determine the place of this activity within their broader social experience. As an institutionalized microcosm of such processes, the art-house audience is clearly a very different context of presentation from general programming. In that respect, it has obvious limitations for capturing the broader and less obviously conceited field of mediaculturalism through which the majority of people encounter a more or less exotic other in symbolic form. Nonetheless, both popular and specialized crossovers provide a useful counterpoint to the insistent 'resident' mode of national media frameworks. At the very least, they allow us to recognize that the visualization of the faraway and exotic has always been a central component within the broad appeal of modern media culture.

Recommended Reading

Ien Ang (1993) *Watching Dallas: Soap Opera and the Melodramatic Imagination*, Abingdon: Routledge.

Elizabeth Ezra and Terry Rowden (eds) (2006) *Transnational Cinema: The Film Reader*, Abingdon and New York: Routledge.

Raminder Kaur and Ajay Sinha (eds) (2005) *Bollyworld: Popular Indian Cinema Through A Transnational Lens*, New Delhi: Sage.

Sukhmani Khorana (ed.) (2013) *Crossover Cinema: Cross-Cultural Film from Production to Reception*, London and New York: Routledge.

Matthias Krings and Onookome Okome (eds) (2013) *Global Nollywood: The Transnational Dimensions of an African Video Film Industry*, Bloomington: Indiana University Press.

Brian Larkin (2008) *Signal and Noise: Media, Infrastructure and Urban Culture in Nigeria*, Durham, NC: Duke University Press.

Tamar Liebes and Elihu Katz (1993) *The Export of Meaning: Cross-cultural Readings of Dallas*, Oxford: Oxford University Press.

Toby Miller, Nitin Govil, John McMurria and Richard Maxwell (2011) *Global Hollywood 2*, Berkeley: University of California Press.

Albert Moran and Karina Ayeyard (2013) *Watching Films: New Perspectives on Movie-going: Exhibition and Reception*, Bristol: Intellect.

7   Media Civilizations and Zones of Consumption

A crossover paradigm for understanding transnational audiences tends to focus upon the ability of media content to cross demographics and thereby 'reach across' cultural spaces. Technically speaking, these kinds of audiences can be created within national spaces or single media markets, but in practice their profusion becomes much more likely in various transnational settings. Diasporic audiences, by contrast, tend to imply demographic consistency paired with physical dispersal. In this chapter, I want to approach transnational audiences at a different scale, one that transcends both individual categorizations and national frameworks but also, much more critically, one that is founded upon the cultural geography of human societies. In making this shift, we will examine a series of arguments that seek to explain various structuring factors that underpin or obstruct the transferability of transnational media flows. These cumulative attempts to reconsider the geography of mass communications over the past twenty years provide us with a useful indication of the extent to which media scholars have moved inexorably away from the paradigm set by the high-tide of national media systems (that is, a tidy mosaic of state-cultural institutions and citizen-publics). In part, this ongoing reorientation exercise is an intrinsic component of a prevailing 'global markets' paradigm, and therefore clearly a matter of political economy. At the same time, the maturation and extension of electronic technologies into the digital age has in itself shifted the perceived affordances of mass media systems from a national to a global reach.

Both the increased density of communication networks and the increasingly intense mediation of commercial transactions imply substantial increases of scale that seem to characterize the epoch in which we live. Nonetheless, the available evidence for determining the cultural basis of media markets inevitably brings to mind a longer term historical perspective that challenges the 'sudden and revolutionary' thesis of globalization that has generally been favoured by technologists and neoliberal economists. When we move from the theoretical premise of McLuhan's medium theory to the complexities of what Graeme Turner and Anna Pertierra (2013) have recently called 'zones of consumption' it becomes immediately obvious that such up-scaling is not (and, indeed, cannot be) established upon a blank canvas. In that sense, the focus for any alternative regionalization of audiences beyond the national must somehow accommodate a world characterized by distinct but overlapping global media systems *and* by equally distinct but overlapping cultural fields. In media studies, it is primarily from the longer term study of broadcast technologies that a larger understanding of media consumption has coalesced around various conceptualizations of cultural affinity, proximity and difference. In this context, extra-national broadcasts are contextualized in terms of their variegated situation within a series of identifiable geocultural regions.

Physical Geography and Cultural Tectonics

The everyday operation of the conglomeration of commercial exchanges, aesthetic forms and modes of transmission across the world's surface is powerfully predisposed by the existing disparity of biological concentrations, idiomatic conventions, ideological platforms, matters of taste and the functional limits of comprehension. These are, if you like, some of the underlying trade barriers that stand in the path of any global media corporation. At the same time, these patterns of differentiation are also the historically constituted treasure house of human culture, without which such a sophisticated media apparatus would be neither necessary nor most likely conceivable. Culture, in this sense, is simultaneously implicated in the reproduction of difference and the necessity of translation and adaptation. Within this circuit of 'civilization', any substantial media system that relies upon mass appeal must be able to conceptualize and deliver a repertoire that accommodates this dual function of cultural diversity. I use the word 'civilization' quite consciously here, since it provides us with a vital basis for the necessary articulation of culture and geography that constitutes a prerequisite for any order of scale pertaining to social communication. The deployment of the term also signposts the continuing influence of the French historian Fernand Braudel, who himself commented upon the semantic confusions caused by the overlapping usage of the terms culture and civilization and their relationship to the concept of society (1995: 3–18).

For Braudel, a civilization represents a cumulative whole that subsumes the cultures within it and operates on a greater timescale than the societies that sustain it. By this reading, French civilization encompasses the regional cultures of Brittany and Alsace and the full range of folk, bourgeois and high cultures and their varied manners. As an historical entity, French civilization outlasts various forms of social organization, as evidenced by the transition from agricultural to industrial society, and equally by a procession of monarchies, empires and republics. It does so because, as much as civilizations assimilate their constituent cultures in the greater whole, they also accrete the creative achievements of their members over the longer sweep of history. As a consequence, civilizations accrue a certain way of thinking as much as a certain way of speaking and this, in turn, inculcates a self-awareness that guarantees their reproduction. Civilizations operate therefore across both scales of time and space, they are bigger than cultures and societies, and in this case they are taken to guarantee the existence of an 'eternal France'. From an Asian perspective, perhaps, Braudel's demarcation of half a dozen distinct European civilizations is incommensurate with his broader argument, not to mention with his delineation of the whole of India and China as single civilizations. What Braudel does argue for successfully, however, is the inherent unity of both the material and expressive pillars of human achievement in each civilization. Even more than that, Braudel is emphatic in propounding the fundamental importance of physical geography to the form of human cultures:

> Civilizations, vast or otherwise, can always be located on a map. An essential part of their character depends upon the constraints or advantages of their geographical situation . . . To discuss civilization is to discuss space, land and its contours, climate, vegetation, animal species and natural or other advantages. It is also to discuss what humanity had made of these basic conditions . . . Every civilization, then, is based on an area with more or less fixed limits. Each has its own geography with its own opportunities and constraints, some virtually permanent and quite different from one civilization to another. The result? A variegated world. (1995: 9, 11)

Under these terms, geography itself predisposes a world of cultural diversity. Each combination of landmass and climatic region serves to shape human civilizations that will eat particular foods, develop particular styles of dwelling and storage and equally particular forms of communication, exchange and marriage. Upon these foundations, a distinctive set of social customs, cosmological beliefs and sciences are built. Due to the prior existence of geographical interruptions such as oceans and mountain ranges, and the intransferability of established agricultural practices to other regions, there are inherent barriers between different zones of habitation. Within the boundaries of each range, however, a critical mass of cultures and societies will evolve a sophisticated interdependence that reflects a common heritage and the boundaries of the larger civilization. This is why humanity speaks in a range of different languages but also why the majority of us speak languages that fall into a relatively small grouping of linguistic families. Consequently, as Gellner also argued, the function of language solidifies the demarcation between one civilization and another. At the same time, however, the physical geography of the world also provides for various bridges between its major zones, notably in the form of navigable waterways and seas. In Braudel's own work, it was therefore possible to describe the interchange between the various civilizations of the mediterranean islands and shoreline as constituting a unique world characterized by cultural and commercial interaction between its constituent parts (Braudel 1996). Where people move, civilizations meet, and this leads to the exchange of both goods and ideas. Thus:

> The stability of these cultural zones and their frontiers does not however isolate them from cultural imports. Every civilization imports and exports aspects of its culture . . . Civilizations continually borrow from their neighbours, even if they 'reinterpret' or assimilate what they have adopted. At first sight, indeed, every civilization looks rather like a railway goods yard, constantly receiving and dispatching miscellaneous deliveries. Yet, a civilization may stubbornly reject a particular import from outside. Marcel Mauss has remarked that every civilization worthy of the name has rejected something. Every time, the refusal is the culmination of a long period of hesitation and experiment. Long mediated and slowly reached, the decision is always crucially important. (1995: 14, 29)

For Braudel, civilizations are not static structures, since they incorporate external influences, experience social change and sometimes even physically move, but as meta-structures of a grand scale they nonetheless also possess their own gravitational mass. Braudel recognizes explicitly, therefore, that the specific boundaries of any civilization are mutable and impermanent. Equally, since the world is finite and our most desirable environmental conditions are unstable, there will be wholesale movement of populations from time to time. These might be triggered by environmental collapse or by the warlike struggle to control natural resources. Even without such periodic upheavals, everyday trade and communication between civilizations forms a vital component of their social and cultural development. In the interchange between civilizations, various forms of knowledge and modes of social organization are either adopted, adapted or discarded for reasons of material practicality or ontological incompatability. Braudel's example is the adoption of European technologies by Muslim civilization matched by its simultaneous rejection of European cultural norms. Another example might be the adaptation of imperial, republican, communist and capitalist social structures by Chinese civilization to suit its underlying Confucian principles. Each culture exerts its own inertia over new ideas and practices, both from within and without, and each of them is substantial enough to cast an influence upon other civilizations, and upon the world as a whole. In that sense, this very particular notion of civilization denotes a form of social and cultural tectonics by which human geography can be explicated.

Linguistic Markets as Media Civilizations

Such a proposition logically destabilizes the primacy of the nation state as the highest unit of culture. In the world of the United Nations, there are many pretenders for states at a civilizational scale, but scarcely a handful of real contenders. Within such a schema, several states may come to occupy a place within a larger civilization, while some states may be situated across areas where different civilizations meet. For our purposes, since cultural preferences can be associated with the larger measure and cultural products are easily transmitted across vast distances, it is reasonable to assume that civilizations might provide the underlying basis for the constitution of transnational audiences. Since the 1990s, the growing reach of transnational television broadcast via satellite technologies has certainly been seen as a critical technological development which supports the formation of transnational audiences at this higher scale (Rinnawi 2006; Sinclair 1999). The vast transmission 'footprint' of satellite broadcasts inherently favours a new supra-national media geography, the limits of which are established somewhat less by the sovereignty of nation states and more fundamentally by the larger map of linguistic and cultural affinities between civilizations. Since much of the evidence for Braudel's model of civilization rests upon the obvious confluence of language and geography, we would naturally anticipate the emergence of a handful of supra-national linguistic markets that import and export content, formats and cultural trends while remaining internally coherent as distinct media civilizations. Indeed, this is precisely the basis of John Sinclair's mapping of the world's television markets within 'geolinguistic regions'.

Over the course of some three decades, John Sinclair (1999) has directed his attention towards the phenomenon of television in the continent of South America. Here, the early dominance of US companies was offset by the overwhelming predominance of Spanish and Portuguese as the native tongues of all of the South American states. This linguistic commonality (coupled with contiguous territories, a shared history, a varying but related blend of Iberian, American and African cultures, and the hegemony of Catholic religion) provided the putative basis for a larger media civilization in Latin America. At the outset, Mexico's position along the US border gifted it a pioneering position in producing Hispanic television for the Americas and both its programming and its organizing structure subsequently came to be exported from Central America to Chile. Notwithstanding interne-cine political conflicts, television programming came to be freely exchanged across this substantial concentration of Spanish-speaking nations. One of the most distinctive, and consistently popular, television formats screened throughout these markets was the epic melodrama of the *telenovela*. The stars from each nationally produced series became recognizable to audiences throughout the southern continent, taking advantage of a common cul-tural market that offered economies of scale to Latin American producers. Brazil's status as the largest Latin American nation, and its Portuguese lan-guage, also provided the basis for a distinctive television market, although due to broader commonalities there are considerable interchanges between Brazilian television and the surrounding Hispanic nations.

The Mexican development of a Spanish-speaking television audience in the United States was an integral part of its commercial operations, and the advent of cable and satellite broadcasting has sought to further integrate the comparatively wealthy Hispanic population of the United States deeper within the Latin American televisual field. As the global television market has matured, Latin American television has also been able to establish both import and export relationships with the old colonial states of Spain and Portugal. Keeping this transnational history in mind, Sinclair proposes that television will naturally expand to serve the broadest market available in a given language. The early decades of terrestrial broadcast located television within a fairly limited range, and thus almost all broadcasters have their origins within a single national space. Once orbital transmission via satellite became a realistic proposition however, large sections of the earth's surface have become available to television producers. In this setting, audiences will watch what they can comprehend, and this is more fundamental to the reception of television than a national structure. This is not to say that the national differences between Mexican Televisa and Venezuelan Venevision are not keenly perceived by their audiences, but it does reflect their common placement within the larger geolinguistic region that these media providers seek to serve. Rather than seeing Latin America as a special case, Sinclair discerns other geolinguistic regions based upon the major world languages, identifying an obvious cultural and commercial concentration for television markets in English, Mandarin, French, Hindi and Bahasa.

We could, to some extent, assume that the primacy of geolinguistic regions for the world of television is a medium-specific condition. The reliance on both oral communication and real-time transmission natu-rally precludes ready participation without fluency in the language. Some other media forms can employ less synchronous and/or more time-bound modes of transmission, thereby allowing for lower (or slower) levels of literacy. However, Sinclair's notion of geolinguistic audiences goes beyond the merely functional aspects of language stipulated by Gellner since he recognizes that 'Language is the vehicle of culture, so it is not similarity of language alone that gives access to foreign markets, but culture more broadly' (2009: 142). It is not enough, therefore, for television viewers to comprehend the language in question. They must also be able to appreciate the themes, motifs and moods through which its narrative structures express the wider culture of each geolinguistic region. The essential fusion with visual language delivers a further layer of culturally specific settings, objects and manners. Thus, geolinguistic audiences necessarily appreciate the wider civilization to a significant extent, and this implies that such audiences would primarily consist of native speakers. Further, the obvious emphasis placed upon their geographic concentration also infers that such audiences would normally inhabit the 'home territories' of the civilization in question. Where geolinguistic regions bear strong affinities with national borders, as in Vietnam, there may be a tidy correlation of Gellner's nationalism and Braudel's civilizationism. The larger geolinguistic audiences, however, are invariably transnational. Accordingly, they inhabit 'border zones', such as Switzerland or the meeting point of English and Spanish regions in North America, but they also inhabit 'heartlands', such as in Anatolia or metropolitan France. Due to the interplay of geography and history, there may also be 'stranded' territories, such as Singapore or Quebec, to which geolinguistic cultures are 'airlifted' by media technologies. Thus, every geolinguistic audience is spatially and culturally unique.

Operating at a civilizational rather than individual or national scale, geolinguistic audiences can be seen to correlate with, and subsume, both national and diasporic audiences with that larger whole. At this level, a geolinguistic location implies a functional compatibility (as matter of literacy), a deep cultural affinity (via Braudel's historical accretions) and a critical mass (in terms of a commercial proposition). These are all, clearly, benefits of scale that are requisite for viable cultural industries operating within a global market system. Nonetheless, to get the full measure of any media civilization, we also need to take the process of cultural interchange seriously. Notwithstanding the fact that bilingual and multilingual populations imply that geolinguistic regions naturally constitute overlapping zones, it is also easy to demonstrate that all geolinguistic regions have various channels by which they speak to their neighbours. Latin America forms a distinctive geolinguistic region, where its own languages and aesthetics predominate and the majority of media content deploys Latin American languages, settings and protagonists. Latin America has nonetheless also been able to assimilate media formats, genres and even direct imports from other regions. Various borrowings from Anglophone film genres, European television formats and transatlantic pop culture are immediately evident. With a mind to such processes, Roland Robertson (1994) famously deployed the term 'glocalization' to describe the process by which foreign cultural products are adapted to suit the needs of the receiving culture.

Cultural Proximity and Relative Affinity

Although some phenomena (like the Beatles) have achieved global popularity in their original formats, a far larger range of imports establish their place in various markets through local reproductions (like the Monkees). Through this process, media producers seek to take advantage of innate audience preferences for 'cultural proximity' between the content on offer and their own cultural background. Cultural proximity is a term developed by Joseph Straubhaar, who also spent several decades studying the phenomenon of television in Latin America (in this case, in Lusophone Brazil). In explaining the transition from imported US television towards domestic production and a range of Hispanic imports, Straubhaar (1991) offers a relativistic approach to the cultural preferences of audiences. Straubhaar concurs that 'countries and cultures . . . prefer their own local or national productions' due to various factors, including the local appeal of celebrities, locally specific humour, locally relevant issues, culturally specific styles and 'the appeal of similar looking ethnic faces'. At the same time, he also notes that 'if countries did not produce certain genres of television, then audiences tend to prefer those kind of programmes from nearby or similar cultures and languages' (2007: 91). The notion of 'nearby' cultures thereby adds a new dimension to cultural geography, because although it identifies cultures as distinctive formations it also suggests that the differences between them are incremental rather than absolute. In that sense, Straubhaar's notion of cultural proximity operates as a putative scale of affinity between cultures. In the context of his own research in Brazil, Straubhaar identifies Brazilian programming as the first choice for television audiences, followed by Hispanic programming which is more culturally proximate than US programming (La Pastina and Straubhaar 2005).

Straubhaar's notion of cultural proximity clearly references the larger map of geolinguistic regions, with its strong links to Braudel's world of civilizations. Proximity creates a form of radial gravity structuring cultural compatibility relative to each region. 'Native' culture comes first, followed by neighbouring (or 'familiar') cultures. More distant formations become marked as exotic, and are only likely to exert an appeal in instances where their singularity implies novelty (as in the worldwide craze for martial arts films in the late 1970s). A concentric notion of proximity can therefore be used to situate cultural preferences among transnational audiences as a whole, referencing a larger scale than the national borders imposed by 'multiculturalism'. A mitigating factor for the proximity effect, however, is the cross-cultural compatibility of particular genres of media content (Straubhaar 2007: 196). While *telenovelas* may be a quintessentially Latin American form, they nonetheless correspond with the common role of melodrama across most of the world's cultures. Thus, even where our sense of distinction between cultures or civilizations is necessarily acute, we should bear in mind Vladimir Propp's proposition that the main features of narrative structure remain surprisingly common across all cultures. The same might certainly be said of the general schemata of television formats (Moran and Keane 2004). It is this 'generic proximity' which allows dubbed or subtitled *telenovelas* to become readily comprehensible to audiences outside of Latin America, although the range of their appeal is still determined to some extent by the cultural proximity of the receiving markets. Mexican telenovelas have proved popular in Brazil and Italy, both of which require linguistic translation, but are more culturally proximate than Sweden and Japan, where *telenovelas* have rather less appeal (Sinclair 2009).

Although primarily transnational in its conception, the notion of cultural proximity has also been employed in some national audience studies. For example, Ksiazek and Webster (2008) used this model to explore the media preferences of Hispanic and non-Hispanic television viewers and radio listeners in Houston, Texas. Their hypothesis was that viewers whose first language was either English or Spanish would gravitate to media sources in their respective languages. They also anticipated that English-speakers of Hispanic origins would access both sources, while gravitating towards Hispanic media as the source of the most culturally proximate content. Findings, obtained from 'people meters' logging media choices, clearly supported the primacy of language in making media choices. For the bilingual population, however, no clear set of preferences emerged, since 'They moved easily between media outlets in each language. In fact, similarity of language explained only a very small amount of the variance in audience duplication amongst this subset of the audience' (Ksiazek and Webster 2008: 498). Bilingualism, obviously enough, offers functional access to multiple geolinguistic regions. Where there is sufficient content available for an omnivorous pattern of media consumption to operate, the likely consequence of bilingualism is an audience with multicultural literacy. This is not to say that cultural proximity does not continue to exert influence. For example, bilinguals who share an ethnic background with the second-language material might develop a more equal balance in their mix of consumption than those whose access to this material is developed strictly through formal language learning. In that sense, the functional requirements of literacy must be correlated with some variance in the 'cultural range' of the audience.

In his Brazilian studies, Straubhaar concluded that 'omnivorous' media consumption was typically stratified by social class. Members of the Brazilian elite were innately cosmopolitan, with regularized access to a broad range of international culture through travel and personal relationships. The upper middle classes aspired to this 'globalized' example, although their engagement with this lifestyle was largely restricted to transnational media consumption and other cultural imports. The middle class proper was much more oriented towards Latin American media and focused their interests within a national scale of reference. Increasing television ownership amongst the urban poor saw them, in turn, seeking to emulate this example. By contrast, the rural poor were more intensely local in their outlook, interests and modes of consumption (Straubhaar 2007: 207–8). Straubhaar relates this relative scale of cultural range in reference to Pierre Bourdieu's notion of cultural capital (2007: 208–13). At the top of the social spectrum, access to greater wealth, education and capacity to travel all serve to mitigate the primacy of proximity. At the bottom of the social spectrum, however, cultural proximity is intense, and even sub-national. If we extrapolate from these findings in the context of mass media systems, we might reasonably assume that the larger an audience becomes, the requirement for it to be socially inclusive increases, and the proximity effect consequently becomes stronger. This assertion might therefore explain the steady 'localization' of television in the developing world, somewhat contrary to the globalization thesis.

Ultimately, what emerges from the complexities of Straubhaar's analysis is an important sense of cultural proximity as an observable effect in media consumption, albeit one that is mitigated by a number of variables arising from differences in cultural range (amongst audiences) and cross-cultural appeal (within content). More niche cultural forms tend to solicit more socially elite audiences and thereby engender more cosmopolitan tastes. Content designed for mass appeal relies on a strong common denominator to reach across social strata, and this tends to give primacy to cultural proximity as a characteristic of audience demand. At the midway point, we could reasonably expect audiences to combine national culture with the most proximate additions, while eschewing the exotic. This pattern would thus tend to fall primarily, if not entirely, within Sinclair's premise of a geolinguistic region. In practice, it is the combination of the two concepts that provides us with a much needed framework for categorizing the logics of media exchange between civilizations. As Straubhaar notes, certain geo-linguistic regions remain culturally proximate to other regions. This then serves to make media imports from those regions preferable to imports from other, more culturally distant, regions. The effect of this 'most favoured' status for certain cultures is amplified in an increasingly prolific and glo-balized media market. When these cultural exchanges reach a certain level, we could argue that a larger regional mediasphere is created from a grouping of proximate cultures. The strength of this integration is notable in Latin America due to a high degree of cultural proximity amongst its constituent states.

Intra-Regional Homologies and Complicated Currents

As a general theory, we should also expect to see other examples of regional groupings organized around cultural proximity. A useful set of studies in this regard has emerged from East Asia over the past two decades. This geo-political region contains three major geolinguistic regions of varying size: Chinese, Japanese and Korean. The Japanese region is more or less contigu-ous with the Japanese nation state, whereas both the Chinese and Korean regions are subdivided into two antagonistic pairings of states (The People's Republic of China (PRC) versus Taiwan and The Democratic Republic of Korea (DRK) versus the Republic of South Korea (RSK)). These lingering political divisions reflect the frontline of the Cold War in the region, with Japan, Taiwan and the Republic of South Korea falling within the capital-ist world system and the PRC and DRK aligned with the former commu-nist bloc. Prior to 1997, the Chinese city-state of Hong Kong remained a British colony and was therefore open to its capitalist neighbours while mainland China was not. Since the end of the Cold War, and the absorp-tion of Hong Kong, the PRC has reoriented its economic system in order to emerge as a major commercial society. While idiosyncratic North Korea remains communist and aggressive towards its capitalist neighbours, its reliance on the patronage of the PRC inevitably puts pressure on its capac-ity to maintain its self-imposed isolation. Eschewing the contingencies of modern politics, however, there are deep and ancient relationships between Chinese, Japanese and Korean civilizations. There are shared philosophical and religious traditions (such as Buddhism) as well as closely related tradi-tions in the arts, statecraft and science. While their linguistic and written systems are mutually unintelligible, they are more akin to each other than they are to any other geolinguistic region further afield. With the obvious exception of North Korea, all of the East Asian states have sought to construct export-oriented economies in the latter half of the twentieth century. Japan, Taiwan, South Korea and, more recently, the PRC have developed manufacturing economies primarily oriented towards global trade.

As a consequence, two of the world's three largest economies are now found within this region. The pursuit of export-oriented cultural industries has been a more recent phenomenon, instigated by Japan, Hong Kong and more recently by South Korea. In his comprehensive study of Japanese popular culture in a transnational setting, Koichi Iwabuchi has noted how Japanese businesses initially pursued a strategy of producing export content that was *mukokuseki*, that is, material free of culturally distinctive elements (2002: 28). In doing so, producers were keenly aware not only of the comprehension gap created by strongly marked Japanese content, but also by the negative image of the country that lingered as a consequence of its imperial past. One of Japan's most obviously successful media exports was in the field of animation, where it would become a global leader by the 1980s. Japan's industrial success in the field of electronics provided further support for the development of a computer games industry that also drew heavily on its well-established animation expertise. Following the peak of Japan's success in consumer electronics, the 'Japaneseness' of its animated exports became more explicit, and even the culturally 'odourless' style itself came to be seen retrospectively as distinctively Japanese. Avant-garde styles such as *manga* and multimedia brands such as *Pokemon* became symbolic of Japan's place in the field of global culture (MacWilliams 2008; Berndt and Kümmerling-Meibauer 2013). During the same period, however, Japan had also become an exporter of television drama and popular music within the East Asian region, products which had little impact further afield.

Research into the regional popularity of Japanese television dramas was conducted in Hong Kong by Anthony Fung (2007). Fung observed the obvious influence of Japanese styles and structures upon the production of local television in the city-state, echoing the equally obvious influence of Japanese animation upon the development of similar content in China and Korea. Fung's finding echoes Iwabuchi's observation that Japanese producers saw themselves as representing the most developed nation in Asia, with a natural role in passing their own version of modern Asian culture on to their neighbours (2002: 66–9). In his content analysis of television dramas, Fung found close similarities in the narrative structures of Japanese and Hong Kong dramas, with these 'Intra-Asian homologies' also making them distinct from Western-produced dramas. In his engagement (via interviews) with their audiences, Fung found that 60 per cent of his respondents believed that the popularity of Japanese dramas rested upon close cultural similarities between Hong Kong and Japan (2007: 282). This intra-Asian proximity consequently offers a basis for understanding the concentration of Japanese media exports within the East Asian region, an understanding based upon the relative proximity of neighbouring civilizations. This greater regional literacy then serves to explain why Japanese pop music (or J-Pop) was another commodity that was successful within the region, but not globally. Unlike the odourless animations and computer games, television and popular music cannot be easily shorn of their Japanese provenance, and even where these styles are clearly Japanese-American hybrids, their Japanese flavour seems to limit their appeal to the most proximate markets.

Following the high-tide of the 1990s, some of Japan's media exports have declined as their neighbours have further developed their own cultural industries, often by reproducing their own versions of these very same formats. Nonetheless, as a trendsetter, Japanese popular culture continues to exert a strong transnational influence within the East Asian region. In the 2000s, building upon the RSK's own post-industrial strategy, it was the 'Korean Wave' that nonetheless achieved the greater visibility across East Asia. At the same time, the influence of J-Pop on K-Pop is obvious, while the 'Korean wave' movies (sometimes known as Hallyuwood) tend to demonstrate a closer affinity with Japanese film aesthetics than they do with the mainstream cinema of China or Hong Kong. Nonetheless, the Korean take on these formats is markedly Korean, notably in their distinctive humour. As the smallest of the three geolinguistic regions in East Asia, the two Koreas are sandwiched between two larger (and historically aggressive) neighbours. As such, the regional success of Korean movies and pop music (and the huge popularity of the latter in China and Japan) occupies a different geopolitical dynamic than Japanese exports. Thus, there are a number of factors underpinning the popular status of K-Pop in China. To some extent, pop culture industries in mainland China remain restricted by the closer political management of public expression in the PRC. As China has opened up commercially, this inertia furnishes market opportunities for its neighbours.

China's engagement with global economy entails close, but culturally problematic, relationships with the Western world. In this context, Asian media imports tend to be seen more favourably than American ones. At the time of the Korean wave, however, the previous popularity of Japanese media imports in China was being tempered by a deteriorating political relationship with Japan. For Korean exporters, therefore, cultural affinity was supported by favourable market conditions and a favourable geopolitical climate. For their audiences, Korean imports were able to provide content that remained culturally proximate with China, while also offering the hybrid and consumerist orientation that characterizes Japan's export productions. At the same time, the cultural proximity between Korea and Japan also furnished access to the Japanese market, where comparable cultural affinity fostered transnational literacy, and cultural difference served as a powerful brand for a Korean 'craze' amongst media consumers. While Korean content proved more palatable in this period for both countries, producers were also able to capitalize upon the transnational markets created by Chinese and Japanese exports. The Korean Wave reached Malaysia and Singapore via the established networks of the Chinese geolinguistic region, while also benefiting from Japan's longstanding exports to Indonesia. In the case of communist North Korea, where imports from the Republic of South Korea are entirely prohibited, the Korean Wave was routed via fixed media formats (such as VCD) replicated in the Chinese market. Thus, all in all, the tripartite relationship between the Chinese, Japanese and Korean geolinguistic regions demonstrates the high degree of interaction in their media markets, where media producers negotiate the 'complicated currents' of their bilateral relationships (Black et al. 2010; Fung 2013).

Zones of Consumption and the Primacy of Place

Within the global economy, the size and importance of East Asian markets are sufficient for major trends to register further afield. Thus, the decade-long success of the Korean wave underpinned the viral popularity (via YouTube) of Psy's pop anthem 'Gangnam Style', which became a chic pastiche taken up at American sports events and by primary school children in New Zealand. In these contexts, however, it became shorn of the meanings and associations established by its satire of Korean social aspirations and its cultural proximity to East Asian audiences. *Gangnam* became mistakenly translated as 'Gangster' and the song was therefore equated with an Asian rendition of the American hip hop genre. Culture, like light, appears to be bent by distance. Within East Asia, and along its borders, this effect nonetheless seems to be gradual enough to facilitate a field of consumption larger than its constituent national and geolinguistic formations. The internal dynamics of this larger market are structured by various linkages and barriers of trade and politics, but the extent of each interlocking zone appears to be fundamentally determined by the underlying forces of cultural proximity. Most recently, Anna Pertierra and Graeme Turner (2013) have explored this broader concept of a 'zone of consumption'. Their analysis stems from an expansive study of the world television that encompasses many different regions (see Turner and Tay 2009). In its exposition, however, the concept is elaborated in concert with their anthropological study of television in Mexico. In this context, we encounter a media culture that is interlaced with the composite cultures of both North and South America. It falls within Sinclair's Latin American geolinguistic region (where it plays a leading role), and its sphere of cultural proximity also extends to Iberian and Mediterranean Europe (and arguably also to the Philippines). Television audiences within Mexico nonetheless also inhabit an overarching national context with strong regional formations. Taking this into account, Mexican television operates within a number of sub-national, national and transnational formations. It is in order to accommodate the cohabitation of the various scales that Pertierra and Turner deploy the terminology of the 'zone', since:

> It can include, if required, the more standard notions of region, nation or locality, but it does not specify either of these as necessary or sufficient in advance. Instead, the 'zone' offers a flexibility and adaptability that allows for a high degree of customization. There is no requirement that all zones of consumption be configured in precisely the same way: the implicit universalism or normatization we have criticized in other accounts of television is no longer an implied imperative. It is not endlessly nor arbitrarily variable, however; the metaphor's invocation of a definable space provides the category with an endpoint – the zone must constitute a particular 'place', with a proposed perimeter and its own body of empirical and cultural content. (2013: 133)

For a study founded upon an ethnographic mode of enquiry, the overlapping scales of cultural geography must also be grounded in the intense locality of consumption. Media consumption is always undertaken by particular individuals within highly specific locations. Thus, a classical cultural studies approach to sampling everyday cultures at the point of consumption necessarily implies that the demographic mix of each household is equally significant to its longitude and latitude. The anthropological arm of the enquiry nonetheless insists upon recognizing more explicitly the structuring forces of cultural geography in terms of both expressive modes and the habituations of differentiated communities and societies. The meanings drawn from media reception are thus contingent upon specific cultural resources being deployed within a preferred cultural range. Subsequently, the primacy awarded to cultural specificity (as an external structure) naturally draws our attention to the other social relationships through which each television setting is formed. Thus, from a more sociological perspective, social class (and most likely the age and gender of viewers) also becomes highly significant in determining the preferences and understandings of audiences. Further, in a world of polymedia as described by Madianou and

Miller, it becomes reasonable to assume that any engagement with television is accompanied and informed by a coterminous engagement with a wider media ecology including the World Wide Web, radio and newspapers. It is within this wider environment that television audiences become located within particular zones of consumption, which offer the capacity to stitch together local specificity and cultural proximity. Consequently, as a particular constellation of social forces:

> the zone resists the notion that the appropriate location within which to examine television rests with any one formation – be it the home, the local community or the nation-state; a zone of consumption can be any one, some or all of these. It is not helpful to categorically locate television within any one kind of media system either, or within any one kind of cultural, political or geo-linguistic space. However, the boundary implied in the phrase also resists the temptation to see the location as utterly arbitrary, or without definition. (Pertierra and Turner 2013: 6)

Compared to the other 'zonal approaches' surveyed in this chapter, Pertierra and Turner's study displays a relative absence of references to large-scale civilizational concepts. At the other end of the scale, one of their stated concerns is to counterbalance approaches to media studies that privilege an individualized consumer 'liberated' by access to a single many-to-many global media system (2013: 61–82). For Pertierra and Turner, the nation still matters and public broadcasting is yet, and indeed unlikely, to become entirely replaced by the fashion for à la carte direct marketing (2013: 42–8). Rather, television has particular attributes which favour the attention of communities, constituted at various scales, as opposed to favouring individuals linked only by common preferences of consumption. The cultural specificity of communities still matters, as does the intimate organization of their internal solidarities. Accordingly, the study of television audiences must still conceive of, and physically encounter, actual communities and the contours of their moral economies (2013: 83–107). The substitution of such physical audiences for broad-sweep linguistic markets or consumer demographics may be sufficient for commercial planning, but it remains insufficient to capture the significance of the media in question. This emphasis upon community and nation is by no means antithetical, however, to the larger frameworks of geolinguistic regions and culturally proximate transnational markets. It is more a case of understanding the necessary interaction between these various scales in the broader cultural geography of television. Transnational exchanges have national constituents, while national media settings incorporate transnational content. Either way, we need to understand 'where consumption occurs and how that location is actually framed by its specific determinants – such as patterns of cultural affinity, industrial and regulatory structures, as well as the particulars of place' (Pertierra and Turner 2013: 82).

Reading Proximate Audiences

The primary focus in this chapter has been upon the television medium, from which the majority of geocultural approaches to audiences have emerged. Nonetheless, the determination of these 'cultural markets' is equally applicable to the formation of transnational publics around radio broadcasts or the geolinguistic concentrations that increasingly characterize the World Wide Web (see Liao and Petzold 2010). With the ongoing mitigation of technological and regulatory barriers, the cultural proximities of audiences seem likely to become a more readily observable factor in delineating the zones within which media content is commonly circulated. By contrast with studies centred on diasporic transmission and commercial crossovers for niche products, the geocultural models essayed here are primarily directed towards detailing the cultural tectonics of transnational media exchanges in total. Equally important for any assimilation of these geocultural approaches by audience researchers is the fundamental importance given to physical geography in setting the terrain for media consumption. The obvious correlation between linguistic concentrations and physical locations, and between cultural affinity and physical proximity, obviously works against trends in medium theory that consider media technologies to be spatially indifferent. In practice, any serious study of transnational audiences that engages 'mainstream' consumption is required to account for these larger configurations within human culture. Regardless of their language, ethnicity or citizenship, it is therefore critical that any study of transnational media reception is able to locate audiences very specifically.

In order to place any given audience within the larger map, we need to establish the linguistic and geographic location that it inhabits, to assess the broader pattern of media consumption within that zone and to gauge the cultural proximity between that location and the origin of a given transnational content stream. Within this more expansive and sophisticated scale of association, the complexities of global media reception become more accessible in specifically relative terms. This relativity becomes critically important as a counterpoint to the strong particularism of nationalist approaches. As a panacea, a Braudelian perspective would suggest that civilizations are relatively immune to the cultural reprogramming so feared by nationalists in the twentieth century, due to historically constituted cultural anchors of astronomical weight. Conversely, the functional primacy of geolinguistic regions appears to suggest that many pretenders to civilizational status are actually composite cultures, and likely to remain so (which may well prove to their benefit). Ultimately, perhaps, what is most significant for our understanding of transnational audiences is the different scales of cultural interaction revealed by these various mapping exercises. Geolinguistic regions, media civilizations and zones of consumption all suggest the potentials for interlacing these reference points with the politically organized institutions of state and the internalized selves that have previously gradated media studies. In turn, the truth of these various grand propositions of cultural geography can only be established when audiences themselves demonstrate an awareness of those relationships in their daily lives.

Recommended Reading

Daniel Black, Stephen Epstein and Alison Tokita (eds) (2010) *Complicated Currents: Media Flows, Soft Power and East Asia*, Clayton: Monash University Press.

Fernand Braudel (1995) *A History of Civilizations*, New York: Penguin.

Anthony Fung (2013) *Asian Popular Culture: The Global (Dis)continuity*, London and New York: Routledge.

Koichi Iwabuchi (2002) *Recentering Globalization: Popular Culture and Japanese Transnationalism*, Durham, NC: Duke University Press.

Youna Kim (ed.) (2013) *The Korean Wave: Korean Media Go Global*, Abingdon and New York: Routledge.

Anna Pertierra and Graeme Turner (2013) *Locating Television: Zones of Consumption*, London and New York: Routledge.

John Sinclair (1999) *Latin American Television: A Global View*, Oxford: Oxford University Press.

Joseph Straubhaar (2007) *World Television: From Global to Local*, Thousand Oaks: Sage.

Part 3

New Formations:
Clouds, Trends, Fields

8   Fan Cultures and User-Led Transnationalism

In the preceding section, we have been primarily concerned with locating transnational media reception within various registers of cultural geography, conceived at a range of scales and inevitably structured in important ways by the historical accretions of our political systems. At the same time, the expanding trajectories of ethnicities, the commercialization of intercultural communication and the constellation of cultural zones as consumer markets are all symptomatic of the triumph of market capitalism, not only geographically but also across the greater breadth of social practices. The peculiarity of the media economy, then, is that it stitches together the purchase of media interfaces, the renting of media access of various kinds and the on-sale of audience viewing time and behaviours to commercial manufacturers, politicians and market researchers. Thus, we interact with media systems at a time in which audiences are not only consumers of media products but are also commodities in their own right. This integrated commodity form is far more encompassing than the early modern logics of industrial production that underpin mainstream economics. Similarly, while Adorno and Horkheimer (1944) famously cautioned against the rise of cultural consumerism in the 1940s, the thrust of their critique failed to anticipate the full significance of media systems in the context of a fully automated information society. It is within this broader framework that the media economy reveals, across its circuitous operations, the multilayered domain of consumption that has emerged since the mid-twentieth century. It is not insignificant, therefore, that the formulation of our advanced stage of consumerism rests in large part upon the twin development of media technologies and the quasi-academic disciplines that strategize the manipulation of the public.

In a consumer society, all social actions are inevitably social transactions, and this necessarily results in the conflation of roles. Thus, viewers, voters, shoppers and subjects have become simultaneous framings that have increasingly dissipated the previous notions of audiences, publics and citizens enshrined in the social contracts of the post-war era. At the tipping point between the two world orders, the great transnational shift of the 1990s rested upon a purposeful union of digital technologies and market expansion. Consequently, the phase of globalization that followed can be characterized not by its internationalism per se, but by its peculiar logics of mass mediation, faux individuation and the commercialization of all speech. All of this tends to sound somewhat sinister, and it has certainly drawn the ire of the socially minded in various guises. Nonetheless, the premise of this programme is unequivocally liberal: the empowerment of individuals through assisted consumption, with their collective aspirations guaranteed by market mechanisms which bring equilibrium to the personal, domestic and political domains. Unravelling this, of course, requires a more detailed account of political economy and contemporary sociology than we can include here. Nonetheless, any recognition of the seismic changes in audience studies across this period must acknowledge the co-evolution of the field with the broader weave of social change and the (typically basic) assumptions upon which our millennial utopias were conceived. To get to that point we have to reach back a little further, to the era in which Adorno's loudly expressed fears of cultural degeneration became manifest in the frenzied consumption of rock 'n' roll.

Rock Music and Transnational Youth Culture

Let's play one that everyone knows. The 1950s was the decade in which the Fordist models of mass consumption pioneered in the United States became the blueprint for the reconstruction of Europe after the Second World War. At a time when the Marshall Plan and the British Loan constituted the major instruments of European reconstruction, the US enjoyed enormous cultural prestige along with more or less unfettered access to markets in Western Europe (Hogan 1989). At the same time, American culture quickly became ubiquitous around the Pacific Rim as the United States became the leading imperial power in that region. For much of the world, this was an era of physical reconstruction, state bankruptcy, shortages of basic necessities, and domestic industries that had either been ravaged by occupation or coerced by military needs. In this context, the arrival of cheap mass-produced recorded music from the United States found a willing audience amongst the generation growing up in the shadow of a global disaster. To a significant extent, the cultural foundations were already in place, with the rock 'n' roll craze building upon the huge popularity of America's glamorous 'movie stars', the radio-friendly song forms of Tin Pan Alley and the earlier success of American Jazz. As a distinctive American form combining black American blues and white American swing, rock 'n' roll quickly became a defining cultural form for the newly minted social category of 'teenagers'. Linked closely to the widespread enthusiasm for a range of Americana from cowboys to Cadillacs, jeans and hamburgers, rock 'n' roll music became emblematic of a new era of consumer affluence in the United States, and the transmission of similar aspirations to young people across the world. Thus, on the face of it, the rock 'n' roll craze constitutes a classic case of American 'soft power'.

Nonetheless, the fusion of black and white performance cultures and the libidinous content of both sound and lyric were deeply shocking to cultural conservatives in the United States as much as anywhere else. The obvious fervour of young people for the music (and the clothes, hairstyles, cars and vices that went with it) was largely inexplicable to an older generation raised on national service and austerity. The whole panoply represented what would later be called a 'subculture', and heralded the advent of 'youth culture' as a central preoccupation of commercial entertainment. In that sense, the transgressions of rock 'n' roll heralded an unprecedented generational shift in the Western world, a shift towards the young that continued into the late 1960s and was made inevitable by the post-war 'baby boom'. As such, rock 'n' roll belongs solidly to those post-war years, but the unique adaptability of popular music and the spread of cheap sound technologies have extended its legacy up to the present day. The energies unleashed in the 1950s and 1960s would go on to transform the aspirations of teenagers across the world, making the formative (and previously nondescript) adolescent years central to the modern lifecycle (see Ruddock 2013; Savage 2008). Similarly, while rock 'n' roll was uniquely American in its original formulation, its multitudinous offspring have been citizens of the world. Between the 1960s and the 1980s, popular music would become a, if not the, predominant form of transnational culture. Enabled by their cultural proximity, and shorn of much in the way of accessible leisure (and certainly glamour), Britain's working-class youth embraced rock 'n' roll to perhaps the greatest degree. As soon as the craze began, British imitators began entertaining their own national publics in the absence of the American originals.

By 1964, the runaway success of the Beatles, enabled by the establishment of transatlantic jet travel and network television, led to a so-called 'British Invasion' in the United States. Throughout the late 1960s, British acts reworked the rock 'n' roll format with black Chicago blues and their own music hall traditions for an enthusiastic American public, inspiring another profusion of musical acts. In the other direction, a boom in American folk music saw the resurgence of interest in English song traditions and, linking up with the American beat poets, introduced Bob Dylan's social commentary to English songwriters. Rapid developments in electronics and recording techniques led to regular changes in the range and sophistication of available sounds, and by the late 1960s, rock 'n' roll had evolved into the rich and diverse forms of modern rock music. Predominantly an Anglo-American hybrid, rock music swiftly became a universally popular genre across the world, supported by millions of record sales and the ubiquitous 'world tours' that took the 'supergroups' of the 1970s to stadia around the globe. As Anglophone rock music extended its popularity, it incorporated a range of other traditions, notably from Latin America and the Caribbean. Rock and lighter pop styles became widely imitated in native languages across Europe and Asia. Thus, at the height of the Cold War, rock music became a powerful symbol of rebellion and illicit Western freedoms for the youth of Eastern Europe and Russia. Rising with the generation that created it, rock music became a major field of consumption that inculcated lifelong behaviours. It is no surprise, then, that marketing professionals quickly took note of the powerful links that young people were forming between popular culture, social identity and everyday consumption (Trentmann 2005).

The Rise of the Fans

The passion of the young not only to buy recordings and attend concerts, but also to imitate the dress and lifestyle of rock stars, to form appreciation societies and attend to the 'message' of their music, all served to demonstrate the potential of popular culture for anchoring meanings within a consumer society. Nonetheless, the obsessive and hysterical behaviours associated with 'Beatlemania' and its many successors fed into prevailing discourses around the pathological nature of cultural consumption. The intensity of devotional sentiments around film stars, musical performers and, in later years, TV 'personalities' clearly jarred with the rational logics of modernity. For the left, the centrality of mass consumption to these practices appeared to underline the dangers of a 'false consciousness' engendered by consumerism. On the right, the behavioural influences of popular culture appeared to support the 'brainwashing' effects associated with the mass media at the height of the Cold War. Thus, in the early decades of audience research, the category of the pop culture 'fan' was broadly associated with psychological disorders and anti-social behaviours (Lewis 1992). It conjured up images of quasi-religious cults of socially dysfunctional and obsessive individuals who gathered together in conventions to engage in fantasies based around popular culture. Science fiction was an early focus of such activity, and 'Trekkies' remain a 'classic case' of fan behaviours (see Drushel 2013). Popular music appeared to replicate this phenomenon on a much larger scale, and much of the activity around computer games in later years would fall into the same pattern (Jenkins 2006).

While the majority of fan cohorts were drawn from young adults, a substantial number of individuals would continue to engage in fan cultures throughout their lives. Because of its obvious excesses, the behaviour of fans remained set aside from the general study of 'audiences', taken to be reasonable and representative samples of the general public. Fans were typified as 'cult' audiences, whose extreme attachments to popular culture were far from normative (Mathijis and Sexton 2011). Nonetheless, as the market for popular culture became more and more sophisticated, the degree of expertise required to achieve literacy in the broader field of consumption became ever more expansive. As a result, the level of investment from consumers in particular genres increased, and most forms of pop culture began to throw up their own cohorts of experts, their own specialist publications and their own series of conventions and events. In the process, fan cultures moved into the mainstream, and offered substantial commercial opportunities. The vast range of merchandise associated with the popularity of the Beatles is a prime example of this shift, as is the vast range of literature available, authored not in the main by musicologists, but by a new breed of critics whose expertise rests upon their detailed knowledge as lifelong fans of the group (e.g., Spizer 2003). Scant on the aural content of the product itself, this genre typically focuses upon the narrative of 'success through struggle' and the most controversial incidents that define the 'larger than life' personas of the artists.

In that sense, the primary role of music literature is the production of a modern folklore that personalizes artists and perpetuates their popularity. Essentially, this is a consumer literature that stitches together the demands of fans for the minutiae of the star story with the marketing machinery of the commercial entertainment business. Despite the pioneering efforts of Hollywood in the pre-war years, the production of celebrities remained a cottage industry in the Beatles heyday. Since then, 'celebrification' has become a central, and well-oiled, constituent of consumerism. The tipping point was the 1970s, as the burgeoning marketing industry responded to the vagaries of successive 'crazes' in popular culture. The conscious inculcation of a 'fan following' became a prime strategy for realizing the commercial potentials of the performing arts. Rather than simply responding to the sudden, but typically brief, popularity of performers with spin-off merchandise, the increasingly corporate music industry constructed formulas designed to premeditate all aspects of a full-blown fan craze. By the 1970s, not only musical acts, but also mainstream movies and television shows would commonly be augmented with a whole range of 'tie-ins' that located the brand value of pop culture at the heart of mass consumption (Austin 2002; Lathrop 2003). For this to make sense, fans had to be regarded not as fringe eccentrics, but rather as the central ideal type for the modern consumer. The implication of this shift is that appeals to consumers will tend to be emotive rather than reasoned, and that the prime goal of any commercial planning is the manufacture of a 'fanbase' that will deliver 'loyalty' to a product.

Whilst such demands were unreasonable, and even downright odd, by the standards of the 1950s, they have become entirely normative by contemporary standards. Indeed, to not be a fan of something would now be considered odd, and even minor artists will consciously refer not to their audiences, but to 'the fans'. In the age of Twitter, it is a common expectation that the stars of sound, screen, sports and politics will maintain daily interaction with their fanbases. Fanbases, then, are distinctive forms of audiences. Their loyalty comes with heightened expectations of personal interaction with their chosen star (Turner 2013). At the same time, their comprehensive consumption of the product range engenders a self-endowed capacity for critique, should their chosen star stray too far from their expectations. Bob Dylan, for example, was a high-profile victim of such sentiments in the mid-1960s (Dylan 2005). For our purposes, it is equally important that larger fan bases tend to be transnational in their membership. There are distinctly national stars, Greece's Michalis Rakintzis and Thailand's Mai Charoenpura come to mind, but in the aftermath of Beatlemania true fame requires international exposure. Within the Anglosphere, the North American market remains commercially essential to major league success in music or film, but the 'big in Japan' test is equally important in gauging the breadth of international appeal. The 'superstars' of popular culture must transcend their primary 'zone of consumption' origins, as Bruce Lee and Bob Marley both did in the 1970s (Morris et al. 2006; White 2006).

Beyond the stars themselves, the broader trends in pop culture commonly cross national boundaries. British genres such as punk and heavy metal have achieved lasting worldwide appeal, exemplified by the popularity of Burmese heavy metal act Iron Cross and the notorious Russian political punk band, Pussy Riot (Savage 2005; Weinstein 2000). American Country Music, and its entire paraphernalia, have become firmly ensconced in rural Australia, whilst nearby New Zealand has demonstrated a lasting passion for Jamaican roots reggae. Black American hip hop has inspired imitators amongst marginalized youth on a global scale, exemplified by Tunisia's El General and Brazil's MV Bill. Mainstream chanteuses like Beyonce and Shakira have a global fanbase and a conveyor belt of imitators, generously supported by their video-oriented presentation on satellite TV channels.

These many sharings and borrowings commonly confound the established explanations of culture founded on ethnic or linguistic singularity. As a cumulative consequence of vinyl and celluloid, satellite broadcasting, the World Wide Web and mobile media, national configurations of popular culture are constantly washed over by the fast-moving tides of global fashions and trends. Each of these movements creates a residual constituency in the form of a fanbase: an audience for a singular product that is more interested in the integrity of the genre than it is in civilizational policing. Further, the consistent replication of fan behaviours across the world makes (so-called) 'fandom' a global phenomenon in popular culture. For researchers, fan cultures, due to their inherent performativity and singular focus, remain easily accessible within an ever-expanding domain of popular culture. As a consequence, perhaps the majority of contemporary 'audience' studies are actually enquiries into fan cultures.

The Activation of Audience Studies

Academic approaches to pop culture have evolved in tandem with the movement of fan cultures to the centre of mainstream media consumption. At the outset, the mass media were assumed to have considerable power in influencing social behaviours, especially amongst the less educated (Gerbner and Gross 1976). Under the influence of Frankfurt School thinkers like Adorno, audiences were more or less positioned as victims of media effects co-ordinated by media producers for commercial or political gain (see Curran 2002). By the beginning of the 1960s, however, doubts were raised surrounding the notion of an all-powerful media. By this time, empirical research had failed to prove conclusively that the mass media had a direct and quantifiable behavioural influence upon their audiences. Joseph Klapper concluded that 'mass communication does not ordinarily serve as a necessary or sufficient cause of audience effects, but rather functions through a nexus of mediating factors' (1960: 8). In practice, the influence of the media was increasingly seen to be dependent upon the pre-existing social worlds inhabited by their audiences, and the social positioning of viewers (structured by age, gender and class) was seen as having primacy over planned 'messages' in terms of determining audience responses to the media they consumed. Much of this analysis focused upon the newly instituted medium of television, and upon general audiences, as opposed to the rising tide of youth culture and popular music. As such, the academy was largely taken by surprise when these movements burst on to the street in the late 1960s.

In the years that followed, the study of popular culture became the central preoccupation of the newly instituted discipline of cultural studies. With its origins in the politics of the British 'new left' of the 1950s and 1960s, British cultural studies had always sought to emphasize the worth of a 'common culture' in the face of cultural elitism (Hoggart 1957; Williams 1961). In light of the pop culture 'revolution' and the arrival of a new generation of practitioners in the 1970s, cultural studies would move its focus to the study of the various 'tribes' or 'cults' being formed around a series of fashions in youth culture. Given British preoccupations with social class, it was the delineation of working-class youth 'subcultures' (such as 'mods', 'skinheads', 'rockers' and 'punks') that would receive the most attention (for example, Hebdige 1979). By applying an anthropological mode of analysis, cultural studies researchers sought to elucidate the various 'ways of life' being constructed around distinct styles of music, dress and sexuality, along with the social and political attitudes that came with them. In the context of economic decline and social conflict, these cults of consumption were seen as providing a useful site of resistance against an established social order that was as hostile to the young then as it is today (Hall and Jefferson 1977). At its heart, cultural studies drew upon a distinct social constructivist position where social meanings were negotiated between the producers of 'discourse' and the audiences who adapted these materials to produce their own 'meanings' about society within the context of a 'counter-culture' (Hall 1980).

Against the backdrop of 'Thatcherism', the sociology of race and the politics of gender would become major foci for cultural studies work in the 1980s, and these topics would characterize the considerable influence of this school of thought in the United States and elsewhere during the same decade (Grossberg et al. 1992). The rise of cultural studies was pivotal in establishing popular culture as a 'legitimate' object of academic study in the domain of universities, who had jealously guarded their role as guardians of 'the classics' and 'the best that has been thought or said' (see Storey 2012). As such, cultural studies became a transnational phenomena in its own right, leading to a great expansion of cultural analysis in numerous academic disciplines, from literature to anthropology. As far as audience research is concerned, it is most critical that both the methodological and the conceptual frameworks of cultural studies would establish the predominant paradigm within academia until the early 2000s. The use of ethnographic methodologies, with an emphasis on the 'thick description' of 'subcultures' defined by their engagement with popular culture characterized the operational logics and training of audience researchers. The theoretical premise that audiences are 'active' participants in the media process displaced the unwitting 'victims' of effects research. The attribution of social and political 'agency' to marginalized groups via (and evidenced by) their participation in pop culture similarly replaced Marxist anxieties about 'false consciousness' with a more optimistic view of 'empowerment' through everyday social practices. An exemplar of this approach can be seen in the work of John Fiske (1989), who argued that British teenage girls effectively contested the marginalization of their youth and their gender through their engagement with the pop videos of Madonna.

Following directly from Fiske, Henry Jenkins (1992) propounded fan cultures as inherently progressive formations, facilitating the self-realization of their members and positive social participation. Going further, Jenkins makes the case that, however it may seem on the surface, the fans of popular culture are much more important, and certainly more powerful, than the media producers or the stars themselves. By this logic, the culture industries belong in effect to the people, since they are compelled, under the direction of the market, to respond to their demands. Pop culture thereby becomes a prime example of the 'consumer democracy' idealized by the marketing industry (which had made its own simultaneous shift from 'selling the product' to 'enhancing the customer experience') (Gournay and Gobe 2002). Perhaps unsurprisingly, then, the arrival of fan studies heralded something of a split in cultural studies. A 'celebratory' strand has been accused of vastly overemphasizing the power of audiences and almost entirely ignoring their concerted manipulation for commercial gain. By contrast, a self-consciously 'critical' approach continues to emphasize popular culture as a site of discursive contest, primarily useful for revealing the actions of disparate social forces in a world characterized by inequality. What nonetheless unites divergent approaches to contemporary cultural studies is the recognition that pop culture provides the raw materials for ordinary people making meaning out of social change, and that this is politically significant.

Digitality and Interactivity

It is upon this basis that cultural studies has been taken up in Asia over the past decade, as that region deals with the accelerated development of consumerism and generational change (Chen and Huat 2007; Sundaram 2011; Otmazgin and Ben Ari 2013). Moving beyond the longstanding arguments concerning the progressive or regressive capacities of popular culture, we must also account for the technological revolution that was intrinsic to the transnational shift of the 1990s. Given that the technologies involved (binary code, information processing and telephony) are explicitly media technologies, it was inevitable that they would reshape the terrain of audience studies as well as the sociology of culture. It is worth recalling that the case for active reception was an argument made at a time when audiences could not easily become producers of popular culture in their own right. Their agency in the 'circuit of communication' rested upon what they did with the symbolic material they consumed, and how this influenced a professional class of media producers and the public and private institutions that controlled the infrastructure of media systems. While audiences could be 'active' at a cognitive level, and they could select purchases and switch channels, their opportunities to become producers of popular culture themselves were necessarily limited. This did not stop them trying. Many bands were formed with each successive craze in popular music, although only a tiny handful would be recruited for recording by the gatekeepers of the music industry.

The onset of 'digitality' changed this scheme of things radically. In the first phase, the arrival of functional interactivity via computer games gave media consumers a direct role in the unfolding of the media content with which they engaged. The compulsive appeal of a stimulus-response relationship was immediately evident in the worldwide craze for electronic games that made fortunes for electronics corporations from the US to Japan in the early 1980s. The steady switchover to digital broadcasting broke the monopolies founded upon limited, and state regulated, analogue bandwidth, thereby empowering 'consumer choice' through a profusion of channels and substantial growth in the availability of 'foreign' media content. The spread of digital audio software broke the monopoly over recording techniques and allowed musicians to produce their own works at a nominal cost, and the skills needed to compose electronic music became easy to acquire. The biggest development by far, however, was the advent of the World Wide Web, which offered both global scale and personal authoring via the Internet. Critically, the medium was offered as an open access and free-to-view platform, with the potential to reach a vast and growing audience, leaving the established cultural industries struggling to find a workable for-profit model until the second Internet decade. In this context, the previously marginal genre of fan production quickly became a predominant format for Internet content.

From UseNet onwards, the World Wide Web has been dominated not by broadcast content, but by the public interaction between its users. A vast and unique field of discourse thereby entered the public domain. Scores of thousands, then millions then billions of Internet users have produced an inconceivably vast store of personal expression, interpersonal communication and creative works. As countless Internet users type out their passion for popular culture in 'cyberspace', the capacity to include interactive scripting in their web pages allows other users to comment upon, interact with and further disseminate the content that they produce. Thus, the previous careful study of audiences in relative isolation had to face the challenge of unimaginable plenitude, as audience responses to popular culture 'go viral' and become available on a previously unimaginable scale. The global ambit of the World Wide Web also means that the conversations taking place are ranging freely across the globe, and thereby creating new forms of long-distance sociability that inevitably transform the very conception of an audience. In the context of our focus in this chapter, it is perhaps unsurprising that the global fashions of popular culture have provided most of the common ground for these vast disembodied debates and electronic interactions. Employing media content and bandwidth for their own purposes, Internet-enabled fans rapidly appropriate, re-purpose and re-shape the 'product'. The ready availability of consumer software for re-working images, sounds and video thereby underpins a giant machinery of perpetual 'post-production' with an almost infinite capacity for the re-use of digital commodities.

With the speed of information transfer increasing over the turn of the millennium, the Internet has since realized its potential as a highly effective mechanism for not simply discussing but also exchanging and distributing the artefacts of pop culture. From Napster onwards, fans everywhere have engaged in an unprecedented frenzy of media swapping, distributing not only their own amateur works, but also building vast collections of pop culture products without paying for them. Naturally, then, the immediate effect of Internet fandom has been to push the cultural industries into an ever-deepening crisis. Similarly, this change in the relationship of audiences to the media, and to the operating environment of audience researchers, has been far-reaching and irrevocable. If we follow the established orthodoxy of the 'active' audience, the rapid growth of Internet users into the world's largest media 'audience' can be taken as the most concrete and radical example of audience power over the media apparatus. In making this shift to 'new media', however, the 'active' concept became separated from its origins in a critique of media representation. Indeed, in the first decade of the public Internet, there was no central source of 'corporate' content upon which to rest such an oppositional criticism. Instead, the active audience concept was dovetailed neatly with the functional interactivity of digital media platforms. As a consequence of this reorientation, audience 'activity' has since become understood primarily as a matter of writing rather than reading, and of doing rather than thinking.

YouMedia and Participatory Culture

In this present configuration of digitality, the 'meaning' of the media culture is taken to exist not so much within the content of various platforms, but within the 'interactivity' (or even 'hyperactivity') of media users. By this logic, audiences realize agency not by choosing to read or think in different ways, but by doing a lot of clicking and commenting. Opportunities to do so have proliferated exponentially, as a procession of multimedia gadgets and software applications have targeted the enthusiasm for online entertainment and interpersonal communication. In the gold rush of the 'Web 2.0' economy of the 2000s, Internet start-ups mushroomed like rock bands in the late 1960s, all seeking to build their own social media fanbases before selling out to entertainment corporates and other major league investors. In that sense, the public love affair with digital technologies has produced its own series of fashions and crazes, with fan cultures building around the styling of personal media devices and the various rituals embedded in platforms such as Twitter, Facebook, Flickr, Viber, WhatsApp etc. In taking part in this vast workshop of communication, Internet users engage with a vast 'participatory culture', an entirely novel media system centred upon the contributions of its audience (Jenkins 2004). For Henry Jenkins, building upon his work in fan studies, the immediate consequence of the digital revolution has been the empowerment of ordinary consumers across the board. The digital media have now made people-power a reality, bringing about the ultimate democratization of culture, which Jenkins (2008) seeks to encapsulate via Alvin Toffler's notion of the 'prosumer', a new form of citizen who is simultaneously both producer and consumer of our contemporary culture.

Digitality, then, has fashioned a union between 'Trekkies' and 'Techies' at a number of levels. As this convergence has been embraced commercially, the new centrality of prosumers to the digital economy has been exemplified by the amateur video-sharing site YouTube and the rich participatory culture it facilitates (Burgess and Green 2009). Launched by a garage band of three in 2005 (albeit one with an $11.5m deal), YouTube was conceived of as a public file-sharing site for video clips. Based on the incorporation of Adobe's Flash Player software, YouTube offers a platform designed for the new era of videophones, as mobile media devices have supplanted desktop computers as the primary means of Internet access during the 2000s. Public participation came on rapidly with thousands of video clips being posted daily in the year before the company was sold on to Google in 2006. After ten years of operation, YouTube now carries the largest collection of audiovisual content in the world, with viewing time outstripping even the largest television providers. In order to manage content at this scale, the visibility of videos on YouTube is organized via a recommendations system that combines Google's search algorithms with the system of customer votes (or 'likes') also seen on social media platforms like Facebook and the customer recommendations system pioneered by Amazon in the 1990s. As with most Web 2.0 platforms, the personal profiles of YouTube users are primarily structured around consumption habits.

The success of Web 2.0 portals over the past decade rests in many respects upon their capacity to build upon the established transnationalism of youth culture, and the rich folklores that have been constructed cumulatively over the last half century. Self-presentation in this domain takes place via our endorsement of particular films, shows and music. Enthusiasts for the participatory culture thesis have also taken note of the phenomenon of 'mash-ups', where fans remix existing materials before circulating them to their network of fellow enthusiasts (Sonvilla-Weiss 2010). More often, however, YouTube is used to simply share existing music, film and TV content, resulting in a long-running struggle between Google and copyright holders such as Viacom. The fair use provisions of the Digital Millennium Copyright Act, under which the site is regulated, allow substantial leeway for the posting of material, although constant transgressions result in thousands of 'take down' orders. However, these barely keep pace with the flood of new materials coming in from millions of users around the world. Time and data volume limits maintain some restriction on the sharing of longer movie features, but recorded music is a free-for-all. As a consequence, YouTube functions as the primary site of contemporary fan culture. Those sharing an interest in a particular artist can use YouTube to quickly gain access to their entire back catalogue, clips of TV appearances, unreleased bootlegs, homemade 'talk to camera' album reviews, cover versions by other fans, documentary features and tutorials providing instruction on how to tune and play specific songs. Attached to all of this material is a string of commentary provided by other YouTube users.

This treasure trove of fan discourse and debate offers a rich mix of personal recollections linked to particular songs, appreciative and amorous statements, queries around particular material, arguments over the relative value of artists and the vigorous correction of erroneous statements by more expert fans (the ubiquitous 'uber nerds'). Although much of the commentary is friendly, there is no shortage of Internet 'trolls' who use the commenting tools to aggravate other users by disparaging their chosen stars or by launching personal attacks upon other users. Thus, participatory culture has proved to be something of a bear pit. Given its universal accessibility, this unruly field of discussion is also a global phenomenon. For example, middle-aged Britons reminiscing about early 1980s gigs at Nottingham Rock City are joined by long-distance fans in Latin America and Asia ('I'm from Japan. I love this!!!!!'). Comment strings on Neil Young's material in the 2000s would often degenerate into a quasi-political discussion around his opposition to the Iraq War, his entitlement to any opinion being loudly denied, on occasion, due to him 'being a Canadian'. These jingoistic comments were invariably countered by other posters reminding fellow Americans that 'Neil has been here a long time' and that 'we should be nice to Canada' (those 'damned liberals' out there . . .). Obviously, this level of invective is entirely mild when compared to the sorts of comments posted about Russia's Pussy Riot. Thus, while it is fair to say that most postings are entirely banal, there is also a clear tendency towards the intense personalization of political disputes.

Leaving aside the procession of 'world's funniest' clips and stunts delivered to your phone handset, YouTube has not become an alternative universe of citizen media, but rather a vast conglomeration of fan culture. Recognizing that YouTube offers a more effective medium than television for reaching an upcoming generation spot-welded to their personal media devices, entertainment corporates have elected to feed the monster. Thus, mainstream promoters use the platform to disseminate trailers and teasers and a whole raft of product promotions and celebrity 'news'. Google sells slots on the pages as part of its core targeted-advertising business. All in all, there are many, many more consumers than prosumers on YouTube. Nonetheless, there are other significant portals that continue to pursue the prosumer ideal. In recent years, SoundCloud has emerged as a major site of amateur music production. Registered in Sweden and based in Germany since 2007, SoundCloud offers paying subscribers the capacity to share and stream hi-definition music files, to offer comments on the works of others and to communicate and share files via the portal. Consequently, SoundCloud has enabled a whole raft of 'virtual' bands, with compositions being worked upon jointly by collaborators spread across the globe. This transnational configuration of dedicated 'semi-pro' creatives aligns with Axel Bruns' (2008) related proposition of 'Produsers' in the digital economy. Even so, their ultimate goal typically remains the same as YouTube's tiny minority of serious video-makers: to 'go viral', to 'get noticed' and to translate amateur passion into paid work. Such a transition has become increasingly unlikely in a world saturated with free music (see Lanier 2010).

User-Led Transnationalism

The phenomenon of popular music provides us with a cogent example of how the cultural presence of transnationalism is facilitated by mass media systems. The parallel replication of fan cultures across the world, and their aggregation via the World Wide Web, is also instructive in terms of how we might understand the innumerable 'public spheres' being constructed around the consumption of popular culture at a global scale. Paying attention to the social life of media artefacts, as much as their formal content, naturally directs us towards the idea of practice being central to cultural transmission (see Couldry 2012: 33–58). What fans say and do around different examples of popular culture offers a prime example of their imaginative engagement with a wider society, notwithstanding the artificially singular focus of each conversation. The fact that such engagements now commonly take place within a unified global media system necessarily inculcates an innate consciousness of the globalization of possibility. Even where these 'virtual communities' maintain a relatively limited referential geography, the vast chamber of the World Wide Web reinforces the grandiose tendencies of youthful expression. At a mundane level, our everyday encounters with the hurly-burly of fan debates in online forums underline the reality of global constituencies. To receive such personalized evidence that your object of self-realization is equally meaningful to someone on the other side of the world is simultaneously both banal and profound. Far more accessible than the complex operations of global value chains, such moments are proof positive of globalization.

This is not always a pleasant experience to be celebrated. In one bulletin board that I viewed, a female YouTube account holder, whose profile picture was taken (unreasonably) to be too raunchy, was assailed by (mostly) male commentators calling her vile names and/or demanding a date. The fact that this collection of Internet 'trolls' were posting from North America, Europe and the Middle East thereby added a transnational experience of misogyny to one young woman's foray into self-realization and fan cultures. Despite its progressive framing, contemporary fandom is a brave new world where you can be sexually abused by a worldwide public via your personal handset. The onset of such attacks seems to be quite random, and appears to require little or no provocation. Neither 'davefrombrooklyn' nor 'AfghanMan' was seemingly interested in this woman's innocuous comments on Peter Jackson's Tolkien movies (although it is common to find a fair amount of abusive material in message strings that do manage to stay on that topic). Nonetheless, the very ubiquity of the message board in 2.0, and the lack of inhibitions that go with it, are intrinsic to the era of the 'prosumer'. They are, in all likelihood, more telling of a consumer democracy than any amateur production or remix. On the surface at least, there are remarkable consistencies between the emotional registers of message boards on popular music and video and those attached to the pages served up by NGOs or providers of international news. Each forum produces its own cascade of armchair experts, narcissists, activists, humanists, bigots, trolls and bunnies.

Across the board, the expansion of conversational scale that such forums represent is quite possibly the most salient feature of the World Wide Web. While the majority of the debates around online audiences have tended to focus on the functional interactivity of the medium, the true significance of its global range rarely receives any substantive interrogation. Arguably, the uniquely transnational nature of online interaction remains an undertheorized aspect of digital culture. Leaving the Chinese case aside, within each self-referential strand of the pop culture fabric, the primacy of national frames is often less determining than other points of commonality or difference between users. Nonetheless, the strategic use of national flags in online debates is itself a perpetual reminder of the global scope of our everyday text debates. People are almost universally compelled to state where they are from in the course of any substantial interchange with other users, and this locative aspect of self-presentation remains tremendously important to the meanings being drawn out by others. From the amicable and cosmopolitan to the jingoistic and barbaric, the online interactions of a vast global public reveal, for the very first time, the operation of grassroots 'international relations' in real time. This is immensely valuable to the privileged few who have access to the bird's-eye data, even as most of us tend to miss its significance in the intense personalization of our media experience.

Of course, the great paradox of a media system increasingly driven by the personal profiles of individual users is that most Web 2.0 portals are presented as entirely generic formats. Barring changes of language and script, YouTube or Facebook present themselves as universal standards for users across the world. This is something that we will return to, but it is worth stating at this point that such a system assumes a remarkable 'cultural convergence' between populations across the world. Far from being culturally neutral, these platforms are infused with the 'Californian ideology' of Silicon Valley, in that they prescribe a certain form of individualism wherein freedom is made synonymous with an expansion of choice. On the screen in your hand, the individual capacity to shuffle your favourites, playlists and address books and to conduct arguments with your own personal public certainly feels very much like the empowerment of a unique personal space.

Just as Raymond Williams saw the television set and the private car as technologies that allowed for the privatization of public space, the era of mobile media takes this to a global scale (Williams 1974). We are now offered a 'roaming' media environment where our media applications and personal profiles operate seamlessly as we move around the world. Regardless of where you travel, your own personal media channels will maintain your personal cultural domain and the privilege of micro-managing it. You can paint your own cloud. It is upon the basis of this promise, seemingly, that we allow our personal data to be moved into the cloud for secondary uses by others. Thus, at one level contemporary digital applications are evidently sites of intensive transnationalism, but at another level the effective personalization of our media environment encourages us to be oblivious of where we are.

Reading Interactive Audiences

Popular music and the rise of fan cultures point towards a very different model of cultural dynamics than we tend to get if we proceed from matching classical cultural formations with general populations. The long-term stability of cultures emphasized by Braudel is pushed to the background, with the rapid interchanges between cultural zones in the here and now becoming our primary interest. The centrality of cultural fusion in the musical field itself naturally tends towards a higher degree of cultural mobility than we might see in other mediums. Whilst lyrics are critically important to modern music, they tend to be relatively simple phrases, and linguistic proximity has more exceptions here than it does in television. The linkages between the various hybrid artistic forms and the broader machinery of popular culture also draw our attention to the ways in which modern youth culture is continually reinvented and circulated backwards and forwards across the world (Buckingham et al. 2014). The modern world has itself been founded upon continuous increases in the velocity of such exchanges, to the point where cultural movements can be seen as originating simultaneously in many locations interlinked by synchronous technologies. In such a context, the transnational is no longer an import-export business but rather a differentiated simultaneity of experience. Over the course of three successive generations, pop culture audiences have moved from the analytical margins to the mainstream, and from London to Lima. Fan culture, whether we take it to be progressive or not, has become normalized everywhere that consumerism has been conjoined with social development (see Sandvoss 2005).

As a consequence, the profusion of transnational interactions via bulletin boards, file shares, creative collaborations and various forms of virtual sociability provides us with a rich and easily accessible field of transnational communication. The individuation of the programming, and its vast cumulative range, offer insights into almost every conceivable topic. Invariably those insights are earthy, emotive, fragmented and inconsistent, thereby getting to the heart of the modern experience. Firmly in the popular domain, the interactions between these new audience formations take us beyond the dry justifications and language of policy and treaty that typically characterize studies in international relations. We should remain aware, of course, that much of this material, tending towards the irrational and the extreme, is unlikely to be representative of the 'considered opinions' favoured by critical theory. Equally, these distinctive disembodied textual exchanges are medium-specific and should not be taken as evidence of 'natural' behaviours. Nonetheless, with their characteristic suturing of the personal, cultural and political, the transnational interactions taking place via the Internet are tremendously valuable as a field of public speech into which the social imagination of globalization is being collectively projected. Thus, while it remains practically difficult for audience researchers to systematically assess such a vast collection of data, the dynamics of transnational interactivity are certain to be a major preoccupation for cultural studies in the twenty-first century.

Recommended Reading

David Buckingham, Sara Bragg and Mary Jane Kehily (eds) (2014) *Youth Cultures in the Age of Global Media,* Houndmills: Palgrave Macmillan.

Jean Burgess and Joshua Green (2009) *YouTube: Online Video and Participatory Culture*, Cambridge: Polity.

John Fiske (1989) *Understanding Popular Culture*, London and New York: Routledge.

Stuart Hall and Tony Jefferson (eds) (1977) *Resistance Through Rituals: Youth Subcultures in Post-War Britain*, London: Routledge.

Henry Jenkins (2008) *Convergence Culture: Where Old and New Media Collide*, New York: New York University Press.

Cornel Sandvoss (2005) *Fans: The Mirror Of Consumption*, Cambridge: Polity.

Patrik Wikström (2013) *The Music Industry: Music in the Cloud*, Cambridge: Polity.

Nabeel Zuberi (2001) *Sounds English: Transnational Popular Music*, Champaign: University of Illinois Press.

9   Alchemy, Numerology and the Global Social

For audience researchers, probably the most discussed 'point of convergence' in the Internet era is that between fan subcultures and mainstream audiences. It appears that the contemporary 'mainstream' is not, after all, a dispassionate and generalized alternative to cult behaviours, but actually a vast field of overlapping fan cultures. Consequently, the devotional and over-invested behaviours of fans can no longer be easily stigmatized. At the same time, this also means that the enabling anthropological concept of subcultures as singular communities is dead in the water. After all, belonging to only one fan culture would scarcely round out anyone's social media profile. In that sense, our intensive interest in interactivity certainly needs to move beyond user-engagement with media content and trendy systems to focus more squarely on the qualities of interaction across a media-rich environment. The comfortable assumptions around agency and activity that currently prevail simply won't be sufficient for much of the work that actually needs to be done in an era of interactive audience research. With digitality, as much as popularity, inflecting our experience of everyday communication, the conceptual distinction between 'active' and 'interactive' audiences needs far greater clarity of purpose. Consequently, some extensive categorical work is required in the coming years, allowing us to distinguish effectively between witting and unwitting interactions, between public speech and trails of data exhaust, and between inputs prompted by users, by interpersonal protocols or by the system itself. This agenda is not specific to the transnational question per se, but the emerging geography of user-led transnationalism further requires that any future epistemology of audience behaviours must also account for interactivity on a global scale.

For qualitative researchers, then, the explosion of scale and the technical complexities of the digital revolution clearly indicate a paradigm shift. Notably, the ethnographic approach that has been predominant for half a century, resting as it does upon close observation and thick description, is fundamentally recast by the sudden abundance of disembodied articulations that threatens to circumvent the careful co-presence of academic collectors of human experiences. For quantitative researchers, however, the global reach of digital systems brings many forms of transnational comparative analysis within almost instantaneous reach. The rapid evolution of collecting and processing algorithms provides readily accessible tools for effectively managing the scale of those systems. With data collection now taking place by and of itself, quantification comes into its own. Thus, the newfound capacities for 'datafication' embedded in our digital architecture offer much promise in terms of underpinning transnational audience research with comprehensive empirical underpinnings. User-tracking allows for the location of specific instances of transnational communication within broader viewing patterns, available for query right down to the individual scale. Automated data harvesting provides the raw materials for the mapping of intricate social networks within media audiences spread across the world. Real-time data management of media streams even allows us to take instantaneous 'temperature readings' of public responses to specific events and media content from anywhere in the world. This, then, is the era of 'big data' presently emerging from two decades of innovative and aggressive information management, and exemplified by the global fortunes of Google and Facebook. In the context of this data arcadia, the need to reconsider our epistemological premise is less apparent than the sudden expansion of the methodological toolkit, but it is no less pressing.

Pinpointing Users

As we have seen in the previous chapter, YouTube (as with other instances of YouMedia) is an exemplar of the digital economy precisely because it is a medium without any content of its own. It relies upon its users to supply the value of the service, and to do so freely and without payment (Andrejevic 2009; Burgess and Green 2009). Such user-led systems have become predominant in an era where media production technologies are cheap and where media distribution has been liberated from both expert intermediaries and costs. Since copyrights are costly to enforce and revenues hard to collect, any substantial media platform must rely heavily upon content which carries no production costs. Equally, the convergence of interpersonal communication and entertainment systems via the Internet means that media products are almost impossible to control within a conventional commercial model. These factors predicate a predominantly user-led media system, but the availability of such inputs is not sufficient in itself to guarantee a profit motive adequate for ensuring the sustained proliferation of digital goods and services. In practice, our passion for consuming 'prosumer' content remains limited, and tends to be concentrated in areas where user content clusters around 'traditional' media products. Thus, the present economics of digital culture relies not only upon the unpaid labour of the audience, but equally upon the systematic exploitation of the back catalogue of popular culture. We know that the global footprint of pop culture established in the twentieth century has facilitated both the scope and depth of user-led transnationalism in its initial phase, but it is also true that the economic incentives to refurbish this treasure trove are rapidly diminishing (see Lanier 2013).

With the digital future looking highly retrospective at the level of content, the primary logics of the 'Web 2.0' era during the 2000s became centred upon capturing the commercial value of the World Wide Web in other ways (O'Reilly 2005). Eschewing the old purchase-driven models of print, film and recorded music, the new capitalists of the Internet looked to the business models arising from its immediate parents: television and telephony. From telephony, we inherit the tradition of a subscription-based service with precisely timed charges. That gets us online via various devices. From television, it is the capacity to carry advertising which has provided the obvious revenue source for Internet start-ups encountering a general resistance to actually pay for any of the services they provide. Some technical modifications were required to make this work. During the 1990s, opportunities for advertising revenues on the Internet were limited, since the audience was dispersed anonymously across a vast range of web pages. Only a tiny fraction of Internet content reached a substantial audience, offering nothing like the aggregation of eyeballs provided by television. However, following the introduction of user-tracking into web browsers and the provision of unique IP addresses, it became possible to individually identify each user. This opened the door to an Internet advertising boom for two reasons: firstly, that a vast body of detailed consumer profiles could be created and, secondly, that individual users could be effectively targeted with advertising upon the basis of those profiles.

Google's growing monopoly on the basic search facilities required to trawl through the vast proliferation of content left the company uniquely placed to build profiles of users' viewing habits. This capability allowed Google to aggressively market the individual addressability of Internet advertising and rapidly become one of the world's largest companies (Levy 2011). With the freedom of expanding bandwidth and greater precision, the commercial re-launch of the Internet rested upon the rapid expansion of the advertising industries throughout the online space. The attractions are fairly obvious. Targeted advertising seems intuitively more efficient than the old 'broadside' approach of radio and television, with the added bonus of eliding the 'timeslot' constraints of these older systems. Equally, compared with other media systems, the World Wide Web provides global reach at very low cost, since a single web page can be viewed from anywhere in the world. At the other end of the scale, user-tracking allows for individual people to be picked out within that vast space, matching universal reach with a unique degree of personalization. Although narrowly conceived, advertising is a behavioural science. Its technicians are not only interested in identifying particular constituencies of consumption, but equally in influencing future choices of consumption. Thus, the shift towards an advertising model on the World Wide Web has naturally brought with it the concomitant interest in gauging media effects and purveying persuasion (a tendency that also characterized early research into television audiences).

Attention to the efficiency of commercial communication has required the intensive collection and correlation of quantitative data regarding consumption patterns. In the early years of audience research, this vocation was limited by the available means of data collection, with surveys, phone polls and focus groups being cost intensive and providing only very limited and artificial insights into consumer behaviour. The Internet, however, is a medium of record where every action produces its own data. At the turn of the millennium, this data became widely available as credit card companies, ISPs and online retailers woke up to the secondary usage of their transaction records. As with any network system the commercial value of such information increases exponentially as the user base expands. An oft-cited example of this is the online retailer Amazon, which initially specialized in selling books. One of Amazon's most innovative features was its recommendation system which used current and past purchases to assess similar products to suggest to its customers. As its inventory and customer base expanded, and the transaction records grew longer and more detailed, the 'accuracy' of the 'recommendations' feature was seen to increase exponentially. This prompted Chris Anderson to make the observation that we should not regard the value of Amazon as a vast online catalogue but rather as an incomparably well-informed salesman (Anderson 2006). By such means, the intense personalization of our media experience becomes, in effect, an apparatus of assisted consumption.

Capturing the Crowd

We could see Web 2.0, as Chris Anderson does, in terms of media efficiency gains for both producers and consumers. In online retail, the consumer benefits from greatly expanded choice, effective price comparison and home delivery. The producer also makes real benefits from direct sales, making savings on storage, distribution and marketing to physical retailers. The online retailer makes its own business by taking a cut from transactions managed through a piece of software that effectively runs itself. By this reading, everyone is happy and everyone makes a saving. A less utopian account may conclude that producers of media content are being paid progressively less, as competition increases and sales drop, and those who rely on employment in 'bricks and mortar' retailers are now visibly out of work in towns full of boarded-up shops. By this reading, the whole edifice of 'price comparison' rests upon the exploitation of cheap labour and the obliteration of specialized businesses by software companies domiciled in low-tax jurisdictions. Any book can, of course, be read in different ways regardless of how you got it. From a material perspective, the emergence of predictive pinpointing constitutes faux individuation, since the vast bulk of actual consumption remains centred upon mass produced commodities. Seen in this light, the rise of user-led media does not signal a triumph of citizen media, but reveals instead the power of automated data to shape strongly guided consumers. Thus user-led media could be alternatively described as 'user is led', given that each of us is increasingly guided by a complex set of algorithms that assess our consumer preferences and make suggestions for future choices.

The larger point, perhaps, is that any standard political economy can only tell us so much about the vagaries of an informational economy. Certainly, the (relatively) simple economic logics of online retail become much less illustrative when we attempt to account for the broader impact of user-tracking. Take Mark Zuckerberg's Facebook, the most notable success of the 'social media' era. Here, the content of the medium is the interpersonal communications of two billion people, as they exchange messages, photos, endorsements and contacts. From a political economy perspective, this is a long way from online shopping since there are no goods being exchanged. Nonetheless, within the highly particular field of digital valuation the commercial ethos of such portals appears to be little different in practice. Like Amazon, Facebook relies on the production of commodities produced by others. Like Google, it relies upon selling user profiles to advertisers and other interested parties. Like both of them, it looks to the vast bodies of data produced by its clients for new ways to generate income. Consequently, the automated shadowing and foreshadowing of our online behaviour inverts Henry Jenkins' (2008) arguments for prosumer power, despite relying precisely on such behaviours for its data inputs. The evidence, then, would appear to suggest that it is not so much the users as those who can aggregate data about users who have become the shakers of the digital economy. In considering this shift at a conceptual level, we come to understand that it is not the audience, nor its time, but the data being produced about the audience that is the actual commodity being realized in these transactions.

For advertisers, the putative big bang occurs when you shift from creating an archive of data about the habits of the past to using this information to make predicative analyses about the future.

The fact that Facebook is primarily a forum for personal communication has raised hackles for many people in ways that Amazon's assisted shopping and Google's arcane back-office algorithms have not (Lyon 2007). Those outraged by the privacy implications of what is essentially a world-spanning phone-tap operation are commonly reminded of the old adage: 'If it's free, then you're the product.' This was, of course, somewhat true of commercial television, but selling slices of your attention span is perhaps more palatable than trawling through your emails, as both Facebook and Google are wont to do. This intense mapping of their audience is rendered precisely in financial terms, via the differential gap between the modest book price of these companies (their assets) and their eye-popping share valuations (their worth). The users of social media certainly derive social gains, in terms of increasing the density of their social networks and their stores of social capital, but for the shakers of social media the value of this labour rests in data gains. That is, the essential value of these online 'products' resides in the datasets they produce for their real clients. Data gains translate far more readily into financial gains, not least because numbers tend to be attracted to each other. The utility, or use value, of data rests in the potentials for subsequent correlation. Price comparison is perhaps the most straightforward way of repurposing numerical data, but the spectre of comparison hovers equally over the more complex data compiled by social media platforms. Facebook, like YouTube, categorizes human beings on the basis of the films, music and sports teams they endorse, while also working hard to establish where they were born, where they work and who they know.

Since this is a global system, everyone in the world must conform to this (let's face it) ridiculous template of human identity as best they can. For the technorati, whose desired crop is readily comparable data, social information must be collected somewhat generically. Further, since the underlying economics of Web 2.0 rely upon the real-time application of targeted marketing via automated algorithms, the input variables must operate in a recognizable series. That is why the prevailing form of 'identity' in digital culture is standardized through this clumsy mash-up of the fan survey, dating ad and CV formats. By firmly anchoring all user activities to a set of profiling systems, this vast audience is systematically captured as an informational commodity (Zafarani et al. 2014). In this context, we should not forget that this systematic capture of the Internet's audience is a direct consequence of an integrated transnational media system. That is, the ambitions of Facebook and Google are only viable because we have already accepted the global domination of the relatively small number of information technology giants who set and maintain protocols and operating standards for the World Wide Web. Portals like Facebook, Google, Amazon and YouTube are all pinch points within the global flows of digital information. They simultaneously provide the means to convey, sort and access the vast realm of content along with easily accessible tools for interpersonal communication. The 'necessary convenience' of these services consequently allows them to operate as gateways to a vast realm of human experience, thereby aggregating a majority of Internet users into the critical mass which allows for their secondary commercialization.

Faith in Big Data

Despite the obvious shortcomings of commercially defined digital profiling, it remains the case that sufficient scale confers value upon even the most clumsy survey instrument. In that respect, the global scale at which contemporary social media platforms operate is inconceivably vast (two billion is an abstraction only tangible, perhaps, to a seasoned quant). Nobody has ever had so much data, nor had it in an individuated and relational structure so purposefully designed for correlation. Unlike an earlier era where market researchers would examine consumers in direct relation to a given product, the vast datasets being constructed in the social media era are purposefully intended to automatically correlate past and potential behaviours in relation to all or any products, activities or actions. This constitutes something of a tipping point in the informational economy. It becomes possible only because processing power has increased exponentially (as anticipated by Moore's law). It becomes possible only because data storage has become inconceivably vast and cheap. It becomes possible only because a user-led medium of record removes the need to employ millions of data-entry clerks to capture the data. With this architecture in place, the engineers of Web 2.0 have consciously initialized a chain reaction in the generation of data. The ultimate output of this vast experiment is a mode of informatics where various logics of correlation can be deployed to create new knowledge from the raw material (Davenport 2014; Neef 2014). To further draw out the analogy between applied nuclear physics and informational physics, this is the point at which more energy is coming out of the process than is going into it.

The recent step-change in the manipulation of information has been usefully explicated in Mayer-Schonberger and Cukier's recent book on the big data revolution (2013). Mayer-Schonberger and Cukier illustrate the implications of pervasive data collection through a series of distinctions, the most central being that between 'digitization' and 'datafication'. We can understand this in terms of the difference between filling the bucket of the World Wide Web and stirring it. In the first phase of the Internet there was a Herculean effort to digitize information. In the current phase, however, our attention has moved to what we want to do with that information. Mayer-Schonberger and Cukier offer the analogy of Amazon's Kindle and Google Books. While Amazon has digitized books for the purposes of selling them as virtual books on Kindle, Google has paired its massive book-scanning programme with text recognition software to create an inconceivably vast automated experiment in linguistic translation. Thus, the print archive becomes adapted for new purposes and new forms of calculation. This is not only a process of digitization, but a process of datafication. For Google, the knowledge gained from parsing all the variants between different language editions of various works generates a new capacity to provide translation services. The creative labour is free, being derived from the previous efforts of human translators working with no realization of the subsequent aggregation, correlation and automation of their knowledge. Similarly, for Facebook the eagerness of users to exchange their digital photographs online, along with their singular capacity to recognize everyone they know, has provided a worldwide test bed for facial recognition software. Every time we are halted by prompts to identify 'friends' tagged in photographs, we contribute to this systematic endeavour.

This, again, is datafication, where the social knowledge of billions of people becomes harvested as a commodity for overarching purposes visible only to the architects of social media systems, their commercial partners, GCHQ and the NSA. Thus, while Web 1.0 was a radical experiment in free speech and global connectivity, the users of Web 2.0 are all participants, witting or otherwise, in a series of universal lab tests exploring the possibilities of big data. This has nothing to do with self-realization, cultural bonding or the uncovering of meaning, but everything to do with the quantification of social behaviours on a global scale. As you might expect, then, this programme has no more time for national sovereignty than it has for personal privacy. A handful of Internet companies now know more about the behavioural patterns of media audiences than every single academic researcher in the world combined and working in harmonious union. What's more, the big data technicians know more than we do about what this vast global audience is doing in real time. It is immediately obvious, therefore, that there is no escaping the implications of big data for audience research as an academic practice. Given the scale of these big data operations, we have to ask the question of whether we should ourselves bother to continue collecting data at all. Perhaps we should simply lobby for greater access to the vast aggregation of big data being generated in digital store-houses across the globe.

If we are turned away by the Silicon Valley landlords, and it is a fairly reasonable assumption that we often would be, we may feel compelled instead to find our own ways to collect data on a similarly global scale. It is not beyond us technically by any means, but we have yet to see free search and file-sharing services being offered by consortiums of universities whose primary interest lies in the secondary usage of user data. One obvious reason is that academics labour under ethical constraints that are antithetical to the big data era. When we collect information on audiences, by whatever means, we have to tell people why we are doing so and for what purpose. Further, in order to mitigate unseen risks to our research participants, we must go to extraordinary lengths to anonymize the data that we collect about individuals. The major portals of Internet traffic in the private sector are under no such compulsion. Their attitude to user data is 'don't tell and freely sell', meaning that our own relationship to audiences is entirely anachronistic when compared to the power relationships that generate big data. Thus, while a loose global network of nationally based universities may have all the necessary programming skills and equipment, it has nothing of the coherence and unity of purpose that characterizes the likes of Google and Facebook. In practice, universities are still struggling to accommodate the step-change in scale which means that they are no longer the major con-centrations of big data in a globalized world.

Data Exhausts are Dirty

Whilst the expanding domain of big data has something of an omnipotent air about it, it remains the case that most of the datafication projects cur-rently in train necessarily suffer from the vast outsourcing operations that make them possible in the first place. Their reliance on a combination of volunteered inputs and the wholesale scraping of such inputs from disparate sources across the World Wide Web has real implications for the integrity of the data being collected. Big it may be, but essentially, this is all stolen data and, as you might reasonably expect, this means it is dirty data. A shop-ping history is not a very accurate rendition of an individual's taste, since the majority of purchases may well be for others. A list of favourite bands or movies is not a very deep reading of cultural orientation, given that people will often tend to 'like' the most popular acts as a result of peer pressure or indifference. The degree of investment, so central to the notion of fan cultures, is absent in the majority of inputs. The standardized format of most 'membership' profiles limits the nature of information collected, and the gaps in this data tend to be very important. In recent years, the more widespread looting of webmail and cloud storage through text searching means that the more standardized formats of profiling have to be correlated with volumes of personal and professional communication, which is by its very nature very complex and context-sensitive data. Such correlations tend to proceed via text-searching mechanisms, which further disembed the data object from its origins.

As always in the social sciences, we also have to account for the knowing qualities of human subjects. Users have become aware of the pervasiveness of data trails, and there is now an obvious 'chilling' effect, where even the most average college student understands that making too many jihad jokes online could make it difficult to take holidays that require air travel. At a more general level however, it is already evident that as our awareness of secondary data processing and the permanency of our user history have started to sink in, people have begun to take evasive action online (Andrejevic 2013). For some users, the constant prompting for elaborate inputs of personal information initiates a tendency towards wilful misinformation. Some users are stepping outside, by turning to private browsing technologies like Duck Duck Go and Tor for reasons that are not so much nefarious as indignant. For the remaining majority, people who enter their personal information in a consistent fashion are probably as rare as the numbers who actually read the terms and conditions agreements when they 'join up'. Even for those who remain willing, it is actually quite difficult to be consistent when responding to innumerable surveys whose questions are preset and ultimate purpose unknown, even to the people designing them. Obviously, there are innumerable ethical issues involved in these developments, but even were we to sort these out it remains the case that the ubiquitous pressures of a global information society are affecting the spirit in which data is solicited and offered. If people suspect that their book purchases are scrutinized for both commercial and paramilitary purposes, then they become naturally more suspicious of the questions put to them by academic researchers, and we in turn become more careful about how we deploy participant information in publications. Inevitably, the rise of blanket collection and retrospective query as a default approach to knowledge production instigates legitimate concerns about the secondary uses of even the most uncontentious student research project.

Against this backdrop, we are reminded that there is nothing innocent about the data that we collect for the purposes of audience research. This places limits upon the integrity of the data itself. At the same time, by falling back upon the scraping of 'free' information provided in less fraught exchanges, as in social media platforms, we become restricted by the cellular architecture of those systems. For example, there is an enormous difference between the viewpoint of a single user moving through the interlinked pages of a social media system and the tiny number of people with access to the bird's-eye view of that system. Collecting data from within the system is very difficult to do in any systematic sense, and the nature of the information is limited by the format parameters and the consistency of inputs. This is particularly frustrating since the scale of data being collected suggests that the answer is probably in there somewhere. At a more fundamental level, audience researchers can become lost in big data because the questions we ask tend to be premised upon the idea that the information 'out there' is descriptive of a social reality that we perceive as human beings. For the serious big data enthusiasts, however, the obvious disconnections between social records and human complexity are largely irrelevant. Data analysts are not interested in the indexical truth of the data (its connection to reality) but almost wholly in the calculative potentials of the data itself. We see this tendency in the distinction that Mayer-Schonberger and Cukier make between causality and correlation – a distinction which marks a rupture between the epistemology (that is, the conceptual world) of science and the epistemology of mathematics.

Alchemy and Geography

Causality is the establishment of a likely reason for an event, via a controlled experiment where all variables are accounted for. Such controlled experiments are inherently difficult when it comes to social science because of the complexity of social variables and the knowing nature of the subjects themselves. Nonetheless, this work is intrinsic to the legacy of natural science and the various 'positivist' traditions in sociology. The essence of positivism is the desire to know why something happens, or why it is as it is, and to establish the answer upon an empirical basis through experiments that can be repeated with consistent results. Essentially, this is how 'social facts' are manufactured (be that about audiences or anything else). Correlation, by clear contrast, is about identifying trends in various forms of information and comparing them to establish patterns. These patterns can then be used to make predictions about what might happen next, even though this does nothing to establish the origin of such trends or the actual reason why any event will occur. In that sense, correlation plots current trends to predict the future, without worrying a jot about causality. Working in this vein, even the dirty nature of our data becomes relatively unimportant. Once the scale of collection becomes sufficiently large, we can just assume the data is all equally dirty and thereby that trends remain valid. Thus, one example could be the harvesting of Facebook 'likes' in order to predict future behaviour in elections and in sexual relationships, which Kosinki et al. (2013) claim to be able to do with 85 per cent accuracy. Without having the slightest idea why people make those choices, big data is numerology rather than science. With its interests in rearranging numbers to see the future, the emerging practices of 'predictive analysis' appear to be trending towards digital alchemy (e.g., Siegel 2013).

It is also critically important to audience researchers that there is little or no mention of cultural diversity in the various explications of big data. There is an implicit assumption that what rings true to a data analyst, programmer or executive in Silicon Valley constitutes the truth everywhere. The various 'universal' platforms of the social media age make scant concession to the complexities of human cultures. Rather, there is a sense that the automated capacity to switch language script within a universal interface addresses the functional aspects of cultural geography, and that this is sufficient for the purposes of standardizing user data. Thus, in marked contrast to the earlier traditions in anthropology and cultural studies, the proponents of big data display a marked indifference to the deeper meanings of the actual content being carried on various platforms and the differing social systems that shape media reception across the world. Because the emphasis is upon functional behaviour rather than cognitive reception, the methodological debates are largely oblivious to the complex matters of form and register that previously concerned disciplines like film studies, for example. Similarly, the use of datafication to 'solve' semantic problems and therefore 'leapfrog' the linguistic barriers that have shaped the television medium implies that cultural difference can be rationalized as a functional rather than subjective obstacle. Nonetheless, every time big data applications functionalize and solve such problems by applying one filter or another, they remove a large portion of the information that we have regarded as central to understanding the phenomena of audiences. Pressed on this, the new audience quants could perhaps provide us with a set of parameters claiming to account for culturally specific viewing patterns if they wished to, but one suspects that colleagues in the humanities might remain unconvinced.

The 'one size fits all' logic of big data notwithstanding, there are also some important questions to be raised when it comes to the geography of big data. Two billion Facebook pages is a big achievement, but this is still only one third of the global population (even assuming that each profile represents a unique and living user). The contours of the digital divide may have changed a good deal over the past decade but the world is not undivided when it comes to Internet access. Even more than that, if we are to rely so heavily on the inputs of shopping carts and pop fandom to establish social identities, then it remains difficult to establish how 'big audience research' of such a kind will capture the perspective of subsistence farmers in Ethiopia, for example, even where they have access to television or Internet. For this reason, uneven geographies and demographies are an inevitable consequence of the narrow interests that govern scraping technologies. The common modes of 'collection' for big data are not sufficiently attuned to populations who remain comparatively less enmeshed in the digital mall that has been packaged as Web 2.0. When it comes to the everyday business of scraping, the Americans and Europeans are the most surveilled people on Earth, but for those who shop less there is less to scrape and, as a consequence, big data is an incredibly skewed sample for any behavioural universe. For our own purposes, therefore, we must always keep in mind that big data is not evenly big, something which becomes readily apparent when we match data inputs to the human geography of the world. As with the broader digital field, it is immediately evident that there are far more Twitter accounts in larger, richer and more densely populated regions than there are in their opposites.

Notwithstanding this uneven capture of human populations, the specific geographies of digital interaction have great potential for audience research and certainly merit further attention. For example, there are at present a range of applications emerging that harvest Twitter streams in order to fashion a barometer of public opinion (Kerns 2014; Kumar et al. 2013). Here, the instantaneous and real-time structure of the medium offers up potentials for continuous political polling, virtual plebiscites, viral civil society 'memes' and other utopias. From a less instrumental perspective, we would be unwise to discount the capacity of Twitter to distribute discursive flows across the space of the globe in real time, and to create fascinating patterns of associational discourse that have both sociological and linguistic significance. Even at a more pragmatic level, the capacity of Twitter to immediately capture what is trending in different parts of the world has provided a new source of impetus for international journalists. This itself becomes highly significant in how we understand the everyday operation of an interactive global media system. We must, nonetheless, recognize the limits of the Twittersphere. Clearly, the Twitter accounts that matter belong to those who are most heavily invested in the promotion of a personality cult, and even an inclusive global network of politicians, pop stars and other public commentators is an extremely limited demography from which to derive a public domain. Equally, as with most online platforms, the Twittersphere is wide open to organized manipulation, and so the formal institution of measures derived from scraping the medium will inevitably produce a lot more dirty data for us to contend with.

Network Correlation

When we think about the secondary potentials of Twitter streams, as with many other applications, the most important starting point is the recognition that we are contending with a network system. As we know, the use value of such systems increases exponentially with the number of users. In the case of social media, the functional gains of hyper-connectivity (the 'convenience' of reaching everyone) are amplified by the simultaneous capture of disaggregated social knowledge (resulting in the contentious 'commercialization' of human sociability). We can see this clearly in the steady rise of social network analysis as a methodology, and ultimately a theory, for understanding society. Beginning as a graphical method for recording kinship relations in anthropology, social network analysis was transformed by computerization during the 1970s (Scott 2012; Wellman and Berkowitz 1988). The capacity to quickly plot even the most complex relationships between individuals in a visual form was then combined with an instrumental view of the social world in which social relationships were essentially transactions in the great game of life (Granovetter 1974). Once networked computing and the Internet became a reality, the distinction between recording networks, exploiting networks and creating networks could not be maintained. Networks beget networks, and their aggregation has been the driving logic of the Internet era. As a medium of communication and of record, the Internet shapes our communications in a network model, but it also captures their form continuously in real time. When we look at network platforms in geographic terms, there is obviously additional value being generated within the spatial information embedded in network communications.

For audience researchers, this means that online audiences are automatically recorded in real time as maps of terminal locations and information flows. When we are able to access this data, we can see the unique spatial record of every audience configuration occurring online. Obviously, to the human eye these maps are a massive jumble of dots and lines that bear little correspondence to a concept of audience that we can easily grasp. From a big data perspective, however, such graphical accounts can be correlated through powerful computers that can compare the almost innumerable records of sociability that now exist. Where patterns begin to emerge, a typology of networks follows, and from this comes a characterization of what audience formations on the Internet 'actually look like'. Critically, such an exercise can be scaled to suit a determined enquiry. If we think back to the example of SoundCloud from the previous chapter: here we have a large number of musicians associating from various points in the globe, with their attendant groups of followers, admirers and critics. Each of these clusters is captured in data-transfer records and can therefore be mapped out visually, revealing in the process the complexity and density of communication in that cluster, along with the physical location of each member. In this form, then, we can now not only conceptualize transnational audiences, but actually see them. To take this exercise to the big data level, it becomes necessary to correlate social network records for every individual subscriber within this system. By doing so, we would hope to identify the predominant configurations of exchange and association within the worldwide field of popular culture.

Social network matching of this kind is a complicated exercise conceptually. It requires careful parameters, sophisticated algorithms and powerful processing (Roy and Zeng 2014). More than that, it requires access to high level data. Nonetheless, while you couldn't do this kind of work on a ten thousand dollar research grant over the Easter recess, it is nothing like the 'Manhattan project' of a global ethnography. Approached in this way, geospatial studies of transnational media audiences are not only conceivable but eminently doable. We can expect, then, that this kind of work will be done more and more in the next few years. As a result, we will be able to learn much about the geographic bias of different cultural forms, from linguistic idioms down to punk bands. In the more finely grained studies, we may be able to capture the kind of inter-group dynamics that inspired social network analysis in the first place. If we then proceed to combine the possibilities of mapping new audience formations with the capacity to scrape and sort digital content, then our spatial knowledge of various networks of association can be augmented with the capture of everyday speech within those networks. Further, the integration of interpersonal communication with entertainment implies that we can also map the varied forms of distribution by which cultural works circulate within social networks (whether by purchase, broadcast, gifting or stealing). Does such usage of big data, then, effectively close the loop between the underlying anthropological premise of audience studies and the emergence of an interactive global media system?

Perhaps not quite. If this was to be our aim, we would have to ensure some capacity to move from the bird's-eye view of big data back to the subjective, environmental and embodied domain of culture as a human experience. In that respect, it is important to read the growing number of works that interrogate digitality within highly particular cultural and material locations. Daniel Miller's studies of social media in Trinidad and the Philippines are exemplary in this regard (Miller 2011; Horst and Miller 2012; Madianou and Miller 2012). At this scale, the fundamental shift from virtual and anonymous Internet profiles to personalized and intimate media platforms clearly signifies the re-embedding of digital networks into the practices of everyday life (not as an 'other life'). In the process, our understanding of these big data platforms becomes subject to material conditions, cultural norms and social rituals where local specificity is everything. It still matters that Facebook is made meaningful in highly specific ways in the Caribbean. This kind of ground-level understanding amongst users requires us to capture not just the local network map, but also the rich interiority of mediated human networks and the environments in which they operate. Thus, at some level, we shift back down to the digitally enhanced village and its workings. At another level, however, the embedding of these vast conjoined systems implies that the presence of the transnational is already endemic within these networks, and thus a mutual awareness of the global scale becomes part of the relative positioning of all the individuals that we encounter. We get the sense that everyone is conceptually mapping global formations from different vantage points within the system. Arguably, it is meaningful evidence of how and why they do this that constitutes the great feedback loop in digital anthropology.

Reading Audience Data

At the most fundamental level, the simultaneous evolution of digital research methods and new audience formations via the Internet signifies the extent to which we may find ourselves increasingly studying data about audiences, instead of the audiences themselves. What could be more tempting than the capacity to sit at your laptop and drop into rich conversations about media culture taking place on the other side of the world? Or the capacity to access a database and get real-time representations of transnational audiences for specific forms of content? The clear and obvious danger of such pleasures is that the essentially human concerns of audience studies could be forgotten in the convenient euphoria of big data. Thus, our longstanding concern with meaning might be ill served by entering this goldmine of functional data without a map of our own. In many respects, it is starting to look like we are coming full circle to a world of 'mass effects' research driven by a priori assumptions and tested on sophisticated correlations of dirty data garnered from a commercially biased trawling operation.

The prevailing emphasis on correlation over causality, and on data manipulation over data integrity, may be suited to behavioural studies of shopping with limited aims, but these are shaky foundations for any understanding of global cultures. Indeed, such tendencies are precisely what the proponents of active audience theory have sought to counter for the past fifty years. In the digital aftermath of cultural studies, then, what we may be left with is a radically decontextualized numerology that begins with the online consumption of popular culture.

If we took such a pessimistic view, the newly automated programme of audience research would doubtless continue without us. If we proceed uncritically across a range of disciplines, then the various data formats now emerging will become self-referential enquiries that increasingly forget the independent existence of the phenomena that they were originally conceived to study. It is in this fashion, very precisely, that data overtakes reality. Thankfully, I don't think we have to take such a pessimistic view. Data is never perfect, nor a natural enemy of humanities research. A more productive approach, then, would be to direct our attention towards the potentials of digital research tools as we see them. In many respects, the real utility of digital data lies not in its sheer bulk but in the fact that it is granular. This means that well-designed studies can operate at several scales, and might therefore be able to furnish understandings in areas that remained practically out of reach just a few years back. For those questions we haven't yet thought to ask, there are also new potentials here for exploratory work, leading perhaps to more sophisticated understandings of key concepts like interactivity, community, crowd and public. For the interests of this particular book, we cannot ignore this emerging capacity to grasp the depth and scope of transnational social interactions in a digital age. This may well prove critical for understanding the cultural geography of the World Wide Web, not to mention the subtle variations in the politics of culture that inevitably point to the future. As long as we remember that audiences are not data, then everything should be fine.

Recommended Reading

Thomas H. Davenport (2014) *Big Data @ Work*, Boston: Harvard Business Review Press.

Heather Horst and Daniel Miller (eds) (2012) *Digital Anthropology*, London and New York: Berg.

Chris Kerns (2014) *Trendology: Building an Advantage Through Data-Driven Real-Time Marketing*, New York: Palgrave Macmillan.

Viktor Mayer-Schonberger and Kenneth Cukier (2013) *Big Data: A Revolution That Will Transform How We Live, Work and Think*, New York: John Murray.

Daniel Miller (2011) *Tales From Facebook*, Cambridge: Polity.

Dale Neef (2014) *Digital Exhaust: What Everyone Should Know About Big Data, Digitization and Digitally Driven Innovation*, New Jersey: Pearson.

Eric Schmidt and Jared Cohen (2014) *The New Digital Age: Reshaping the Future of People, Nations and Business*, New York: John Murray.

Eric Siegel (2013) *Predictive Analytics: The Power to Predict Who Will Click, Buy, Lie, or Die*, New Jersey: John Wiley and Sons.

Reza Zafarani, Mohammad Ali Abbasi and Huan Liu (2014) *Social Media Mining: An Introduction*, New York: Cambridge University Press.

10 Transnational Spectrum and Social Imagination

Here we are, then, with a wide range of examples, concepts and contexts spread out across the floor. In the preceding chapters, we have managed to pick up most of them and situate them within certain patterns and scales of transnational communication. To a significant extent, many of these pieces are defined by the varying aspects of what we call 'culture' in the twenty-first century. Within the considerable breadth of this term, the predominant approaches to mapping culture all tend to privilege a particular vantage point for comprehending the whole. Consequently, there are a number of registers which situate transnational culture within geographic, demographic, linguistic, political, technical or economic frames. It is notable that, for all the talk of a 'global culture' during the past three decades, very little seems to have been done upon any workable aesthetic distinction between forms of cultural expression that are global and forms of cultural expression that are not. The most we have in this regard is a global-local dialectic, which is itself a factor of scale rather than a cultural comparison as such (for example, Wilson and Dissanayake 1996). Over the past half century, we can also see that there has been an important discursive shift within 'academic culture', as it has repositioned itself from valorizing various 'national' brands of high culture (that were perhaps less distinct from each other than was presumed) to valorizing the triumphant rise of various shards of popular culture in a universal framing more attentive to individual expression (albeit in a rather unconvincingly generic form). It will be necessary, then, to take some kind of stand on culture in this final chapter.

What we have also been able to illustrate in the various case studies of transnational media phenomena is the extent to which the great 'transnational shift' from 1991 to 2007 has to be understood equally as a technological shift and a geopolitical shift. The advent of a global media apparatus and the consequent rise of audience interactivity took place amidst the triumph of a new world order (and its tragic aftermath in the early years of this century). Since 2007, we have begun to recognize a further substantive shift in power towards a more multi-polar world, with new political realities following the ripples of the global financial crisis. At the same time, it is equally clear that the prevailing trends towards the popular and from broadcast to network media have continued to gather pace. The reach of media systems, both old and new, and the size of their audiences also continues to expand, primarily via economic and population growth in the developing regions. In a diverse world, this technical and cultural amplification plays out differently, as global media trends intersect with powerful regional con-figurations of culture, commerce and technology. Some of these forces are national, although many are not, and so this is an environment in which transnational communication necessarily proliferates. Our everyday experi-ence of long-distance mediation inevitably implies social conditions where new ways of knowing the world become possible. In that sense, the ongoing enquiry into transnational media reception within the academy necessarily rests upon our capacity to interrogate the dynamics of the social imaginaries by which audiences situate themselves within a world of media flows. It will also be necessary, then, to consider these imaginative processes throughout this final chapter.

The Transnational Spectrum

As if these two prerogatives, of culture and imagination, were not enough to contend with in drawing out the common lessons from the various examples we have considered, we must also address the questions of scale that have arisen with such regularity throughout this book. At the outset, I noted that the pairing of the cultural and the social in transnational com-munication is going to be very different from the uniform but bounded conditions implied by the nationalist paradigm. As we saw in chapter 2, the consolidation of the national in our present world system engages various aspects of ethnicity, language, history, geography and cultural idiom in the pursuit of sovereign legitimacy. In the subsequent chapters, we have seen how all of these aspects, taken by themselves, tend to break the frame of the national in various ways. Ultimately, nations in their modern form are about attempting to draw lines around a zone where these forces overlap. They do so by leaving out (or otherwise marginalizing) the various bits that don't fit. That is why approaching the transnational as a compara-tive enquiry between nation states built of necessity upon such partial and pragmatic foundations is unlikely to engender an adequate understanding of global culture and communication in the broader sense. For our pre-sent purposes, what is required instead is a scaleable model that addresses the global-local dialectic in a rather different fashion. The *spectrum* of the transnational, as I will present it here, is not about big and small nations, or about the effective range of media flows or the volume of markets. Rather, it seeks to encapsulate the subjective inter-relationship between the personal, communal, political and civilizational positionings of various viewers, users, readers or fans.

The aim of this exercise is to conceptualize an everyday experience of the transnational. Most of us now live in a densely mediated world where national media institutions, regional media markets, multinational media corporations, local community media and far-flung mediated communities all interject their content into our personal experience. They do so via an expanding array of what Madianou and Miller called 'polymedia' (2012). In such a setting, it becomes imperative for audience researchers to approach the transnational as a full spectrum of communicative relationships, where exchanges are taking place simultaneously at a number of scales. In order to understand the conditions of reception within which audiences make sense of these competing registers, we therefore have to account for their relative understandings of individuals, localities, cultures, nations and civilizations. As such, transnational media reception is most productively approached as an act of social imagination undertaken across this broad spectrum of relational understandings. In the production of meanings from acts of mediation, various signifying configurations of the local, national and global (or indeed the familial, social or civilizational) are obviously recognized by those participating as audiences. For each individual, these different frequencies of media content must be juxtaposed against each other in order to bring semantic order to this universal scale of the familiar and the strange. For this reason, the personal positioning of individuals in relation to the constituent forces of cultural signification and the trajectory of their personal experiences remains critical to any substantive understanding of their worldview.

Inhabiting the Cultural Field

It is at the micrological scale of social imagination, then, that we will seek to enter the transnational spectrum. One of the most forceful arguments made by cultural studies researchers during the 1970s was that people read and watch things in different ways, and that they draw different conclusions from the same material (Hall 1980). At one level, of course, this seems pretty obvious. Nonetheless, the research emerging from the cultural studies school served as a powerful corrective to the idea that media programming could achieve cultural homogenization (in the fashion suggested by Gellner) or easily manufacture consent (as in Chomsky's account) (Gellner 1983; Herman and Chomsky 1994). Instead, interpretation of media content tended to differ on the basis of differences of class, race, age, gender, education and other salient factors. We should also recognize, however, that early cultural studies researchers were able to interrogate the diversity of the audience precisely because they could rely upon the unity of the message. In an era where national broadcasters were largely hegemonic, the differentiation of meanings could be observed systematically from responses to a single source (as in the famous *Nationwide* study by Brunsdon and Morley, 1978). As a consequence of the expansion, integration and/or collision of media systems over the past twenty years, we can no longer assume a unified media message or even a similar media mix for members of the audience. The pluralism of content, in both form and origin, means that we now have to situate media users within a much more personalized media environment. This amplifies the importance of their subjectivity considerably, typically taking them beyond the various social categories into which they fall.

To illustrate this point, I am going to juxtapose Pierre Bourdieu's influential notion of the 'cultural field' with observations on standpoint theory from Marcel Stoetzler and Nira Yuval-Davies (Bourdieu 1993; Stoetzler and Yuval-Davies 2002). For Bourdieu, the cultural field represents a struggle for hegemony between cultural producers, whose respective idioms are determined by their *habitus* (the literacy derived from their familial, institutional and experiential learning). At the centre of the field is a rarefied space where cultural expression has a value inverse to its economic value. This aesthetic ideal is contested by the class formations which seek to advance within the field and privilege their own cultural idioms. As such, Bourdieu's field is something like a rugby pitch, where lumbering social strata face off against each other in a contest for cultural legitimacy. The 'rules' of this field rely upon an absolute demarcation of 'high' and 'low' cultures, an antithetical relationship between art and commerce, and the unity of social origins amongst the contesting parties. Unlike the liberal paradigm of the present, Bourdieu sees no scope for individualism. Equally, he rejects any correspondence between audience demand and the operation of the cultural field. Ultimately, this is a very French field, and not intended for understanding a world of transnational media flows. Nonetheless, the central idea of a differential positioning around cultural practices has obvious merit for understanding the world of pluralism and difference that we now seem to inhabit, in France as much as anywhere else. Across this larger set of fields, the class struggle is not the only game that we are playing at any given time.

This brings me to the evolution of standpoint theory, which established an initial paradigm during the oppositional feminism of the 1970s. In that context, the privileged social position (male) was contested by the victims of patriarchy (female) whose uniform oppression gave them a unique perspective on inequality, and a legitimate claim to wrest the speaking staff from the establishment (e.g., Hartsock 1983). Since then, standpoint theory has evolved to account for the recognition of many other factors (such as class, race, age, faith, et al.) which determine our social experience in different ways. Consequently, the location of any particular standpoint (marginal or otherwise) must account for a number of different vectors. In this model, every subject possesses a different standpoint, constructed around their own imaginative interactions with various ideological and material articulations of the social. The agency of subjects, then, stems from their ability to creatively imagine the complex interfaces between individual *experiential* and collective *relational* ontologies. In the first iteration of standpoint theory, a woman could speak only as a woman, but also speak for all women. In the latter, more relative account, subjects must of necessity articulate their multi-dimensional relationships to others in order to describe their own unique position. On this basis, Stoetzler and Yuval-Davies describe a 'situated imagination' where social knowledge is produced and contested, in a form which might be defined as anchored 'in actual social practices (that are linked, but not reducible to certain social positionings)' (2002: 317). Taken beyond the frame of gender alone, this 'situated imagination' of individual subjects suggests a far greater degree of subjective agency for individuals than that which might be measured by class consciousness (as suggested by Bourdieu) or by choices of consumption (as suggested by Facebook).

If we incorporate this more sophisticated account of social positioning into the conceptualization of the cultural field, we end up with something rather more like a cricket ground. In the first place, the setting of the field depends upon who is out in the middle. What subsequently happens depends upon what kind of ball is being delivered (the message) as much as it does upon the stroke that is played (the reception). Where the ball ultimately ends up depends not only upon this exchange but upon where others are positioned in the field (that is, upon a relative social imagination). It does matter whether the message is a deft piece of Sri Lankan spin or a classic Hollywood Yorker, and different strokes will be played depending upon the content and origins of the message as well as our perception of where others are standing. This reworking of the cultural field, then, is all about relative proximity. In essence, this is Straubhaar's cultural proximity mapped out at the micro scale. Given the many factors involved in the constitution of our individual subjectivity, and the mixture of content, we cannot reasonably expect anyone to play in exactly the same way, even where the team as a whole tends to perform better in home matches (that is, under 'resident' conditions). Familiar bowling will be played with ease and the more exotic stuff with more erratic results, but we would anticipate a bit of both in the course of a day. On occasion, some balls will be unplayable.

Consequently, many outcomes (meanings) are possible from a varied media diet and a diverse set of players.

Dispensing with the metaphors, the model of the cultural field that I propose here in the context of transnational communication is conceived as a radial zone of influence within which viewers engage with various media streams from particular standpoints, thereby generating different meanings and pleasures (see Athique 2008a). It is increasingly useful to think of media audiences in this way because, under the aegis of 'globalization', our media experience is likely to be shaped by a multiplicity of actors, practices and sources of information. As we have seen in the course of this book, positionality within such a field has many constituents, and is not easily restricted to the model of centre and periphery that prevailed thirty years ago. With a greater range of media sources, and a growing awareness of the intertextuality amongst content as a whole, we must account for a more sophisticated, and context-sensitive, viewer. Further, if our social experience is subject to many different factors, we also need to recognize that some of these will change over time, as we move around physically, as we age, as we encounter new forms of expression and social actors different from ourselves. It is important, therefore, to recognize that subjectivity at an individual scale cannot be essentialized or static. It will tend to move. Critically, in amidst the convergence of entertainment and interpersonal communication, participation in the cultural field will always be understood in relative terms (indeed, often in direct conversation). Consequently, the position-taking of agents will be articulated relative to the presence of other agents within the field. When we consume media, we are always aware that others are doing so, no matter how remote or asynchronous that activity is. This, perhaps, is the key point in Anderson's (1991) original exposition of the imagined community.

Situating the Local

Reconsidering the orientation of the cultural field has obvious benefits for the simultaneous differentiation of both the audience and the message. It also brings into focus the cumulative presence of large numbers of people in any act of mediation. Awareness of this larger social dimension inevitably structures the encounter between media content and individual viewers. Taking this line, our attention to field placements would apply equally to identification at a number of scales. In moving up from the individual scale to the interrogation of the local, Stoetzler and Yuval-Davies' other point of emphasis comes to the fore. That is, the 'situatedness' of individuals within complex relational fields. In that sense, cultural identity (which has been a major focus of academic enquiry for the past thirty years) has to be understood as a relative and outward-looking process. As an act of social imagination, we orient our own position in reference to our perception of other positions. Equally, in everyday life, we don't just identify with a position in a symbolic sense, we also inhabit it within a particular set of social conditions. In order to account for this, it becomes necessary to bridge the gap between the subjective and the material. That is, whatever your subjective response to a world of symbolic differences is, that response is always fashioned within a definite social environment: where you sleep, eat, meet with others and from where you access mediated accounts from other places. It is this simple fact that underpins the continuing presence of the local in any discussion of the global.

In the face of increasing anxieties about global interconnectivity and its relationship to unravelling economic fortunes and intensifying political conflicts, there is a natural tendency to romanticize the local, just as the early sociologists romanticized pre-industrial societies. If value judgements are needed here, then, it is worth pointing out that some local contexts are particularly unpleasant for their inhabitants, and no locality is an arcadia for everyone in it. Nonetheless, while the local should not be an unqualified good, it is obvious that transnational media flows will get different responses in Kratie or Krakow and, even, within their various districts or neighbourhoods. Fernand Braudel (1995) would argue for their distinct historical, climactic and linguistic orientations, but he also made the point that the material conditions of everyday life are major contributors to the formation of any culture. We would expect this to be true, then, as much at the local scale as at a civilizational scale. The nature of our dwellings shapes the timing and organization of media use, as does what, when, where we eat and who we take meals with. The prevailing economic activities and the patterns of employment and consumption that stem from them also impose routines and relationships that influence our engagement with representations of the wider world. The need to account for all these factors suggests the continuing relevance of ethnographic approaches to media audiences. Arguably, the need to account for the wider social environment in such depth is what marks the transition point between media studies and cultural studies.

At one end of the spectrum, the 'situation' of media reception occurs at an individuated scale and, at the other end of the spectrum, it operates across a world of differences. Located reception, then, is a larger concept than simply accounting for local conditions in great detail. Nonetheless, in any exploration of local conditions, it quickly becomes apparent that each and every place has a particular material environment, a particular population mix and a particular media mix. These provide immediate reference points for the decoding of any incoming media stream. During the 1990s, Manuel Castells (1996) placed considerable emphasis upon the uneven distribution of media flows in the global network society. He pointed out that not only was there an enormous disparity between the density of media flows in different parts of the world, there were also hot and dark spots within single cities. In that respect, our attention to locality tends to encounter the uneven presence of transnational communication in a quantitative sense. Take, for example, the South Indian city of Bangalore. Here, the concentration of multinational corporations, Internet connectivity, smartphone ownership, cable subscriptions and travel opportunities for those living around the campus developments in the south and east of the city indicate a greater density of transnational communication than you would find in the old native city, or *Pettah*, to the West (see Stallmeyer 2011; Mascarenhas 2012). Some years ago now, and keeping with the Indian theme, I investigated the consumption of imported films in different suburbs of Sydney. In that study, it was clear that localized differences in material conditions and demography led to different social practices and different sets of meanings being derived from the same transnational content (Athique 2005).

Working at the local scale naturally tends to privilege the influence of material conditions, and it favours ethnographic methods and a presence on the ground. By engaging audiences within a well-defined social context, the subjective positioning of respondents can be usefully juxtaposed with a range of environmental factors that frame their engagement with various media sources. Thus, while a focus on individual positioning directs us towards the idea of the cultural field, a focus on the local environment directs us towards Pertierra and Turner's (2013) proposition of 'zones of consumption'. Zones of consumption can be taken to represent environmental conditions that emerge from the material and discursive forces that predominate in any given location. The nature of these forces, and their relative importance, may vary in any given case, but their common effect is to produce a distinctive set of conditions within which media content and media practices are contextualized. These conditions are commonly accessible within the zone, and they rely upon a similarity of options and reference points. These options may well include a substantial range of transnational and intercultural modes of communication, and the population of each zone need not be homogeneous in any sense. Nonetheless, each zone of consumption is constituted in a definite place, and is thereby defined primarily by geography rather than demography. In my reading of the cultural field, individual subjectivity takes the centre of the pitch.

By contrast, Pertierra and Turner's approach to situated media reception emphasizes the environmental conditions in the broadest sense. These two exercises in boundary-setting also scale in different ways. While the notion of a cultural field seeks to account for the individual differentiation of global proximities, the zone concept is directed more firmly towards the central bands of the transnational spectrum. That is, towards defining the common sociability of media environments at the local, national and regional scales.

Nations at the Fulcrum

During the 1990s, the proposition of the global-local dialectic was often accompanied by the proposition that the national was being superseded in a globalized world. More recently, some approaches to transnational media studies have rejected the old 'national media' paradigm and concentrated instead upon the most explicitly cosmopolitan or multinational content they can hire from the video store. Both approaches to the transnational are flawed. In fact, the national is not going away, and it continues to occupy the central position in the transnational spectrum. This is necessarily so, because the nation continues to demarcate a relational polity positioned somewhere between the experiential world of the face-to-face and the abstracted, but undeniable existence of a vast heterogeneous world. Set between a localized world of personal experience and the cacophony of a global media apparatus, the national constitutes a zone of consumption aligned with the division of sovereignty in the world system, and with the practical boundaries of political administration. The sovereignty of nations and the legislative powers of states are not inconsequential. As a basis for power and the construction of a state, the domain of the national is considered distinct from both the personal and the universal, but lays claim to a measure of authority over both. For all these reasons, the vagaries of nations continue to structure the trajectories of transnational media flows and to dominate the social imagination of media audiences. As such, within the broader scheme of things, the 'national' is by no means an alternative to the 'local' or the 'global', since it operates as the fulcrum between the two.

Critiques of the notion of the national audience as an 'imagined community' by scholars such as Andrew Higson (2000) have pointed out that audiences do not display the subjective homogeneity implied by nationalist arguments. Benedict Anderson, however, claimed in *Imagined Communities* that print-capitalism allowed participants in mass culture to imagine social formations as comparable and related. That is, they imagined the presence of other readers, places and ideal types and this laid the foundations for various nationalisms to emerge in pursuit of statehood. He did not claim that they *necessarily* imagined those nations in the same way, or for the same reasons. Rather, it seems that any accepted 'sameness' of perspective figured on nationality only really emerges when the nation is juxtaposed against an imagined, generic community of outsiders. Taking this position, we could say that it is likely not the eternal 'ethnie' proposed by Anthony Smith (1999), but rather the existence of the 'anti-ethnie' of an opposing nation that really cements national belonging. This, perhaps, is why nations tend to be born in blood. It is equally true that national identity, as such, is always a largely symbolic construction, that nations are internally differentiated in numerous ways, and that their inhabitants spend more time arguing with each other than anything else. In that sense, internal diversity and transnational cultures are part of the everyday national experience. These things are not an obvious problem for nation states as civic bodies, but they do pose an existential threat to cultural nationalism as a political ideology, and this is where the problem lies.

Without labouring the point too much, what I am seeking to establish here is that transnational media systems are not antithetical to national cultures. Indeed, transnational media systems are becoming a major site for the articulation of national cultures, national politics and nationalist sentiment. As a quick example, the unfolding events in Ukraine during 2014, as presented by the nationally branded, post-imperial BBC World website, were plastered with reader postings on this most contentious issue. At various points in this bulletin string, quintessentially British armchair experts were joined by American Cold War warriors and a host of pro-Putin and anti-Putin Russians, pro-Russian, pro-German and pro-Ukrainian Ukrainians, with the occasional Polish and Serbian interjection. Thus, what has long been a decidedly national 'mouthpiece' has somehow become an operative space for multilateral debate, which garners a massive global audience from attaching itself to a well-funded national apparatus. Some of it is jingoistic and some of it is conciliatory, and doubtless much of the content is furnished by the teams employed by various states to doctor and distort online forums. The larger implication is that national identification remains strong in most transnational forums, especially (but not exclusively) where national interests are at stake. Instead, the national intrudes into local and global media spaces every bit as much as 'foreign' content interjects itself into the national space. It is equally evident that the articulation of the national amongst audiences is always at its strongest when mobilized in contrast to another national sphere.

In that sense, Anderson's later observations in *The Spectre of Comparisons* (1998) ring true. Nations must be imagined in explicitly comparative terms, as a series of relativities by which the human geography of the world is imaginatively located. On that basis, it is obvious from the user-generated content of the World Wide Web more broadly that the national looms large in the social imagination. More prosaically, the national imaginary continues to be promoted by an array of institutions and mechanisms in ways that other points of scale along the transnational spectrum are not. Mediaculturalism has yet to develop a sorting mechanism outside of the national scale. Thus, the nation is the only point on the scale where there is an effective mechanism of power over cultural practice. Nonetheless, in a more densely mediated world driven by international debt, it is no longer a simple matter for states to regulate national audiences into existence and then police them. Their naturalized existence was, perhaps, a fleeting historical combination of terrestrial broadcasting and Cold War politics. As one might expect, the growing inconvenience of a global media apparatus does not prevent state authorities from pursuing such a cause, and it seems likely that the fortunes of the Chinese experiment will be pivotal in this regard. For those who are choosing instead to adopt a laissez-faire approach, it may well prove that erstwhile 'national' audiences spend an increasing amount of their time seeking out transnational media sources, but that they will also continue to engage with national media systems.

The Mixed Fortunes of Mediated Regions

To all intents and purposes, nations continue to be perceived as social actors, and their imaginaries dominate the identification of the adjacent scales within the transnational spectrum. Although there has been a tendency to privilege the global as the counterpart to the national, our most common experience of supra-national culture tends to be located within the cultural tectonics established around cultural, geographic or linguistic proximities. That is, what John Sinclair (1999) would call geolinguistic regions, what Braudel (1995) would call civilizations, and what media executives would call regional markets. If we follow Joseph Straubhaar (2007), the compatibility of cultural production at this regional scale rests upon a relative proximity of culture. All of this suggests a clear bias in transnational communication towards our near neighbours in cultural terms, compounded by the preponderance of trade between physically proximate economies. In the twenty-first century, digitality negates distance but not the concentration of populations, and hence interactions, around cultural proximities. As such, the density of communication at a regional scale proves critical. This is a matter of volume, with clear links to population size, language capacity and levels of access. Consequently, formations at the regional scale vary considerably in size and scope. The configuration and depth of their imaginaries is also highly variable, ranging between implicit recognition, tacit approval and, more rarely, public enthusiasm. Some regional zones are constituted by explicit political programmes, while others operate at a more informal level.

Our perception of the regional scale is commonly refracted through the national concept and the massive upscaling of 'neighbourliness'. In that respect, close neighbours tend to have the most in common culturally, but they also tend to have the most bitter disputes. The South Asian region springs to mind here, but the obvious success of the transnational media market in East Asia would not lead anyone to downplay the ambivalence in the political relationship between the various countries involved. Thus, the sense of a general homology between neighbouring cultures is always accompanied by an acute sense of national differences. In that regard, the various attempts to integrate the media markets of the European Union have been fruitful at a financial, regulatory and technical level, but it would be a stretch to say that a European media system has really taken hold of the popular imagination (see Papathanassopoulos and Negrine 2013). The idea of Europe certainly endures but it has, perhaps, become more closely linked in the social imagination to a particular set of political institutions than it is to a sense of fraternity. There appears to be a critical difference, then, in the threshold of commitment fashioned by latent cultural proximity and the requirements of pan-regionalism as a political programme. Another region to watch in this respect is the ASEAN grouping, which is now pursuing initiatives designed to cement an awareness of the larger regional framework amongst national populations with very different cultural, social and historical referents.

Although there is no straightforward comparison between the two regions, we could venture that the degree of cultural diversity within them implies that intra-regional mediation will take precedence over pan-regional mediation. By comparison, it is not insignificant that the largest supranational 'zone' in the global media system rests upon cultural rather than physical proximity. Despite the internecine rivalries and the eternal grumbles about cultural imperialism by the smaller members, the pan-regional integration of media systems in the English-speaking countries confers mutual advantage. The size and wealth of the 'Anglosphere' and the scale of its audiences convey a natural advantage in the global media trade. With an established market leader position serving as a multiplier, Anglophone dominance over the audiovisual environment has always been a given for studies in transnational communication. Unlike the Latin American states, the English-speaking group of nations constitutes the founding core of the United Nations system and most other international bodies. With the United States at its heart, the 'Anglosphere' continues to exert a massive presence in the global system. Indeed, no other 'media civilization' has invested as much infrastructure and effort in injecting its presence into the social imagination of other parts of the world. In recent years, the focus of this 'media imperialism' has retreated in some areas and expanded in others, but it is obvious that the interaction of cultural proximities within that zone operates alongside a wider agenda for commanding a worldwide audience. Taking this line, we might be inclined to see the thickening of the regional scale as primarily a commercial and political strategy directed towards occupying ground at the global scale.

A decade ago, there was some sense that regional groupings were superseding nations as the dominant force in international affairs. This notion has not survived the definitively national fallout of the global financial crisis. Nonetheless, it is probably fair to say that the density of intra-regional interactions continues to increase, and that mediation necessarily forms a large part of this process. Transnational communication within proximate regions gives visibility to the regional scale, even in the absence of a strong pan-regional consciousness. That visibility inevitably provides stimulus for social imagination with an international focus. Interactive media systems also provide the vehicle for the attendant responses to regional issues, with the regional scale being the hothouse of user-led transnationalism. Broadcast media, where cultural gravity is strongly felt, also tend to be delimited at the regional scale by the mass effect of cultural geography. Even putatively global media brands are commonly franchised via the regional markets that constitute the global economy. Thus media interests often supersede the national, but the audiences they engage are more commonly regional than global. Although we tend to approach the regional scale via the domain of international relations, it is worth recognizing that interpersonal relationships are also concentrated within the regional scale. Despite the huge distances involved, our comparative imagination of regional dynamics is subject to a sense of proximity that is absent in the 'othering' of more distant cultures. As a consequence, the global scale itself is heavily structured by the cultural tectonics that have evolved at the regional scale. This is true politically, but also true when it comes to the concentration of audiences.

Mapping the Global

When we attempt to think about the global scale, we tend to imagine even broader groupings such as 'The West', 'Asia', the 'Islamic World' or suchlike. These polyglot entities are larger than the strictly regional and often play a significant role in our imagination of the global space, but they are still not global configurations as such. The global scale, being everything, defies categorization by any comparative measure. In determining culture at a global scale, therefore, we must address a question that only becomes operative at the poles of the transnational spectrum. That is, should global culture be taken as the aggregate of all the lesser scales or should it be approached upon the basis of a universal set of principles that transcends them? In the first instance, the profusion of transnational exchanges implies integration and/or a dialogic relationship between different nations and regions. In the second instance, the prevalence of transnational exchanges may suggest a level of human exchange that goes beyond the compartmentalized logics of the current world system. In other words, sovereign cultural diversity may be offset by a wide-reaching humanism that furnishes communication between people everywhere. For either to occur, or both of them, there must be an adequate infrastructure in place. In that respect, when we consider the global scale in functional terms, we are focusing upon systems and forums that demonstrate a universal presence and a worldwide audience. At the outset of modernity, print publication provided such a mechanism, at least to the literate, with nationalism seen as being a consequence of the confluence between a relatively lean form of media and an expansive human imagination.

In the present epoch, it becomes reasonable to ask whether global telecommunications and the World Wide Web are furnishing a new set of communicative relationships that occur only, or predominantly, at the global scale. In making the shift from a comparative international or intercultural model to a global one, there is a necessary change in conceptual register. That is, we shift from framing our analysis in terms of 'zones' and 'crossovers' to looking at various 'networks' and 'trends' recorded across a universal canvas. Previously, to take on audiences at this scale (whether in aggregate, universal or discrete terms) has been a practical impossibility. In the twenty-first century, common media formats, universal communication protocols and the incredible aggregation of users by contemporary web portals have brought the top end of the transnational spectrum into focus. Thus we are held to have entered an era of big data, where an automated account of audience activity is being collected on a universal scale, and not predominantly by national actors. For those able to access and effectively manage such information, there is now a real possibility of recording transnational interaction as a percentage of media consumption, of monitoring indicators of its activity levels as a live feed, of mapping the communicative structures of transnational interactions, and of tracking processes of cultural translation in real time. Our field of enquiry seems poised for a shift from musing in detail on small samples to brainstorming new ways to sift and present data on a vast scale.

The practical challenge is how to granulate the harvest. The methodological challenge is how to unstack the Russian doll of the transnational spectrum in an illustrative fashion. The conceptual challenge is how to situate the individuals and the social formations encapsulated in big data. These issues must be resolved because, taken by itself, it is hard to see how scraping away at the big picture can tell us much that is meaningful. Certainly, correlation can give much in the way of context, but that is not the same thing. As such, we must maintain a critical awareness of the implications of a universal numerology. Will this be the final outcome of the expanding functional integration described by Gellner, or will it constitute a Brahmanical code that only a global technorati will ever be able to read? What kinds of social imagination are being fostered by the primacy of data, and how will they differ from the human relationships that have been conceived through the preceding eras of reading and viewing? The first of these questions requires a detailed ethnography of the digital elite, whose social perspectives often seem awkwardly confined to business-oriented publications. The second question might be productively tackled by focusing upon the strictly mediated communities that only exist at this scale. That is, those networks of interactants who share nothing in terms of intimacy, geography, culture or polity. There are now numerous examples of transnational formations oriented primarily by enthusiasm for a particular set of mediated practices (variously receptive, collaborative, distributive and/or dialogic).

Such online engagements between participants here, there and everywhere cannot properly be considered as media communities, as mediation itself is their only instance of communality. Most likely, these activities are only fragments of a wider multi-channel experience for their members, and scarcely a major trope of social identity. Nonetheless, some of the larger portals on the World Wide Web have memberships that rival nation states, and we have not yet established the extent to which this mobilizes new supra-national sensibilities or whether it merely constitutes a banal transnationalism. This is a vitally important question. If we were to take our lead from Marshall McLuhan (1964), we would determine the implications of the World Wide Web for the social imagination in terms of the scale that the system introduces into human affairs. Evidently, the 'wired world' represents an exponential increase in human mediation in terms of the sheer volume of users in a single system. Acting upon the dimension of time-space, its reach over physical distance is entirely unparalleled and a fundamental reworking of temporality can also be deduced from the simultaneity of its operation. IT providers casually offer us a world at our fingertips, and promise that 'Your World' can speak to you through your personal handset. The intensity of this global personalization rests upon a ubiquitous technical system through which any location can be accessed, and where each user can themselves be precisely located (see Wilken and Goggin 2014; Frith 2015). As of now, armed with your own 'cloud', you can apparently inhabit a privatized universalism as 'You' traverse the globe without leaving the comfort of your own mediatization.

Tipping the Scales

For audience researchers, the cloud proposition initiates a direct link between the individual and the global, thereby circumventing the intervening scales that have previously dominated mass communication. In this fashion, the contemporary configurations of digital communication threaten to upset the balance of the transnational spectrum. It becomes reasonable to ask whether the increasing prevalence of global systems is symptomatic of a bridge being built over newly obsolete scales of functional communication further down the spectrum. Personally, I think not. The various frequencies of the transnational spectrum all continue to influence the demarcation of our cultural fields, and they all serve to determine the boundaries of the various zones of consumption that we experience as fully fledged social environments. Indeed, my explicit argument would be that the different scales of transnational orientation are interdependent. Without the social imagination that orients the individual, the various components of a world system could not be grasped. Similarly, the national could not be conceived without the capacity to locate others imaginatively within a global order. Since our social experience operates within material conditions, local and regional geographies also remain indispensable referents for our necessary sense of scale. In many respects, it is increasingly volume rather than distance that seems to present the greater cognitive challenge for transnational audiences. The many configurations of communication now taking place require complex exercises of information management and heavy investments of time in order to make sense of our expanding reach. Amidst the complexity and density of such mediation, should we expect world-spanning algorithms to expand our capacity for social imagination or to swamp it?

In this final chapter, I have attempted to organize the key concepts of this book within a rising order of scale. The underlying objective of this exercise has been to move away from Vertovec's (2009) definition of the transnational as a set of extraordinary disruptive conditions. I have instead worked to establish the transnational dimensions of mass communication as an entire spectrum. I have also sought to emphasize the human capacity to locate the different frequencies of the transnational spectrum within a sense of scale appropriate to our own social experience. Since this larger proposal hinges upon a particular concept of culture, I made a foolhardy promise at the beginning of this chapter to take a 'stand' on culture itself. To summarize briefly, culture, as I understand it here, is the product of social imagination. That is, cultural production can be most usefully defined as the various actions and articulations which seek to return our social imagination to the realm from which we draw our inspiration. In linking the interiority of experience with the primacy of social relationships, the sum of cultural production constructs the order of social life. Clearly, culture in this overarching sense is as vast and unknowable as the imagination of humanity. It is not invisible, however, since it has to be formulated through expression. Culture, then, can be understood as *manifest* imagination. We can see this process of manifestation operating in the production of works, the social organization of cultural practices, and the ways in which relational meanings are articulated at the level of reception. As a set of communicative and cumulative processes, culture structures social interaction across all scales of human experience.

Culture and imagination are both cumulative rather than collective forces, for the simple reason that everyone participates from a unique situation within the whole. The whole is itself important, as this is where the social imagination becomes fundamental to connecting humanity in a very practical sense. It is the capacity to understand ourselves in a relational framework that enables our collaboration in wider social formations and in their steady transformation. The function of media technologies, at its deepest level, is subject to that purpose. Mediation becomes so significant, in and of itself, because of the enormous increase in the range of information, and the sheer number of relationships, that it enables us to perceive. When C. Wright Mills (1959) expounded the sociological imagination in the twentieth century, he talked of an individual's capacity to see their own state of employment as part of a larger set of national economic structures, and as a consequence of the forces of global trade. In recent years, many of us have been prompted to do just that in the context of an even more integrated world system. In doing so, it becomes apparent to people everywhere that the present crisis of globalization, and the supposed remedies, go well beyond the purely economic. Wherever we are, the meanings that we draw from events naturally rely upon our comprehension of the forces at work in the world and of our own place in the scheme of things. Consequently, the final point that I will make on transnational media reception is that everyone's worldview matters. Not because we are individuated subjects living under our own cloud, but because our relative perception of the world shapes our social actions at every scale.

References

Adorno, Theodor and Horkheimer, Max (1944/2006) 'The Culture Industry: Enlightenment as Mass Deception', in Meenakshi Gigi Durham and Douglas M. Kellner (eds) *Media and Cultural Studies: Keyworks*, Malden, MA: Blackwell, pp. 41–72.

Alonso, Andoni and Oiarzabal, Pedro (eds) (2010) *Diasporas in the New Media Age: Identity, Politics, and Community*, Reno: University of Nevada Press.

Anderson, Benedict (1991) *Imagined Communities: Reflections on the Spread of Nationalism*, London: Verso.

Anderson, Benedict (1994) 'Exodus', *Critical Enquiry*, 20:2, pp. 314–427.

Anderson, Benedict (1998) *The Spectre of Comparisons: South East Asia and the World*, London: Verso.

Anderson, Chris (2006) *The Long Tail: How Endless Choice is Creating Unlimited Demand*, New York: Random House.

Anderson, Stewart and Chakars, Melissa (2014) *Modernization, Nation-building and Television History*, London and New York: Routledge.

Andrejevic, Mark (2007) *ISpy: Surveillance and Power in the Interactive Era*, Lawrence: University Press of Kansas.

Andrejevic, Mark (2013) *Infoglut: How Too Much Information is Changing the Way We Think and Know*, London and New York: Routledge.

Ang, Ien (1985/1993) *Watching Dallas: Soap Opera and the Melodramatic Imagination*, London: Routledge.

Ang, Ien (1991) *Desperately Seeking the Audience*, London and New York: Routledge.

Appadurai, Arjun (1996) *Modernity At Large: The Cultural Dimensions of Globalisation*, Minneapolis: University of Minnesota Press.

Appadurai, Arjun (2013) *The Future as Cultural Fact: Essays on the Global Condition*, London: Verso.

Arvidsson, Adam (2005) *Brands: Meaning and Value in Media Culture*, London and New York: Routledge.

Athique, Adrian (2005) 'Watching Indian Movies in Australia: Media, Community and Consumption', *South Asian Popular Culture*, 3:2, pp. 117–33.

Athique, Adrian (2008a) 'Media Audiences, Ethnographic Practice and the Notion of a Cultural Field', *European Journal of Cultural Studies*, 11:1, pp. 25–41.

Athique, Adrian (2008b) 'The Global Dynamics of Indian Media Piracy: Export Markets, Playback Formats and the Informal Economy', *Media, Culture and Society*, 30:5, pp. 699–717.

References

Athique, Adrian (2008c) 'The "Crossover" Audience: Mediated Multiculturalism and the Indian Film', *Continuum: Journal of Media and Cultural Studies*, 22:3, pp. 299–311.

Athique, Adrian (2008d) 'Non-resident Consumption of Indian Cinema in Asia', in Youna Kim (ed.) *Media Consumption and Everyday Life in Asia*, London and New York: Routledge, pp. 145–54.

Athique, Adrian (2011) 'Theorising the Diasporic Audience: The Case of Indian Films', *Participations: Journal of Audience Research*, 8:2, pp. 1–23.

Athique, Adrian (2013) *Digital Media and Society: An Introduction*, Cambridge: Polity.

Austin, Thomas (2002) *Hollywood Hype and Audiences: Selling and Watching Popular Film in the 1990s*, Manchester: Manchester University Press.

Axel, Brian Keith (2002) 'The Diasporic Imaginary', *Public Culture*, 14:2, pp. 411–28.

Bailey, Olga G., Georgiou, Myria and Ramaswami, Harindranath (2007) *Transnational Lives and the Media: Re-Imagining Diasporas*, Houndmills: Palgrave Macmillan.

Balnaves, Mark, O'Regan, Tom and Goldsmith, Ben (2011) *Rating the Audience: The Business of Media*, London: Bloomsbury Academic.

Banaji, Shakuntala (2006) *'Reading Bollywood': The Young Audience and Hindi Films*, Basingstoke: Palgrave Macmillan.

Barker, Martin and Mathijs, Ernest (eds) (2007) *Watching the Lord of the Rings: Tolkien's World Audiences*, Bern: Peter Lang.

Barnouw, Erik and Krishnaswamy, S. (1980) *Indian Film*, New York: Oxford University Press.

Baron, Nancy (2008) *Always On: Language in an Online and Mobile World*, New York: Oxford University Press.

Baumann, Zygmunt (1998) *Globalization: The Human Consequences*, Cambridge: Polity.

Baym, Nancy (2010) *Personal Connections in the Digital Age*, Cambridge: Polity.

Beckett, Charlie and Bell, James (2012) *Wikileaks: News in the Networked Era*, Cambridge: Polity.

Berndt, Jaqueline and Kümmerling-Meibauer, Bettina (eds) *Manga's Cultural Crossroads*, London and New York: Routledge.

Billig, Michael (1995) *Banal Nationalism*, London: Sage.

Black, Daniel, Epstein, Stephen and Tokita, Alison (eds) (2010) *Complicated Currents: Media Flows, Soft Power and East Asia*, Clayton: Monash University Press.

Bolter, Jay David and Grusin, Richard (2001) *Remediation: Understanding New Media*, Cambridge, MA: MIT Press.

Bourdieu, Pierre (1984) *Distinction: A Social Critique of the Judgement of Taste*, Cambridge, MA: Harvard University Press.

Bourdieu, Pierre (1993) *The Field of Cultural Production*, Cambridge: Polity.

Boyd-Barrett, Oliver (2014) *Media Imperialism*, London: Sage.

Braudel, Fernand (1995) *A History of Civilizations*, London: Penguin.

Braudel, Fernand (1996) *The Mediterranean and the Mediterranean World in the Age of Philip II*, Berkeley: University of California Press.

Brinkerhoff, Jennifer (2009) *Digital Diasporas: Identity and Transnational Engagement*, Cambridge: Cambridge University Press.

Bruns, Axel (2008) 'The Future is User-Led: The Path Towards Widespread Produsage', *The Fibreculture Journal*, 11, at: http://eleven.fibreculturejournal.org/fcj-066-the-future-is-user-led-the-path-towards-widespread-produsage (accessed 17 September 2015).

Brunsdon, Charlotte and Morley, David (1978) *Everyday Television: 'Nationwide'*, London: British Film Institute.

Buckingham, David, Bragg, Sara and Kehily, Mary Jane (eds) (2014) *Youth Cultures in the Age of Global Media*, Houndmills: Palgrave Macmillan.

Burch, Elizabeth (2002) 'Media Literacy, Cultural Proximity and TV Aesthetics: Why Indian Soap Operas Work in Nepal and the Hindu Diaspora', *Media, Culture and Society*, 24, pp. 571–9.

Burgess, Jean and Green, Joshua (2009/2015) *YouTube: Online Video and Participatory Culture*, Cambridge: Polity.

Butcher, Melissa (2003) *Transnational Television, Cultural Identity and Change: When STAR Came To India*, London: Sage.

Canclini, Nestor Garcia (2014) *Imagined Globalization*, Durham, NC: Duke University Press.

Cardoso, Fernando and Faletto, Enzo (1971) *Dependency and Development in Latin America*, Berkeley: University of California.

Carstens, Sharon A. (2004) 'Constructing Transnational Identities? Mass Media and the Malaysian Chinese Audience', *Ethnic and Racial Studies*, 26:2, pp. 321–44.

Castells, Manuel (1996) *The Information Age: Economy, Society and Culture, Vol. I: The Rise of the Network Society*, Cambridge, MA and Oxford: Blackwell.

Castells, Manuel (1997) *The Information Age: Economy, Society and Culture, Vol. II: The Power of Identity*, Cambridge, MA and Oxford: Blackwell.

Castells, Manuel (1998) *The Information Age: Economy, Society and Culture, Vol. III: The End of Millennium*, Cambridge, MA and Oxford: Blackwell.

Castoriadis, Cornelius (1987) *The Imaginary Institution of Society*, Cambridge: Polity.

Cavanagh, Allison (2007) *Sociology in the Age of the Internet*, Buckingham: Open University Press.

Chalaby, J. K. (ed.) (2005) *Transnational Television Worldwide: Towards a New Media Order*, London and New York: I. B. Tauris.

Chapman, Adam (2004) 'Music and Digital Media Across the Lao Diaspora', *The Asia Pacific Journal of Anthropology*, 5:2, pp. 129–44.

Chaudhuri, Shohini (2005) *Contemporary World Cinema: Europe, Middle East, East Asia and South Asia*, Edinburgh: Edinburgh University Press.

Chen, Kuan-Hsing and Huat, Chua Beng (eds) (2007) *The Inter-Asia Cultural Studies Reader*, London and New York: Routledge.

Cohen, Robin (2001) *Global Diasporas: An Introduction*, London and New York: Routledge.

Cohen, Stanley (1987) *Folk Devils and Moral Panics: The Creation of the Mods and the Rockers*, Oxford: Wiley-Blackwell.

Couldry, Nick (2012) *Media, Society, World*, Cambridge: Polity.

Couldry, Nick and Hepp, Andreas (2013) 'Conceptualizing Mediatization: Contexts, Traditions, Arguments', *Communication Theory*, 23:3, pp. 191–202.

Coyle, Diana (1999) *The Weightless World: Strategies for Managing the Digital Economy*, Cambridge, MA: MIT Press.

Cunningham, Stuart (2001) 'Popular Media as Public "Sphericles" for Diasporic Communities', *International Journal Of Cultural Studies*, 4:2, pp. 131–47.

Cunningham, Stuart (2002) 'Theorising the Diasporic Audience', in Mark Balnaves, Tom O'Regan and Jason Sternberg (eds) *Mobilising the Audience*, St. Lucia: University of Queensland Press.

Cunningham, Stuart and Sinclair, John (2000) *Floating Lives: Media and Asian Diasporas*, St. Lucia: University of Queensland Press.

Curran, James (2002) *Media and Power*, London: Routledge.

Curtin, Michael (2003) 'Media Capital: Towards the Study of Spatial Flows', *International Journal of Cultural Studie*s, 6:2, pp. 202–28.

Curtin, Michael (2007) *Playing to the World's Biggest Audience: The Globalization of Chinese Film and TV*, Berkeley: University of California Press.

Curtin, Michael and Shah, Hemant (2010) *Reorienting Global Communication: Chinese and Indian Media Beyond Borders*, Champaign: University of Illinois Press.

Das, Dilip K. (2004) *Financial Globalization and the Emerging Market Economy*, London and New York: Routledge.

Davenport, Thomas H. (2014) *Big Data @ Work*, Boston: Harvard Business Review Press.

De Grazia, Victoria (1998) 'European Cinema and the Idea of Europe 1925–95', in Geoffrey Nowell-Smith and Stephen Ricci (eds) *Hollywood and Europe: Economics, Culture and National Identity: 1945–95*, London: British Film Institute.

Desai, Jigna (2004) *Beyond Bollywood: The Cultural Politics of Diasporic South Asian Film*, London and New York: Routledge.

Drushel, Bruce E. (2013) *Star Trek*, Bristol: Intellect.

Dudrah, Rajinder Kumar (2002a) 'Vilayati Bollywood: Popular Hindi Cinema-Going and Diasporic South Asian Identity in Birmingham (UK)', *Javnost*, 9:1, pp. 19–36.

Dudrah, Rajinder Kumar (2002b) 'Zee TV-Europe and the Construction of a Pan-European South Asian Identity', *Contemporary South Asia*, 11:2, pp. 163–81.

Durovicova, Nataa and Newman, Kathleen (2009) *World Cinemas: Transnational Perspectives*, London and New York: Routledge.

Dylan, Bob (2005) *Chronicles: Volume One*, New York: Pocket Books.

Ezra, Elizabeth, Rowden, Terry, Cohan, Stevan and Hark, Ina Rae (eds) (2006) *Transnational Cinema: The Film Reader*, London and New York: Routledge.

Fanon, Franz (1967/2001) *The Wretched of the Earth*, London: Penguin.

Featherstone, Mike (1990) *Consumer Culture and Postmodernism*, London and Thousand Oaks: Sage.

Feldman, Christine Jacqueline (2009) *We are the Mods: A Transnational History of a Youth Subculture*, Bern: Peter Lang.

Fiske, John (1989/2010) *Understanding Popular Culture*, London and New York: Routledge.

Fortunati, Leopoldina, Pertierra, Raul and Vincent, Jane (eds) (2013) *Migration, Diaspora and Information Technology in Global Societies*, London and New York: Routledge.

Frith, Jordan (2015) *Smartphones as Locative Media*, Cambridge: Polity.

Fuchs, Christian (2008) *Internet and Society*, London and New York: Routledge.

Fukuyama, Francis (1992) *The End of History and the Last Man*, New York: Free Press.

Fung, Anthony (2007) 'Intra-Asian Cultural Flow: Cultural Homologies in Hong Kong and Japanese Television Soap Operas', *Journal of Broadcasting & Electronic Media*, 51:2, pp. 265–86.

Fung, Anthony (2008) *Global Capital, Local Culture: Transnational Media Corporations in China*, Bern: Peter Lang.

Fung, Anthony (2013) *Asian Popular Culture: The Global (Dis)continuity*, London and New York: Routledge.

Fung, Anthony Y. H. and Erni, John Nguyet (2013) 'Cultural Clusters and Cultural Industries in China', *Inter-Asia Cultural Studies*, 14:4, pp. 644–56.

Gates, Bill (1995) *The Road Ahead*, 2nd edn, London and New York: Penguin.

Gauntlett, David (2007) *Creative Explorations: New Approaches to Identities and Audiences*, London and New York: Routledge.

Gellner, Ernest (1983) *Nations and Nationalism*, Oxford: Blackwell.

Gellner, Ernest (1998) *Nationalism*, London: Phoenix.

Gerbner, George and Gross, Larry (1976) 'Living With Television: The Violence Profile', *Journal of Communication*, 26, pp. 172–99.

Giddens, Anthony (2002) *Runaway World: How Globalisation is Reshaping our Lives*, London: Profile.

Giddens, Anthony and Sutton, P. W. (2013) *Sociology*, 7th edn, Cambridge: Polity.

Gillespie, Marie (1995) *Television, Ethnicity and Cultural Change*, London: Routledge.

Gitlin, Todd (1998) 'Public sphere or Public Sphericules?', in T. Liebes and J. Curran (eds) *Media, Ritual and Identity*, London: Routledge.

Gittings, Christopher E. (2002) *Canadian National Cinema*, London: Routledge.

Goggin, Gerard (2011) *Global Mobile Media*, London and New York: Routledge.

Goldsmith, Ben and Lealand, Geoff (2012) *Directory of World Cinema: Australia and New Zealand*, Bristol: Intellect.

Gournay, Patrick and Gobe, Marc (2002) *Citizen Brand: 10 Commandments for Transforming Brands in a Consumer Democracy*, New York: Allsworth Press.

Granovetter, Mark (1974) *Getting a Job: A Study of Contacts and Careers*, Cambridge, MA: Harvard University Press.

Greenwald, Glenn (2014) *No Place to Hide: Edward Snowden, the NSA and the Surveillance State*, New York: Penguin.

Grossberg, Lawrence, Nelson, Cary and Treichler, Paula (eds) (1992) *Cultural Studies*, London: Routledge.

Habermas, Jürgen (1989) *The Structural Transformation of the Public Sphere: An Inquiry into a Category of Bourgeois Society*, Cambridge: Polity.

Hake, Sabine (2002) *German National Cinema*, London: Routledge.

Hale, Constance (ed.) (2006) *Wired Style: Principles of English Usage in the Digital Age*, San Francisco: Hardwired.

Hall, Stuart (1980) 'Encoding/Decoding', in Stuart Hall et al. *Culture, Media, Language*, London: Hutchinson.

Hall, Stuart (1988) 'New Ethnicities', in Kobena Mercer (ed.) *Black Film/British Cinema*, ICA Document 7, London: Institute of Contemporary Arts.

Hall, Stuart (1990) 'Cultural Identity and Diaspora', in Jonathan Rutherford (ed.) *Identity: Community, Culture, Difference*, London: Lawrence and Wishart.

Hall, Stuart (1993) 'Culture, Community, Nation', *Cultural Studies*, 7:3, pp. 349–63.

Hall, Stuart, Clarke, John, Crichter, Chas, Jefferson, Tony and Roberts, Brian (1978) *Policing the Crisis: Mugging, the State and Law and Order*, Basingstoke: Macmillan.

Hall, Stuart and Jefferson, Tony (1977/2006) *Resistance Through Rituals: Youth Subcultures in Post-War Britain*, London: Hutchinson.

Hall, Stuart, Morley, David and Chen, Kuan-Hsing (1996) *Stuart Hall: Critical Dialogues in Cultural Studies*, London and New York: Routledge.

Hamm, Bernd and Smandych, Russell (2005) *Cultural Imperialism: Essays on the Political Economy of Communication*, Peterborough: Broadview.

Hartsock, Nancy (1983) *Money, Sex, and Power: Toward a Feminist Historical Materialism*, New York: Longman.

Hayward, Susan (1993) *French National Cinema*, London: Routledge.

Healey, Jason (ed.) (2013) *A Fierce Domain: Conflict in Cyberspace 1986–2012*, Arlington: Cyber Conflicts Study Association.

Hebdige, Dick (1979) *Subculture: The Meaning of Style*, London: Methuen and Co.

Hegde, Radha (2011) *Circuits of Visibility: Gender and Transnational Media Cultures*, New York: New York University Press.

Hepp, Andreas and Krotz, Friedrich (eds) (2014) *Mediatized Worlds: Culture and Society in a Media Age*, Houndmills: Palgrave Macmillan.

Herman, Edward S. and Chomsky, Noam (1994) *Manufacturing Consent: The Political Economy of the Mass Media*, New York: Vintage.

Higson, Andrew (2000) 'The Limiting Imagination of National Cinema', in Mette Hjort and Scott Mackenzie (eds) *Cinema and Nation*, London and New York: Routledge, pp. 63–74.

Higuchi, Naoto and Inaba, Nanako (2012) 'Migrant Workers Enchanted with

Consumer Society: Transnationalism and Global Consumer Culture in Bangladesh', *Inter-Asia Cultural Studies*, 13:1, pp. 22–35.

Hjort, Mette and Mackenzie, Scott (eds) (2000) *Cinema and Nation*, London and New York: Routledge.

Hoffman, Donna and Novak, Thomas (1998) 'Bridging the Racial Divide on the Internet', *Science*, 280, pp. 390–1.

Hogan, Michael J. (1989) *The Marshall Plan: America, Britain and the Reconstruction of Western Europe, 1947–1952*, Cambridge: Cambridge University Press.

Hoggart, Richard (1957) *The Uses of Literacy*, London: Chatto and Windus.

Hopkins, Antony (ed.) (2002) *Globalization in World History*, London: Random House.

Horst, Heather and Miller, Daniel (eds) (2012) *Digital Anthropology*, London and New York: Berg.

Howard, Philip (2011) *Castells and the Media*, Cambridge: Polity.

Hudson, Dale and Zimmerman, Patricia R. (2015) *Thinking Through Digital Media: Transnational Environments and Locative Places*, Houndmills: Palgrave Macmillan.

Huffer, Ian (2013) 'A Popcorn-free Zone: Distinctions in the Spaces, Programming and Promotion of Independent Cinemas in Wellington, New Zealand', in Albert Moran and Karina Aveyard (eds) *Watching Films: New Perspectives on Movie-going, Exhibition and Reception*, Bristol: Intellect.

Huntingdon, Samuel (1996/2002) *The Clash Of Civilizations: And the Remaking of World Order*, New York: Free Press.

Innis, Harold (1951) *The Bias of Communication*, Toronto: University of Toronto Press.

Innis, Harold (1952) *Changing Concepts of Time*, Toronto: University of Toronto Press.

Iwabuchi, Koichi (2002) *Recentering Globalization: Popular Culture and Japanese Transnationalism*, Durham, NC: Duke University Press.

Jaikumar, Priya (2006) *Cinema at the End of Empire: A Politics of Transition in Britain and India*, Durham, NC: Duke University Press.

Jarvie, Ian (2000) 'National Cinema: A Theoretical Assessment', in Mette Hjort and Scott Mackenzie (eds) (2000) *Cinema and Nation*, London and New York: Routledge, pp. 75–87.

Jenkins, Henry (1992) *Textual Poachers: Television Fans and Participatory Culture*, London and New York: Routledge.

Jenkins, Henry (2004) 'The Cultural Logic of Media Convergence', *International Journal of Cultural Studies*, 7:1, pp. 33–43.

Jenkins, Henry (2006) *Fans, Bloggers and Gamers: Essays on Participatory Culture*, New York: New York University Press.

Jenkins, Henry (2008) *Convergence Culture: Where Old and New Media Collide*, New York: New York University Press.

Julian, Roberta (2003) 'Transnational Identities in the Hmong Diaspora', in Timothy J. Scrase, Joseph Todd, Miles Holden and Scott Baum (eds)

Globalization, Culture and Inequality in Asia, Melbourne: Trans Pacific Press, pp. 119–43.

Jung, Sun and Shim, Dooboo (2013) 'Social Distribution: K-Pop Fan Practices in Indonesia and the "Gangnam Style" Phenomenon', *International Journal of Cultural Studies*, 17:5, pp. 485–501.

Karim, Karim H. (ed.) (2003) *The Media of Diaspora*, London and New York: Routledge.

Katz, Elihu and Liebes, Tamar (1985) 'Mutual Aid in the Decoding of *Dallas*: Preliminary Notes from a Cross-Cultural Study', in Phillip Drummond and Richard Patterson (eds) *Television in Transition*, London: British Film Institute, pp. 187–98.

Katz, James E. and Aakhus, Mark (2002) *Perpetual Contact: Mobile Communication, Private Talk, Public Performance*, Cambridge: Cambridge University Press.

Kaur, Raminder and Sinha, Ajay (eds) (2005) *Bollyworld: Popular Indian Cinema Through a Transnational Lens*, London: Sage.

Kerrigan, Finola and Ozbilgin, Mustafa (2002) 'Art for the Masses or Art for the Few?: Ethical Issues of Film Marketing in the UK', *International Journal of Nonprofit and Voluntary Sector Marketing*, 7:2, pp. 195–203.

Kerns, Chris (2014) *Trendology: Building an Advantage Through Data-Driven Real-Time Marketing*, New York: Palgrave Macmillan.

Khorana, Sukhmani (ed.) (2013) *Crossover Cinema: Cross-Cultural Film From Production to Reception*, London and New York: Routledge.

Kim, Youna (2013) *The Korean Wave: Korean Media Go Global*, London and New York: Routledge.

Kirlantzick, Joshua (2007) *Charm Offensive: How China's Soft Power is Transforming the World*, New Haven: Yale University Press.

Klapper, Joseph (1960) *The Effects of Mass Communication*, New York: Free Press.

Kohl, Uta (2007) *Jurisdiction and the Internet: Regulatory Competence Over Online Activity*, Cambridge: Cambridge University Press.

Kosinski, Michal, Stillwell, David and Graepel, Thore (2013) 'Private Traits and Attributes are Predictable from Digital Records of Human Behavior', *Proceedings of the National Academy of Sciences*, 110:15, pp. 5802–5.

Kozinets, Robert (2010) *Netnography: Doing Ethnographic Research Online*, London, Thousand Oaks and New Delhi: Sage.

Kraidy, Marwan (2002) 'Hybridity in Cultural Globalization', *Communication Theory*, 12:7, pp. 316–39.

Kraidy, Marwan (2005) *Hybridity, or the Cultural Logic of Globalization*, Philadelphia: Temple University Press.

Kraidy, Marwan (ed.) (2013) *Communication and Power in the Global Era: Orders and Borders*, London and New York: Routledge.

Krings, Matthias and Okome, Onookome (eds) (2013) *Global Nollywood: The Transnational Dimensions of an African Video Film Industry*, Bloomington: Indiana University Press.

Ksiazek, Thomas and Webster, James (2008) 'Cultural Proximity and Audience

Behavior: The Role of Language in Patterns of Polarization and Multicultural Fluency', *Journal of Broadcasting & Electronic Media*, 52:3, pp. 485–503.

Kumar, Ranjit (2011) *Crossovers and Makeovers: Contested Authenticity in New Indian Cinema*, unpublished PhD thesis, University of Wollongong.

Kumar, Shamanth, Morstatter, Feed and Liu, Huan (2013) *Twitter Data Analytics*, New York and Heidelberg: Springer.

Kuotsu, Neikolie (2013) 'Architectures of Pirate Film Cultures: Encounters with the Korean Wave in "Northeast" India', *Inter-Asia Cultural Studies*, 14:4, pp. 579–99.

Lanier, Jaron (2010) *You Are Not a Gadget*, London: Allen Lane.

Lanier, Jaron (2013) *Who Owns the Future?*, London: Allen Lane.

La Pastina, Antonio and Straubhaar, Joseph (2005) 'Multiple Proximities Between Television Genres and Audiences: The Schism between Telenovelas' Global Distribution and Local Consumption', *Gazette: The International Journal for Communication Studies*, 67:3, pp. 271–88.

Larkin, Brian (1997) 'Indian Films and Nigerian Lovers: Media and the Creation of Parallel Modernities', *Africa*, 67:3, pp. 406–40.

Larkin, Brian (2003) 'Itineraries of Indian Cinema: African Videos, Bollywood and Global Media', in Ella Shohat and Robert Stam (eds) *Multiculturalism, Postcoloniality and Transnational Media*, New Brunswick, NJ and London: Rutgers University Press, pp. 170–92.

Larkin, Brian (2008) *Signal and Noise: Media, Infrastructure and Urban Culture in Nigeria*, Durham, NC: Duke University Press.

Lathrop, Tad (2003) *The Business of Music Marketing and Promotion*, New York: Billboard Books.

Leadbeater, Charles (2000) *Living On Thin Air: The New Economy*, London and New York: Penguin Books.

Leslie, Daniel Adeoyé (2014) *Legal Principles for Combatting Cyberlaundering*, Heidelberg and New York: Springer.

Levy, Steven (2011) *In The Plex: How Google Thinks, Works and Shapes Our Lives*, New York: Simon and Schuster.

Lewis, Justin (1990) *Art, Culture and Enterprise: The Politics of Art and the Cultural Industries*, London: Routledge.

Lewis, Lisa A. (1992) *The Adoring Audience: Fan Culture and Popular Media*, London and New York: Routledge.

Liao, Han-Teng and Petzold, Thomas (2010) 'Analysing Geo-Linguistic Dynamics of the World Wide Web: The Use of Cartograms and Network Analysis to Understand Linguistic Development in Wikipedia', *Journal of Cultural Science*, 3:2, at: http://cultural-science.org/journal/index.php/culturalscience/article/viewArticle/44 (accessed 15 September 2015).

Liebes, Tamar (1984) 'Ethnocriticism: Israelis of Moroccan Ethnicity Negotiate the Meaning of *Dallas*', *Studies in Visual Communication*, 10:3, pp. 46–72.

Liebes, Tamar (1988) 'Cultural Differences in the Retelling of Television Fiction', *Critical Studies in Mass Communication*, 5:4, pp. 277–92.

Liebes, Tamar and Katz, Elihu (1993) *The Export of Meaning: Cross-cultural Readings of Dallas*, Oxford: Oxford University Press.

Lyon, David (2007) *Surveillance Studies: An Overview*, Cambridge: Polity.

MacKinnon, Rebecca (2012) *Consent of The Networked: The Worldwide Struggle For Internet Freedom*, Philadelphia: Basic Books.

McLaughlin, Jance, Phillimore, Peter and Richardson, Diane (eds) (2011) *Contesting Recognition: Culture, Identity and Citizenship*, Houndmills: Palgrave Macmillan.

McLuhan, Marshall (1962) *The Gutenberg Galaxy: The Making of Typographic Man*, Toronto: University of Toronto Press.

McLuhan, Marshall (1964) *Understanding Media: The Extensions of Man*, New York: McGraw Hill.

McLuhan, Marshall and Fiore, Quentin (1968) *War and Peace in the Global Village*, New York: Bantam.

MacWilliams, Mark (ed.) (2008) *Japanese Visual Culture: Exploration in the World of Manga and Anime*, London and New York: Routledge.

Madianou, Mirca and Miller, Daniel (2012) *Migration and New Media: Transnational Families and Poly-Media*, Routledge: London.

Mascarenhas, R.C. (2012) *India's Silicon Plateau: Development of Information and Communication Technology in Bangalore*, Hyderabad: Orient BlackSwan.

Mathijs, Ernest and Sexton, Jamie (2011) *Cult Cinema*, Malden: Wiley-Blackwell.

Mayer-Schonberger, Viktor and Cukier, Kenneth (2013) *Big Data: A Revolution That Will Transform How We Live, Work and Think*, New York: John Murray.

Mhihelj, Sabina (2008) *Media Nations: Communicating Belonging and Exclusion in the Modern World*, Basingstoke: Palgrave Macmillan.

Millard, André (2012) *Beatlemania: Technology, Business, and Teen Culture in Cold War America*, Baltimore: Johns Hopkins University Press.

Miller, Daniel (2011) *Tales From Facebook*, Cambridge: Polity.

Miller, Toby, Govil, Nitin, McMurria, John and Maxwell, Richard (2011) *Global Hollywood: No. 2*, Berkeley: University of California Press.

Mills, C. Wright (1959) *The Sociological Imagination*, Oxford: Oxford University Press.

Moran, Albert and Aveyard, Karina (eds) (2013) *Watching Films: New Perspectives on Movie-going: Exhibition and Reception*, Bristol: Intellect.

Moran, Albert and Keane, Michael (eds) (2004) *Television Formats Across Asia: TV Industries, Programme Formats and Globalization*, London and New York: Routledge.

Morley, David (1980) *The Nationwide Audience: Structure and Decoding*, London: British Film Institute.

Morris, Meaghan, Li, Siu Leung and Ching-Kiu Chan, Stephen (2006) *Hong Kong Connections: Transnational Imagination in Action Cinema*, Durham, NC: Duke University Press.

Naficy, Hamid (1993) *The Making of Exile Cultures: Iranian Television in Los Angeles*, Minneapolis: University of Minnesota Press.

Naficy, Hamid (ed.) (1999) *Home, Exile, Homeland: Film, Media and the Politics of Place*, New York and London: Routledge.

Napoli, Philip (2010) *Audience Evolution: New Technologies and the Transformation of Media Audiences*, New York: Columbia University Press.

Neef, Dale (2014) *Digital Exhaust: What Everyone Should Know About Big Data, Digitization and Digitally Driven Innovation*, New Jersey: Pearson.

Negroponte, Nicholas (1995) *Being Digital*, Rydalmere: Hodder and Stoughton.

Nightingale, Virginia (2011) *Handbook of Media Audiences*, Oxford: Wiley-Blackwell.

Nilan, Pam (2003) 'The Social Meanings of Media for Indonesian Youth', in T. Scrase, T. J. M. Holden and Scott Baum (eds) *Globalization, Culture and Equality in Asia*, Melbourne: Trans Pacific Press, pp. 168–190.

Norris, Pippa (2000) *Digital Divide: Civic Engagement, Information Poverty and the Internet Worldwide*, New York: Cambridge University Press.

Norris, Pippa and Inglehart, Ronald (2009) *Cosmopolitan Communication: Cultural Diversity in a Globalized World*, Cambridge: Cambridge University Press.

Nowell-Smith, Geoffrey and Ricci, Stephen (eds) (1998) *Hollywood and Europe: Economics, Culture and National Identity: 1945–95*, London: British Film Institute.

Nye, Joseph (2004) *Soft Power: The Means to Success in World Politics*, New York: Public Affairs.

Nye, Joseph (2005) 'Soft Power Matters in Asia', *Japan Times*, 5 December 2005, at: http://belfercenter.ksg.hardvard.edu/publication/1486/soft_power_matters in_asia.html (accessed 10 December 2009).

Nye, Joseph (2008) *The Powers to Lead: Soft, Hard and Smart*, New York: Oxford University Press.

Nye, Joseph (2011) *The Future of Power*, New York: Public Affairs.

O'Reilly, Tim (2005) 'What is Web 2.0: Design Patterns and Business Models for the Next Generation of Software', O'Reilly Media, at: http://www.oreilly.com/web2/what-is-web-20.html (accessed 15 December 2011).

Orgad, Shani (2012) *Media Representation and the Social Imagination*, Cambridge: Polity.

Otmazgin, Nissim and Ben-Ari, Eval (eds) (2013) *Popular Culture Co-Productions and Collaborations in East and Southeast Asia*, Singapore: NUS Press.

Panagakos, A.N. (2003) 'Downloading New Identities: Ethnicity, Technology, and Media in the Global Greek Village', *Identities: Global Studies in Culture and Power*, 10, pp. 201–19.

Papathanassopoulos, Stylianos and Negrine, Ralph (2013) *European Media*, Cambridge: Polity.

Parmar, Inderjeet and Cox, John (2010) *Soft Power and US Foreign Policy: Theoretical, Historical and Contemporary Perspectives*, London and New York: Routledge.

Parrenas, Rhacel Salazar (2006) *Children of Global Migration: Transnational Families and Gendered Woes*, Quezon City: Ateneo De Manila Press.

Peitz, Martin and Waldfogel, Joel (eds) (2012) *The Oxford Handbook of the Digital Economy*, Oxford: Oxford University Press.

Pendakur, Manjunath (2003) *Indian Popular Cinema: Industry, Ideology and Consciousness*, Cresskill: Hampton Press.

Pendakur, Manjunath and Subramanyam, Radha (1996) 'Indian Cinema Beyond National Borders', in John Sinclair, Elizabeth Jacka and Stuart Cunningham (eds) *New Patterns in Television: Peripheral Vision*, Oxford: Oxford University Press.

Pertierra, Anna and Turner, Graeme (2013) *Locating Television: Zones of Consumption*, London and New York: Routledge.

Poster, Mark (1995) *The Second Media Age*, Cambridge: Polity.

Postill, John (2006) *Media and Nation-building: How the Iban became Malaysian*, New York: Berghahn Books.

Propp, Vladimir (1984) *Theory and History of Folklore*, Manchester: Manchester University Press.

Pugsley, Peter (2013) 'Hong Kong Film as Crossover Cinema: Maintaining the HK Aesthetic', in Sukhmani Khorana (ed.) *Crossover Cinema*, London and New York: Routledge, pp. 51–64.

Ragnedda, Massimo and Muschert, Glenn W. (2013) *The Digital Divide: The Internet and Social Inequality in International Perspective*, London and New York: Routledge.

Rainie, Lee and Wellman, Barry (2012) *Networked: The New Social Operating System*, Cambridge, MA: MIT Press.

Rajadhyaksha, Ashish (2003) 'The "Bollywoodization" of the Indian Cinema: Cultural Nationalism in a Global Arena', *Inter-Asia Cultural Studies*, 4:1, pp. 25–39.

Ramaswami, Harindranath (2006) *Perspectives on Global Culture*, Buckingham: Open University Press.

Reese, Stephen D., Rutigliano, Lou, Hyun, Kideuk and Jeong, Jaekwan (2007), 'Mapping the Blogosphere: Professional and Citizen-based Media in the Global News Arena', *Journalism*, 8:3, pp. 235–61.

Rheingold, Harold (1993) *The Virtual Community: Homesteading on the Electronic Frontier*, Boston: Addison Wesley.

Rinnawi, Khalil (2006) *Instant Nationalism: McArabism, Al Jazeera and Transnational Media in the Arab World*, Lanham: University Press of America.

Robertson, Roland (1992) *Globalization: Social Theory and Global Culture*, London: Sage.

Robertson, Roland (1994) 'Globalization or Glocalization?', *Journal of International Communication*, 1:1, pp. 33–52.

Robins, Kevin and Webster, Frank (1999) *Times of the Technoculture: From the Information Society to the Virtual Life*, London: Comedia.

Roy, Suman Deb and Zeng, Wenjun (2014) *Social Multimedia Signals: A Signal Processing Approach to Social Network Phenomena*, Heidelberg: Springer.

Ruddock, Andy (2013) *Youth and Media*, London: Sage.

Said, Edward (1978) *Orientalism*, New York: Pantheon.

Said, Edward (1993) *Culture and Imperialism*, London: Chatto and Windus.

Salinas, Racquel and Paldan, Leena (1979) 'Culture in the Process of Dependent Development: Theoretical Perspectives', in Kaarle Nordenstreng and Herbert Schiller (eds) *National Sovereignty and International Communication*, Norwood: Ablex Publishing, pp. 82–99.

Sandvoss, Cornel (2005) *Fans: The Mirror Of Consumption*, Cambridge: Polity.

Savage, Jon (2005) *England's Dreaming: The Sex Pistols and Punk Rock*, London: Faber and Faber.

Savage, Jon (2008) *Teenage: The Creation of Youth, 1875–1945*, London: Random House.

Schiller, Herbert (1969) *Mass Communications and American Empire*, New York: Augustus M. Kelly.

Schiller, Herbert (1976) *Communication and Cultural Domination*, White Planes: International Arts and Sciences Press.

Schiller, Herbert (2000) *Living in the Number One Country: Reflections from a Critic of American Empire*, New York: Seven Stories Press.

Schlesinger, Philip (2000) 'The Sociological Scope of National Cinema', in Mette Hjort and Scott Mackenzie (eds) *Cinema and Nation*, London and New York: Routledge, pp. 63–74.

Schmidt, Eric and Cohen, Jared (2014) *The New Digital Age: Reshaping the Future of People, Nations and Business*, New York: John Murray.

Scott, John (2012) *Social Network Analysis*, London: Sage.

Shohat, Ella and Stam, Robert (1996) 'From the Imperial Family to the Transnational Imaginary: Media Spectatorship in the Age of Globalization', in Rob Wilson and Wimal Dissanayake (eds) *Global/Local Cultural Production and the Transnational Imaginary*, Durham, NC: Duke University Press.

Shohat, Ella and Stam, Robert (2000) 'Film Theory and Spectatorship in the Age of the "Posts"', in Christine Gledhill and Linda Williams (eds) *Reinventing Film Studies*, London: Arnold.

Shohat, Ella and Stam, Robert (eds) (2003) *Multiculturalism, Postcoloniality and Transnational Media*, New Brunswick, NJ and London: Rutgers University Press.

Siegel, Eric (2013) *Predictive Analytics: The Power to Predict Who Will Click, Buy, Lie, or Die* , New Jersey: John Wiley and Sons.

Sinclair, John (1999) *Latin American Television: A Global View*, Oxford: Oxford University Press.

Sinclair, John (2009) 'Latin America's Impact on World Television Markets', in Graeme Turner and Jinna Tay (eds) *Television Studies After TV: Understanding Television in the Post-Broadcast Era*, London: Routledge, pp. 141–8.

Sinclair, John and Cunningham, Stuart (2000) 'Go With The Flow: Diasporas and the Media', *Television and New Media*, 1:1, pp. 11–31.

Singhvi, L.M. (2000) *Report of the High Level Committee on the Indian Diaspora*,

New Delhi: Ministry of External Affairs, Foreign Secretary's Office, Government of India.

Skinner, Rob (2001) 'Natives Are Not Critical of Photographic Quality – Censorship, Education and Films in African Colonies Between the Wars', *University of Sussex Journal of Contemporary History*, at: http://www.sussex.ac.uk/Units/HUMCENTR/usjch/rskinner2.html (accessed 9 August 2004).

Sklair, Leslie (1995) *Sociology of the Global System*, Baltimore: Johns Hopkins University Press.

Smith, Anthony (1988) *The Ethnic Origins of Nations*, Oxford: Blackwell.

Smith, Anthony (1998) *Nationalism and Modernism*, London and New York: Routledge.

Smith, Anthony (1999) *Myths and Memories of the Nation*, Oxford: Oxford University Press.

Smith, Anthony (2000) 'Images of the Nation: Cinema, Art and National Identity', in Mette Hjort and Scott Mackenzie (eds) *Cinema and Nation*, London and New York: Routledge, pp. 45–60.

Sonvilla-Weiss, Stefan (2010) *Mashup Cultures*, New York: Springer-Wien.

Soros, George (2002) *On Globalization*, Oxford: Public Affairs.

Sparks, Colin (2007) *Globalization, Development and the Mass Media*, London: Sage.

Spizer, Bruce (2003) *The Beatles Are Coming! The Birth of Beatlemania in America*, New York: Four Ninety-Eight Productions.

Srinivas, S. V. (2013) 'Rajnikant in Japan: Indian "Superstardom" and Low Value Markets', *Inter-Asia Cultural Studies*, 14:4, pp. 615–34.

Stallmeyer, John (2011) *Building Bangalore: Architecture and Urban Transformation in India's Silicon Valley*, London and New York: Routledge.

Standage, Tom (1999) *The Victorian Internet*, New York: Walker Publishing.

Stiglitz, Joseph (2003) *Globalization and its Discontents*, New York: Penguin.

Stoetzler, Marcel and Yuval-Davies, Nira (2002) 'Standpoint Theory, Situated Knowledge and the Situated Imagination', *Feminist Theory*, 3:3, pp. 315–33.

Stokes, Simon (2014) *Digital Copyright: Law and Practice*, Oxford: Hart Publishing.

Storey, John (2012) *Cultural Theory and Popular Culture: An Introduction*, London and New York: Routledge.

Straubhaar, Joseph (1991) 'Beyond Media Imperialism: Asymmetrical Interdependence and Cultural Proximity', *Critical Studies in Mass Communication*, 8:1, pp. 33–59.

Straubhaar, Joseph (2007) *World Television: From Global to Local*, London: Sage.

Stremlau, John (1996) 'Bangalore: India's Silicon City', *Monthly Labour Review*, 119, pp. 21–47.

Sun, Wanning (2006) *Media and the Chinese Diaspora: Community, Communications and Commerce*, London and New York: Routledge.

Sundaram, Ravi (2011) *Pirate Modernity: Delhi's Media Urbanism*, London and New York: Routledge.

Tapscott, Don (1995) *Digital Economy: Promise and Peril in the Age of Networked Intelligence*, New York: McGraw-Hill.

Taylor, Charles (2002) 'Modern Social Imaginaries', *Public Culture*, 14:1, pp. 91–124.

Thompson, Kristin (1985) *Exporting Entertainment*, London: British Film Institute.

Thussu, Daya (ed.) (2007) *Media on the Move: Global Flow and Contra Flow*, London and New York: Routledge.

Thussu, Daya (2013) *Communicating Soft Power: Buddha to Bollywood*, New York: Palgrave Macmillan.

Tomlinson, John (1991) *Cultural Imperialism: A Critical Introduction*, London: Continuum.

Tomlinson, John (1999) *Globalisation and Culture*, Cambridge: Polity.

Trandefoiu, Ruxandra (2013) *Diaspora Online: Identity Politics and Romanian Migrants*, New York: Berghahn.

Trentmann, Frank (2005) *The Making of the Consumer: Knowledge, Power and Identity in the Modern World*, Oxford: Berg.

Tunstall, Jeremy (1977) *The Media Are American: Anglo-American Media in the World*, London: Constable.

Tunstall, Jeremy (2007) *The Media Were American: US Mass Media in Decline*, New York: Oxford University Press.

Turner, Graeme (1994) *Making It National: Nationalism and Australian Popular Culture*, St Leonards: Allen and Unwin.

Turner, Graeme (2002) *British Cultural Studies: An Introduction*, London and New York: Routledge.

Turner, Graeme (2013) *Understanding Celebrity*, London: Sage.

Turner, Graeme and Tay, Jinna (2009) *Television Studies After TV: Understanding Television in the Post-Broadcast Era*, London and New York: Routledge.

Vasudevan, Ravi S. (2000) 'The Politics of Cultural Address in a "Transitional" Cinema: A Case Study of Indian Popular Cinema', in Christine Gledhill and Linda Williams (eds) *Reinventing Film Studies*, London: Arnold.

Vertovec, Steven (1999) 'Conceiving and Researching Transnationalism', *Ethnic and Racial Studies*, 22:2, pp. 447–61.

Vertovec, Steven (2009) *Transnationalism*, London and New York: Routledge.

Wallerstein, Immanuel (1974) 'The Rise and Future Demise of the World Capitalist System: Concepts for Comparative Analysis', *Comparative Studies in Society and History*, 16, pp. 387–415.

Wallerstein, Immanuel (2004) *World Systems Analysis: An Introduction*, Durham, NC: Duke University Press.

Weinstein, Deena (2000) *Heavy Metal: The Music and Its Culture*, Boston: Dacapo Press.

Wellman, Barry and Berkowitz, S. D. (1988) *Social Structures: A Network Approach*, Cambridge: Cambridge University Press.

White, Amanda and Rughani, Pratip (2003) *ImagineAsia Evaluation Report*, London: BFI.

References

White, Timothy (2006) *Catch a Fire: The Life of Bob Marley*, London: Owl Books.
Wikström, Patrik (2013) *The Music Industry: Music in the Cloud*, Cambridge: Polity.
Wilken, Rowan and Goggin, Gerard (eds) (2014) *Locative Media*, Abingdon and New York: Routledge.
Williams, Raymond (1961) *The Long Revolution*, London: Chatto and Windus.
Williams, Raymond (1974) *Television: Technology and Cultural Form*, London: Collins.
Williams, Raymond (1983) *Keywords: A Vocabulary of Culture and Society*, London: Fontana.
Wilson, Rob and Wimal Dissanayake (eds) (1996) *Global/Local Cultural Production and the Transnational Imaginary*, Durham, NC: Duke University Press.
Winston, Brian (1998) *Media, Technology and Society: A History From the Telegraph to the Internet*, London and New York: Routledge.
Yau, Esther C. M. (ed.) (2001) *At Full Speed: Hong Kong Cinema in a Borderless World*, Minneapolis: University of Minnesota Press.
Yusufzai, Rahimullah (2001) 'In Which Lollywood Gives Bollywood Those Ones', *Himal South Asian*, at: http://www.himalmag.com/march2001/analysis.html (accessed 7 July 2006).
Zafarani, Reza, Abbasi, Mohammad Ali and Liu, Huan (2014) *Social Media Mining: An Introduction*, Cambridge: Cambridge University Press.
Zhang, Xiaoling and Zheng, Yongnian (eds) (2009) *China's Information and Communications Technology Revolution: Social Changes and State Responses*, London and New York: Routledge.
Zuberi, Nabeel (2001) *Sounds English: Transnational Popular Music*, Champaign: University of Illinois Press.

Index